Teams Win Championships

How to Create, Lead and Contribute to

High Performance Sales Teams

Teams Win Championships

How to Create, Lead and Contribute to High Performance Sales Teams

The Paradigm Shift from "I" to "We" in Sales

Authors: Andreas (Andy) Jaffke, Eduardo (Eddie) Baez, James Craig, John Di Marzio, Mattia Bruzzi and Pablo Escobar de la Oliva

Foreword: Mike Weinberg

Published by: Andreas (Andy) Jaffke, Eduardo (Eddie) Baez, James Craig, John Di Marzio, Mattia Bruzzi and Pablo Escobar de la Oliva.

Copyright© 2021 by Andreas (Andy) Jaffke, Eduardo (Eddie) Baez, James Craig, John Di Marzio, Mattia Bruzzi and Pablo Escobar de la Oliva

Cover design by: Pablo Escobar de la Oliva

Interior book design by: Pablo Escobar de la Oliva

Identifiers: ISBN 9798565264869

Names of the authors: **Jaffke**, Andreas (Andy); **Baez**, Eduardo (Eddie); **Craig**, James; **Di Marzio**, John; **Bruzzi**, Mattia; **Escobar de la Oliva**, Pablo

Foreword: **Weinberg**, Mike

Title: Teams Win Championships: TWC–1

Description: How to Create, Lead and Contribute to High Performance Sales Teams

Madrid, Spain: Teams Win Championships, 2021.

Teams Win Championships is exclusively available on Amazon.

Please send your inquiries at: http://www.teamswinchampionships.org

/

Early Praise

What others think about "Teams Win Championships"

Within the context of our **Teams Win Championships** book project, the following people have supported our project by granting us their valuable time and openly sharing their experiences. The end result is an extraordinary compilation of knowledge from both the business and academic worlds. We wholeheartedly owe them all a world of thanks for their invaluable contribution.

Thank you!

Dan Veitkus, CEO, Corsica Partners | Amazon Best Selling Author, Straight Talk your Way to Success | Broadway Producer, Dream Big!

"'Teams Win Championships' (TWC) is THE playbook that should be a standard issue for all professionals – leaders and individual contributors – and especially those in the noble profession of sales.

What sets this book apart from the countless titles in this category?

The authors are true champion practitioners of the principles they illuminate and the inspiration they impart across the pages of TWC. Forged through experience – successes and failures – the practitioner authors have succeeded in shining a bright light on the attitude and aptitude required to demonstrate how the "Shared WHY" is 10x more effective than the "Individual WHY".

The shift to the "we paradigm" is what really separates good from sustainably great performances as teams and organisations, and TWC offers high performers the framework and inspiration to reach for their own championship achievements."

Prof. David Clutterbuck, One of Europe's most prolific and well-known management writers and thinkers, author of 65+ books and hundreds of articles on cutting-edge management themes, Co-Founder of the European Mentoring & Coaching Council, Practice Lead at Coaching and Mentoring International LTD

"Of all the "teams" in an organisational structure, sales teams find it most difficult to function as a genuine team. The traditional culture of sales encourages and rewards individual focus. But it doesn't have to be like that. This book explores practical ways in which salespeople can employ high-quality teamwork and teaming skills — to both their own benefit and everyone else's."

Gerard O'Donovan, Owner and Founder–The Noble Manhattan Group

"As someone who has been heavily involved in coaching and building teams for many years and who has read countless books on the subjects, I was delighted to read this.

It is one of the clearest and most comprehensive books I have come across regarding building, growing and managing teams.

It is complete in almost every way, covering all major points and issues that would be of interest and relevance to any manager or team leader.

The six authors have put together a remarkable and deeply insightful guide, covering most of the key aspects of teambuilding, team management, motivation and, more importantly, achievement.

In a world with over 1,000 books right now on leadership and management, many of which contradict each other, some of the key leadership messages here are not only succinct and powerful but incredibly relevant in today's world when it comes to developing and leading high-performance teams."

Santiago Campuzano, Senior Director EMEA Hyperscalers Alliance at Citrix

"Sales is experience, and experience is success. There are too many books about sales, but most of them are based on theories and methodologies; only a few reveal the path to success through Experience and Leadership.

'*Teams Win Championships' contains thousands of hours of experience learnt and acquired by prominent leaders who understood that the real secret to success lies with their teams and the way you may inspire them.*"

James Muir, CEO of Best Practice International and bestselling author of The Perfect Close

"'*Teams Win Championships' is critical reading for every sales leader because it cuts right to the highest-leverage, most underutilized aspect in sales – leadership. The insights are both brilliant and timeless and will take your game to a whole new level. Two big thumbs up!*"

Chris Champagne, CEO, Champagne Consulting Group Inc.

"*TWC is a book written by the sales community (6 authors from 5 countries in a variety of sales roles) for the sales community. From front-line sellers to sales leaders, TWC has provided a thoughtful and well researched book including interviews with sales thought leaders. Selling from a Channel perspective was also valued as this role continues to play a vital role in B2B2B sales.*"

Dennis Sorenson, Senior Vice President Revenue & Sales at Alegeus, Senior Transformational Tech Executive

"*A must-read inspirational account of how real sales leaders do the critical, detailed work of connecting strategy to execution to get things done! Teams Win Championships is full of practical advice and true gold nuggets from the experience of some of the best real sellers in the business.*"

Dr. Solange Charas, Founder and CEO at HCMoneyball, LLC, Adjunct Professor Columbia, USC and NYU

"*Andy and his fellow authors have created awareness about the criticality of teams in achieving desired outcomes – not just for sales teams, but for all teams in an organization. Teams are critical "systems" to any enterprise, and this book goes a long way to show how to develop, manage, and nurture teams to achieve success.*"

Chris Ortolano, Chris Ortolano works with technical account managers to develop their account growth plans and can be found at OutboundEdge.com

"*Teams Win Championships (TWC) will help you rethink your revenue process. The*

TWC process will help you promote knowledge transfer, collaborate with your peers, and create a strong sense of community within your organization. Embrace the TWC philosophy to root out sales communication problems, increase effectiveness, and create a culture of transparency and consistency."

Sami Suni, CEO at Showell

"Teams Win Championships is a very comprehensive take on how teams should be built and supported in a modern company. As a growth company CEO I've started from sales that consisted of founders and gradually step by step by hiring more people to form a sales team that can scale sales. This book is a valuable asset for any business leader regardless of company size, industry or stage. It contains lots of detailed hands-on tips and best practices that covers almost every single aspect of sales. I wish I would have had this book in my hands earlier. Strong recommendation."

Prof. Malcolm McDonald, One of the world's foremost authorities on strategic marketing, market segmentation, sales and strategic/key account management, author of 45+ books on the subject of marketing, 30+ years researching and helping many of the world's leading organisations profit from being more market driven, Chairman at Malcolm McDonald International

"As an expert in business books, it is a real pleasure to come across one that is so full of wisdom, practical advice and common sense. It is a great read for anyone in a sales leadership role or being a part of a sales team."

Fernando Mateo, Vicedean, Higher Polytechnic School & Nebrija Business School, Universidad Nebrija, Madrid (Spain)

"In almost all human activities, being successful is not an individual job, but this is especially true in sales. Throughout the book the authors share their experiences about "Do's" and "Don'ts" of the commercial processes, setting the principles and guidelines needed to become a successful sales professional.

I would like to point out the importance of 'trust' to building high performance teams, something not always easy to find, but certainly it is one of the key factors to winning championships.

Inspiring and pragmatic, a must-read book!"

Contents

To: Victor Antonio

Victor, I want to thank you for all that you do for the Sales Community. Despite having a million things on your plate, you still found time to contribute to our project and make a tremendous impact. For this, we are all extremely grateful. Writing this to you seems pretty surreal, because it's the equivalent of writing a note to someone like Zig Ziglar, but better! I have the picture and I got an opportunity to work with you on something. Like I've always told you, you are one of my sales super heroes, and having worked with you has felt like a dream come true.

— Eddie Báez

Teams Win Championships

Why "Teams Win Championships" And Who is it for?

Teamwork is at the heart of everything in our lives. Look around you and you will notice how everything that has ever been created was originally done by a team of some sort. When people join forces and form partnerships or collaborate on projects, creativity and ingenuity combine to achieve the most incredible goals.

Every human being strives to win in life and overcome the challenges, competitions or goals they face. Teams come together from all walks of life to form winning teams in sports, business, science, the arts, government and cultural affairs, to name but a few. Championships are certainly not just limited to sports. Quite simply, teams win championships in all aspects of our lives.

This team-based concept also applies to sales teams–the intended audience for this book. Sales is not about CRM's, processes, methods, tools, social selling or artificial intelligence. Sales is about people, and most sales decisions are influenced and decided between people; real people with real emotions and motivations and with actual results that can be measured.

Sales is a team sport, and outstanding results are almost always achieved through the collaborative efforts of a group of talented and driven individuals. Everyone puts in the effort, but unfortunately, the world being the way it is, awards and compensations are not often distributed fairly across sales professionals which may discourage some from seeking better results.

While many sales teams are content with reaching their quotas, others struggle to hit their numbers and can't figure out how to raise the bar a notch. These teams cannot aspire to much more unless they take a proactive approach to change for the better. In contrast, upper-tier sales teams often make it look so easy–at least to the observer–that their seemingly effortless methods become the envy of their competitors.

So, what makes them better? How do they stay consistent at higher levels? What is their secret sauce? Are they just on a lucky streak?

Who is Part of the Sales Team?

Every single company whose entire existence relies on clients must be filled with people who contribute directly or indirectly to the value offered through the products and services it sells. From the CEO to the receptionist and everyone in between, everybody in an organisation sells. In some way or another, every person is connected to the clients and is either connected to or collaborating directly with the organisation's sales team. So, if everybody sells, how can we make them accountable for sales success?

One thing is clear: without sales, there is no business. Or as author Jeb Blount succinctly put it in the foreword of **Mike Weinberg's** book "*Sales Management. Simplified.*":

"*Without sales, without clients, you have no company. Period. End of story.*"

Sales teams are complex social organisms with unique individuals who each have their own unique identities; therefore, each sales team is distinct and unlike any other. Despite their differences, each and every sales team has, by definition, unlimited potential. Potential for improvement. Potential for greatness. Potential for world-class leadership in their space.

The project that led to the publication of this book is about just that: "*Achieving world-class performance by creating, nurturing and developing exceptional sales teams*". It is this premise that has led to our mission.

This project also attempts to promote the *Paradigm Shift in Sales from "I" to "We" and from "Me" to "Us"*, discarding the antiquated image of the me-first salesperson–the pushy "Always Be Closing" type of lone wolf–chasing his next commission cheque above all else and where the goal justifies the means.

This project was originally meant to be a single book project written by a few authors. It turned into an open team project anchored by the idea of creating something never really seen before, an idea that finally evolved into a co-authored framework project to provide a series of practical books to the Global Sales Community.

The six authors, originally from five different countries across Europe and North America, came to the project from diverse cultural and professional backgrounds – not to mention the substantial time difference for the weekly meetings. They have a combined 150 years of experience in sales, sales team management and leadership in more than 50 different start-ups, SME's, and global and multinational companies. The authors' areas of expertise in sales, coaching, marketing, general management, engineering, consulting, product management, and individual and team sports have been immensely beneficial.

The process of how this team–the "Teams Win Championships" team–emerged suddenly during the early days of the COVID-19 crisis of 2020 is quite remarkable. The ability to begin such a project and sustain it for well over a year is the cornerstone of the framework presented in this book. From the outside looking in, someone may not fully comprehend the level of commitment this took, but we can attest to it being quite massive.

We, the co-authors of this book, are testament that the process and key concepts developed and explained in this book do actually work; we were able to maintain focus, keep the project together and follow through on our commitments. This process is described in Part I, Chapter 7, "The Process – How We Created Teams Win Championships". The following concepts provide the foundation for any big aspirational idea: Values (Individual–Collective), Vision (Purpose–Why), Mission (Goals–What), Execution (How), and Culture encouraging open communication and feedback. These were also used to maximum effect in our project.

Our vision for this book project is that it adds educational value for the readers to:

"Provide you with both an inspirational and practical framework towards cultivating consistently top-performing sales teams."

We are confident that if you work through our framework, put in the effort and consistently plan, prepare, practice and adjust, then you and your sales team can achieve the ambitious goals you set yourself.

When you achieve – as you see, we didn't say "If you achieve" – your aspirational sales goals, you will have proven your ability to execute and persevere. You will have shown resilience on your journey as a team truly united around a powerful purpose, aligned and supported by a great leader and its organisation.

"Everything is impossible until it's done."

This famous quote by one of the most outstanding political leaders of the 20th century, Nelson Mandela, conveys this sentiment exceptionally well.

This book's framework explains how world-class sales teams are created, nurtured, transformed, led and managed over time until the seemingly "impossible" goal is achieved: A championship! The context also requires you to set "Championship goals" for your team and organisation.

Regarding team building, the most important task for team development is to have the right people in the first place. We call this the People Factor; others call it "The People Process" or simply the need to have "*The right people in the right role*". Just as important as the people you select is identifying the required roles and profiles – the required skills and levels of experience. Only after those roles and profiles have been well defined should you start searching for the best people to match. The People Factor is the most important aspect of any world-class sales team, and we review this thoroughly throughout each part of the book.

We discuss team psychology – the mindset of the individuals who make up the team as well as the collective mindset of the team—as a system of its own. We analyse how goals are set, how plans and tasks are adjusted and completed, and how failure, setbacks and early successes are handled.

We discuss how to set new goals once the first championship (sales success) has been won and how to maintain the motivation and momentum for future successive wins.

The book is further enriched by insights acquired through interviews carried out with a dozen global leaders from both the corporate and academic worlds.

We use real examples from our own hands-on experiences of successes and failures. It would be unfair to promote the notion that every path leads to glory and success. 95%+ of teams that aspire to win a championship may not achieve their goals.

Finally, we have included a list of great books that will inspire and help you—the reading sales practitioner—develop your knowledge base further, and explore the power of teams, teamwork, coaching, and mentoring.

We wrote this book for the coach, the leader, the manager, the trainer, and any other individual who seeks to achieve success with a group of people as a team. You are that leader, and you have unlimited potential. Always remember that if you believe in yourself, you are halfway there!

Perhaps you've just been promoted to a new sales role in your company, or you're starting your own business with your first hires. Maybe you're a seasoned manager struggling to lead your team, and you simply need a new perspective. Or, perhaps you're just searching for answers to some of the following questions:

Right People in the Right Role

- How do we choose the right people, and which key criteria do we need to consider?

- Have we identified and clearly defined the right roles in the team?

- Who does what?

- How do we assure efficient coordination among all team members so they contribute in the best way to the overall goal?

Culture

- How can we establish the right team culture and spirit?

- How do we keep creativity, motivation and energy at high levels for the team and the individuals?

- How do we, as a team, manage success and failure?

Goals and Accountability for Performance

- How do we define the right goals?

- How do we hold the team and each individual accountable?

- How do we measure team performance and communicate progress to the team and each individual?

Leadership and Leadership Roles

- What are my standards of hard work, discipline and success?

- What are my key responsibilities and tasks as a leader?

- What are my key functions and tasks as a manager?

- What should my own key habits and leadership actions be?

- What should I do if things go wrong, team morale drops, or I experience self-doubt?

Sales Process

- What methods and processes need to be defined, implemented, and executed to ensure continuous improvement?

- What does it mean to be a role model in and for my team, and what impact does it have on the team?

- How do we manage results versus process?

- When and how do individual team members evaluate their own performance?

- How can we measure team performance as opposed to individual performance?

- What are the key aspects of an effective sales team compensation plan?

No matter your situation, we are confident this book is for you!

Foreword by Mike Weinberg

There is this captivating (false) romantic narrative about successful entrepreneurs and business leaders, athletes in individual sports, and even sales professionals:

"She did it on her own."

"He was a maverick and accomplished this all by himself."

While these success stories are certainly appealing, the problem is that, at best, they are incomplete and, more accurately, they are a myth!

We don't win in business or sales "all by ourselves", and neither does the professional golfer or tennis player win major championships completely on their own. Did these champion athletes not have parents who invested in their pursuits and sacrificed time and money to support their development? Were there not coaches along the way? Physical trainers? Nutritionists? Equipment suppliers? Practice partners? Mentors? Sports psychologists? What about ball boys and ball girls, caddies, drivers, pilots?

In my own sales career and as an author/speaker/coach, my success is very much a product of the support I received and the teams with whom I was surrounded. On the Acknowledgment pages in my books, there are paragraphs upon paragraphs dedicated to thanking teammates for their enormous contributions because the undeniable truth is: "Teams Win Championships."

How perfectly fitting it is that this insightful, impactful book was written by a team – a wonderfully diverse group of individuals from different countries and continents with varying backgrounds, roles, and areas of expertise who, for a worthy cause, became a championship-caliber book-writing team!

Teams Win Championships is so valuable because it confronts us with this harsh reality: we need others to succeed, and while individual talent is a wonderful blessing, it is often not enough to produce a champion. And I'm confident that every reader (or listener) can quickly rattle off a litany of sports teams that have shelled out (wasted) millions of dollars on superstar players but never achieved the ultimate prize – winning the championship.

The inspiration for this book you are now reading (or listening to) came from my good friend, sales executive Andy Jaffke, an über-talented, German-born resident of Spain whose tremendous success with leading sales teams to victory prompted him to recruit this talented and passionate group of co-authors…

- A proud Puerto-Rican-born sales star from New York City with a passion for mentoring;

- A former Canadian naval officer, engineer, serial entrepreneur;

- A Montreal, Quebec based super successful company president;

- An EMEA star sales director who is a self-proclaimed smile dispenser and "prima donna destroyer"; and

- An optimistic, digitally-native Spanish millennial who loves data analytics and thrives by creating winning teams.

…to deliver exactly on the promises set out in the subtitle of this book: How to Create, Lead, and Contribute to High-Performance Sales Teams!

As much as I love "simplifying" sales … today's world has become more and more complex, and the reality is that complex sales require teams. An individual rarely, if ever, wins a big, detailed, complex deal by him/herself. This truth dictates that creating and maintaining successful teams is not optional if we want to win big in business – it's a necessity!

This book not only drives home the importance of teams but it will also help you to become both a better leader and a better teammate. Open your mind (and heart) to the process, the interviews, the stories, and the lessons as the authors intentionally tackle the BIG topics.

As critical as you may already be of team culture, prepare to be pushed even harder on the reality that culture permeates every aspect of a team. Be ready to convert the pleasant and overused term servant leader into much more than a mere platitude. And if you dare to think that you communicate clearly and often enough with your teammates, then buckle up; the authors are about to confront you with an undeniable truth: Communication is the lifeblood of a successful team. It's the "oil" that lubricates, reduces friction, cools tensions, engages hearts, and provides longevity.

The reader (listener) will very much appreciate the authors' humility and honesty. Instead of bragging and chest-beating, they simply tell their stories, share their successes and struggles, and allow their interview subjects to shine. I particularly appreciated their refusal to pretend that they have all the answers when it comes to leading championship teams. The authors' refreshing admission that a topic as enormously important as sales team compensation remains a massive unresolved challenge. There appears to be universal agreement that no one has truly quite figured out how to fairly and appropriately compensate cast members (engineers, consultants, etc.) who support the sales function.

Teams are an integral part of selling and business. All of us long to be part of something bigger than ourselves, and we can all agree that there is nothing quite like the elation of celebrating a hard-won championship with your teammates. If you're ready to become a better leader, a more valuable teammate, and truly understand why and how the best (sales) teams win championships, grab a pad and a highlighter and dig in!

Mike Weinberg

Author of *New Sales. Simplified.* and *Sales Management. Simplified.*

St. Louis, Missouri, USA

Acknowledgements

This book could not have been possible without the support of our families. For over a year, we have taken time away from them with our weekly Saturday calls (4 pm CET/10 am EST) and our research and writing during the rest of the week. We appreciate all your patience, valuable feedback and advice on our scripting/writing/reading. Thank you from the bottom of our hearts!

A very special thank you goes to the leaders who selflessly donated their time to the **Teams Win Championships Interview Series.** Your valuable contributions, perspectives and insights are priceless.

We are honoured and humbled that our friend **Mike Weinberg** offered to write the foreword to this book. We also greatly appreciate what you are doing for the global Sales Community. Thank you so much!

Thank you, **Desh Deshpande**, for providing insights from mentoring and coaching hundreds of start-ups to your own leadership skills as a seasoned founder and CEO of successful tech companies.

Thank you, **Dr Solange Charas**, for contributing to the measurement of team performance through your PhD research and practical applications on hundreds of boards, C-Suites and sales teams. You provided one critical correlation between sales teams and performance: the proof that a team's performance level can be measured as an integrated system, as opposed to the aggregation of individual performance - basically still calculated as a simple roll-up of the achieved sales results.

A very special Thank You goes to **Prof. David Clutterbuck**, author of **"Coaching the Team at Work"** and recognised as one of the founding fathers of modern coaching who provided his views on sales teams and sales teams coaching. At the end of the interview, he raised the following challenging question: "How do

11

we actually turn the sales function into a function for universal good, that people perceive as being the archetype of a benefit to society?". Today's sales literature doesn't even go near this topic!

We are very grateful for the contributions of **Sami Suni**, founder and CEO of *Showell*. He provided a unique perspective with his history of heading a smaller but internationally growing technology company out of Helsinki, Finland.

We would like to thank **Chris Ortolano** for his thoughts and contributions around the concept of the middle of the funnel activities and building collaborative experiences with clients. Chris offered our community a diagnostic approach to collaboration with a framework focused on empowering sales contributors to be more prescriptive in their recommendations to clients.

Thank you to **Victor Antonio** for guiding us through one of the most difficult conversations in sales – compensation! Victor shared his thoughts on the lack of continuity with respect to sales compensation plans and their potential to unlock stellar sales performances.

Thank you to **Mike Figliuolo** for walking us through the leadership mindset and the behaviors leaders need to cultivate to achieve consistent overachievement. In his interview, Mike walked us through how to effectively build a strong culture and lead by ensuring that it translates positively to your employees.

We would like to thank **Scott Ingram** for guiding our audience through the "you vs you" mindset of high-performing salespeople. Scott goes on to speak out on the challenges of mental health and the difficulties of working through the constant rejection in the field and how to cope with these challenges.

We would like to thank **Marta Martínez** who quickly and enthusiastically responded to our invitation and highlighted the importance of always aspiring to be the best you can be and working relentlessly to achieve it.

We are thankful to **Cesar Cernuda** for helping us understand the importance of building and nurturing trust in the team and across all companies.

Santiago Campuzano, we really appreciate your dedication and contribution. Your experiences in enterprise sales leadership and sales team management are vital to our book, and we hope we have done it justice.

Our Vision and Mission for this Project

The mission of the concept of "*Teams Win Championships*" is to create a team of writers who each provide a unique and practical framework to the sales world. We aim to encourage a paradigm shift in today's sales world from "I" to "We" and from "Me" to "Us", fully supported with real-life experiences, practical advice, proven methods, and our collective experience.

In our attempt to provide a comprehensive practical guide to sales leaders and their teams, we also encourage them to rethink their overall processes and recognise the contribution of extended sales teams.

We can only reach new heights by seeking out new ideas and perspectives on established norms; therefore, we invite the reader to join us on this learning journey. By aiming to build highly consistent sales teams and forming solid bonds within a core group, successful teams strive to support one another when difficult situations come their way.

When team members actively support one another during trying times, imagine the thrill of seeing them perform when times are good! By embracing new thoughts and new theories, we can all aim for better teamwork and appreciate that '*Always Be Learning*' is more relevant today than ever before. When everyone contributes towards a common purpose, the sum is greater than the parts, and the sky's the limit.

This book also serves as a reminder of the often forgotten and undervalued fundamentals of human collaboration that profoundly impact who we are and what we finally become during our lifetime journey: Values, character and principles.

Part I

The Team Genesis and Definition

The Big, Collective "WHY" – Vision and Mission

Shared Values for You and Your Team

Magical things can happen when people come together and form the necessary partnerships to collaborate on shared and valued causes. When individuals form a team with a common goal, the power of teamwork can be harnessed to get things done in an efficient and effective manner.

One of the basic team archetypes is an entry-level team which can easily be formed when individual talents and expertise are combined to form groups within an organisation. There are also more effective teams that focus on learning to work together and elevating their skills beyond the basic company requirements. However, even greater teams can be formed when employees elect to expand their notion of "working together" and as a result begin to work collectively with a set of shared values. In our opinions, the pinnacle of team archetypes is a team that chooses to be best-in-class and consistently developing and expanding their high-performance qualities like having a well-thought-out vision, sharing an ethical culture from within, and having a clear mission to drive everyone's work efforts.

Our book focuses on building and nurturing teams with the specific intent of elevating revenue-generating teams (sales teams) to greater heights. We encourage sales teams to reconsider their current sales logic as it relates to team building, and look towards a future that embraces a new and innovative high-performance outlook.

We will begin our discussion by establishing a set of core values to direct and encourage team members to break out of their current habits and set a new course driven by elevated standards.

Before creating the team's ideal vision and mission, we encourage sales teams to reflect on how their individual and collective values should look. The team values are the foundation on which the team can be built. For the TWC team, the most important value (and the paradigm that we aim to shift) is the need to think of the sales team as a cohesive unit rather than alpha wolves on the hunt.

As salespeople, we have all experienced the isolation and pressure of being an individual performer and the expectation of having to be a sales superstar. Some of us, however, have had the privilege of experiencing the strength of a team-centric sales process where egos are set aside, and the many hands of the team join in lightening the load.

The "We" focused paradigm is why we wrote this book. It is what got us to sit in front of our keyboards and keep writing for 15 consecutive months. Under this paradigm shift, sales engineers, product specialists, subject matter experts, managers, senior leadership, and individual contributors alike are all participants in making equitable contributions to the sales process as a team.

At the beginning of writing this book, our TWC team used word clouds, whiteboards, and intentional discussions to help draw out our individual goals. We then took a vote on the ones we felt the greatest affinity for and decided on nine values that best expressed our collective feelings and attitudes towards the project and the impact we wanted to make.

Only a few of us on the team are engineers, but even a layperson will tell you that nine foundation beams is overkill.

We encourage you to carry out this collective value elicitation exercise at the start of your team journey. Aim to pick out the most meaningful values and focus on the impact that each one will have on what you, as a team, hope to achieve.

Our goal was not on volume but on choosing the values that resonated most with us and called us to action. When thinking about your team's values, we invite you to consider the same notion and push the team to find values that truly speak to everyone and drive them to action.

TWC's Team Values:

1. We-focused (As opposed to "I" focus)

2. Honesty

3. Integrity

4. Accountability

5. Always keeping the goal in mind

6. Discipline

7. Empathy

8. Learn from each other

9. Passion and energy.

Defining the Team's Purpose

Every good story we've ever heard typically follows the same consistent format; a strong beginning with a unique proposition, a detail-oriented and supportive middle, and an ending with a call to action that motivates the reader to act. When building the foundations of a consistently top-performing sales team, we think that the process should be the same. When thinking about your sales team's "Big Collective Why", we invite you to start thinking with the end in mind.

The team's WHY should consider the team's unique sales identity, individual strengths, and overarching objectives. However, before starting any whiteboard sessions and jotting down collective values and vision/mission statements, we encourage you to start with your primary goal as a unit. What does the team want to be known for in the marketplace? What does the team aim to achieve for their clients? What are your team's brand and identity?

"Identity cannot be found or fabricated but emerges from within when one has the courage to let go."

Doug Cooper[1]

When we embarked on writing "*Teams Win Championships*", we started by letting go of our individual egos and personal agendas. Instead, we focused on defining our team's identity as a group of writers coming together to write a book and forwarding all proceeds to charitable organisations. Our team defined our literary audience, the gap we were trying to fill, and the impact we wanted to make within our communities. The impact will be determined by our ability to reach our audience.

Defining our identity, objectives, and audience helped us define our purpose and create a focal point for converging our efforts. This manifested in the person across the table having a coffee with us and talking through these recommendations. For many of us, it felt like the voice of the people with whom we were looking to connect. It is what guided our thoughts through every word we've written.

When applied to a sales team, this is the same voice that guides individual contributors on a team to provide clients with exceptional service and lead with servant leadership. It is also the same voice that compels the sales leader to diversify the team, hire the best talent and drive everyone through the most difficult sales challenges. The team's purpose is the wireframe for the rest of your collective vision and mission.

Individual Strengths and Motivations

Like any new relationship, we all spent quite a bit of time on our initial calls getting to know one other, discussing the project, and our individual WHYs. This is also how most sales teams start building their initial relationships. It is important to get to know who you are working with and what their interests are.

At the start of our project, we focused on the project plan and all the different stages to get the book started. During the process, we all got tunnel vision and lost sight of the relationship and the reasons why we came together in the first place. Once we acknowledged that we needed to spend time getting to know each other, we realised what a significant impact the building of relationships had on the fluidity of our writing. Not stopping to take stock of who we were outside of this project could

---

[1] Doug Cooper–Quotes

19

very well have been the kiss of death for this project.

We all banded together and prioritised getting to know each others' stories, what their lives looked like at home and who they were as individuals. This knowledge launched us into hyperdrive; it was the fuel we needed to spark the team's chemistry.

Collectively, we agree that sales has a lot to do with process and science; however, when it comes to the art and intangible elements that make selling truly special, there is nothing more powerful, in our opinion, than the chemistry of a unified and cohesive team. We invite our readers to get to know their teammates well and in a way that respects and augments their humanity. This is the point at which science ends, and the magic begins!

As part of our due diligence, we provided each other with a brief biography of ourselves, highlighting our strengths and interests concerning the project. We reviewed this together to understand our collective breadth of knowledge and experience. This approach allowed us to map out who would be best suited for the individual contributions that would make up the book. In sales, we can't be a one-person band and expect to make things happen by themselves. Even sole proprietors and start-ups lean on the help of small business development centres, networking contacts, and friends to turn their dream into reality.

Taking Inventory of Your Teams' Capabilities is Essential[2]

Recognising our capabilities helped us to identify gaps in our experience and what we needed to improve. Identifying and acknowledging these boundaries and limitations are factors that sales leaders can leverage to raise their own team above plateaus and help them improve.

When thinking about career paths, using mid-year and annual performance reviews against these boundaries are great indicators of growth areas to be worked on individually and as a group. As individual contributors, the mid-year and annual reviews may, at times, fall flat and feel like busy work. However, this may signify that the questions being asked are not addressing the individuals' unique needs and the goals they aspire to reach.

---

[2]   9 Sales Weaknesses That Cripple a Sales Rep's Ability to Qualify–Pete Caputa @ pc4media–HubSpot

Sales leaders trying to better understand the employees on their team can employ valued techniques like reviewing intrinsic motivators, asking about professional development, developing stretch goals, and a vision for their team's professional aspirations. Activities such as conferences, book projects, hobbies, team outings, and volunteering opportunities are all phenomenal things to ask your team members.

These are the topics that help us truly understand the areas of improvement, intrinsic motivators, and the personal boundaries within a team that make for legendary performance and unyielding team chemistry.

Building Your Vision Statement

Unlike a mission statement, a vision statement is focused on the team's future state and its accomplishments. It's the idealistic and inspirational picture of what your team's future holds and what will fuel the group's collective passions. The vision should be thought of as the long-term dream waiting to be realised.

We think the vision statement should invoke powerful feelings that push each person to rise above their station in life and make a meaningful impact on the world. To accomplish this, the team will need to use its collective imagination and creative intelligence, for imagination and creativity are two of the most underutilised assets on a team. Don't be afraid to let your vision statement run wild within the boundaries of your mission.

When we embarked on creating our vision statement for **"Teams Win Championships"**, many of our ideas seemed extremely lofty, and almost instilled a bit of fear because in the moment, it was seemingly out of reach, but it wasn't unattainable. As the saying goes – *"If your dreams don't scare you, they simply aren't big enough"*. You must be willing to escape your comfort zone, if you have any hope of reaching your full potential.

For the people who might be asking us to reign it in and provide some boundaries, there are some parameters that we encourage teams to observe to make this exercise more focused and impactful. When creating a vision statement for your sales team, we encourage you to focus on impacting your target audience. Try putting yourself in the clients' shoes to feel what their challenges are, and what the implications of those challenges look like for their business. What might their world look like without that problem?

As the guide to the protagonist in this epic tale of client vs business problems, how are you helping your clients defeat the villain that is hardship? This isn't an exercise in how big you can inflate your team's ego or describe how differentiated your products are, but instead, we encourage you to think of this as a Venn diagram.

At the heart of the circles is a perfect marriage between your unique value proposition, the scope of the capabilities of your product or service, and the most significant impact your team can deliver with its collective abilities.

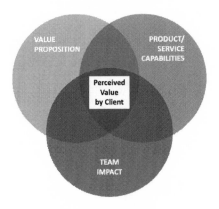

Figure 1: Venn Diagram

The team's vision should stretch the boundaries of its collective breadth of knowledge and push you to reach for something greater; however, it should never result in a falling out of bounds. If we had to describe what we think the vision statement should look like for your team, it would honestly be a gigantic paradox.

For us, it's a matter of dreaming as big as you possibly can within the limitations of your product's or service's capabilities. It should also provide room for the products and services to evolve and have more of an impact as they mature.

22

TWC Team's Vision Statement

"Provide both the most inspirational and practical framework towards cultivating consistently top performing sales teams"

Building Your Mission Statement

After establishing your vision statement, there comes a set of "We Will" claims that helps to formulate your mission statement. A mission statement encapsulates the most important assignments your team needs to complete to make the vision statement a reality.

"We Will" claims are meant to answer the "5 W's and the How" by which your team will accomplish its goals and achieve its vision. We encourage our readers to start by taking stock of (1) WHY they have embarked on this journey, (2) WHO they expect will be the beneficiary of their vision, (3) WHAT is it exactly that you are looking to accomplish, from a day-to-day perspective, (4) WHEN will these activities start, (5) WHERE will they begin, and finally, HOW do you aim to achieve these milestones consistently? When you have addressed these questions effectively, you can then begin to identify what your team needs to realise the vision.

For the TWC team, this was a combination of our project plan and the framework we developed to help our fellow sales partners achieve repeatable success. We encourage you to think of the mission statement as the blueprint, and document the calls to action.

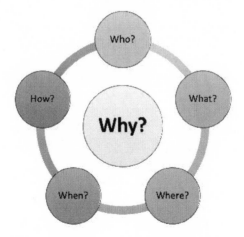

Figure 2: The 5 "W" and the "H"

The following are the TWC team's 5W's for the collective mission statement of the project:

TWC Team's Mission – Why and for Whom?

Why: There is a clear need in the Global Sales Community to amplify the message of adopting a "We"-focused mindset to sales, where the lone-wolf is no longer the norm, and the sales leaders proportionately share the responsibility of sales at all levels across the sales process.

for Whom: We focus on client-facing and non-client facing people involved in sales – both individual contributors and management.

TWC Team's Mission – What, Where, When and How?

What: With "*Teams Win Championships*", we provide a simple and easy-to-apply framework that reflects the current sales environment and the challenges teams face throughout the sales cycle worldwide. We explain, illustrate, and provide the process on how to achieve consistent top sales performance as a fully integrated team, driven by and built on a strong culture of mutual trust and accountability.

Where and When: After initial planning, the book will finally be launched in June 2021 on Amazon. Throughout the creative and writing phases, the team began generating and drumming up interest in and around the book, announcing that it would be exclusively published on Amazon.

How: We will create a single book, in both eBook and paperback formats, made up of three distinct parts. We have included additional supporting audio-visual content that offers diverse and valuable real-life perspectives of the six co-authors of the "*Teams Win Championships*" project team, as well as ten interviewees. Furthermore, we are opening the project up to, and calling for, input and active participation from the global Sales Community.

Team Fundamentals and Values

"He who has a WHY to live can bear almost any HOW."

Nietzsche

In the previous chapter, we presented our thoughts on the collective "WHY" of an organisation as seen from a macro level. This chapter expands on this idea a little further from the perspective of the teams themselves. The importance of an aligned purpose to a collective WHY was popularised by **Simon Sinek,** the author of the widely popular book "*Start with Why*"[3].

Mr Sinek describes the importance of having all teams and their individual team members aligned with the ultimate organisational WHY. He presented the idea that great leaders inspire others by putting the WHY (the purpose) before the HOW (the process) or the WHAT (the product); his view and suggested approach has influenced organisations worldwide and is considered a fundamental starting point when building a team.

Building and Assembling the Right Team

When building a team from the ground up, having a shared purpose is undoubtedly great to have, but for a team to make a serious impact, the structure must provide clarity and generate consistency above and beyond the WHY, HOW, and WHAT.

Organisations that lack clarity and consistency in their team-building processes will soon realise it. Without these two qualities, how can they ever hope to get a team off the ground, get it to work cohesively, or determine which skill sets are needed? Things will also get more complicated when you need different teams to collaborate.

---

[3] "Start with Why: How Great Leaders Inspire Everyone to Take Action", *Simon Sinek*, 2011

You can publicly announce your WHY, HOW and WHAT, but unless the different teams work in sync, the company may simply end up failing in its overall mission. Just saying it won't make it so.

A company's clearly defined and consistent vision and mission can overcome these complications. We can create a roadmap. The roadmap will enable people to perform at their very best with a series of predetermined actions aligned to the company's WHY, HOW and WHAT. And the effort they invest will reflect directly on the company's overall performance.

Building or reorganising a sales team may seem like an overwhelming task, with so many factors to consider and duties to manage, cognizant that things could go very wrong very fast. However, we can take a pragmatic approach and focus on the really important things. Thus, we can ensure that the sales team will be built to support the company's business goals in collaboration with other departments.

You could fill up a personal library just with the books and studies on the importance of culture and its lasting impact on team building. However, the reality in companies today tells a very different story; business literature rarely reflects reality. Probably less than 1% of companies are extremely high performing and seek to attain perfection; therefore, there is always room and opportunity for improvement. Getting everyone involved to define the mission clearly is a great place to start. In the early stages of team building, senior executives may consider using a defined set of personal and professional characteristics to look for in team members.

We have dedicated a full chapter of this book to our external support teams in "Part III: The Right People in the Right Roles". Suppose we use the analogy of a football team (soccer for our North American readers) whereby we compare the players to the employees of the company: strikers make up the sales team, goalkeepers provide back-up (admin, finance, legal and HR), defence provides support (support, operations and IT), and midfield always remain active (R&D, professional services, pre-sales and marketing).

Clear Rules of Engagement and Process

A basic definition of a team is: "*A collection of people with a shared identity who collaborate to achieve a common mission or goal*". That is easier said than done. Wharton School Professor **Adam Grant**[4] states, "*Putting people in a group doesn't make them a team*". To transform a group into a team, we must first identify the core values, goals, and roles to achieve the company's mission.

The personal dimension of the team is the most powerful aspect to getting people to commit truly to seeking higher performance, but it is also the hardest to manage. The personal dimension includes attitude, behaviours and verbal skills, which dramatically impact interactions between sales professionals and their clients. Suppose an employee is going through a stressful period – or just having a terrible day – their personal dimension will affect their performance which may become a burden to the rest of the team.

Clarity of the team's personal dimension will help reduce uncertainty, unnecessary friction and ultimately facilitate cooperation and interaction inside and across the various teams.

It may prove helpful to have everyone on the sales team – especially those on the front line of sales – go through an agreed-upon process. It would be equally beneficial to review this process periodically.

This way, the team can review if the process works and helps move the business forward. The process should not slow anyone down; sometimes, over-processing can do that. The rules of engagement should be fair, efficient and most importantly, effective.

---

[4] Adam M. Grant is an American psychologist and author who is currently a professor at the Wharton School of the University of Pennsylvania specialising in organisational psychology . He received academic tenure aged 28, making him the youngest tenured professor at the Wharton School.

Trust is a Must

Once we have defined each employee's role, we must ensure that everyone is clear on team expectations and communication styles. Expectations for the entire team can be reached when congruent with the employees' ability to trust one another, and a transparent messaging system is used for everyone.

As part of our TWC Interview Series, **Ms Marta Martinez**[5] (IBM EMEA General Manager) expressed the basic need for trust. You can listen to the full interview through the link in the footnote.

You may believe you have the best products and sales professionals on the market, but success will be difficult to sustain unless trust is shared equally within the group. You may initially sell your products very well based on the quality of your offerings, but time will eventually erode your win rate if the team can't work together in good faith.

Trust is a simple concept to understand, yet extremely difficult to build up and, unfortunately, so easy to lose. You may have had dozens of deals that went well for a client but, if the most recent one didn't, you can be sure it's also the one your client will remember.

This also applies to interpersonal relationships, such as a work environment, where personal agendas can make it more challenging to sustain strong relationships, ultimately leading to a complete breakdown.

Ms Martinez provided us with an interesting and intuitive approach to building trust within a team. She suggested that the first step needs to be clarity between participants.

Clarity is the crucial prerequisite for building strong bonds between people, particularly during difficult times when we inevitably tend to soften the truth to lighten a situation.

---

[5] Marta Martinez is a seasoned top executive who, like many others, kindly agreed to support this project by sharing her experience and key values to lead top performing teams.

The sentiment may be well-intended, but sugar-coating the reality of a situation also changes it. If the message is unclear, the audience gets confused, leading to frustration and mistrust. However, when we relay a truthful message with complete transparency, we show that we trust our teammates to form their own independent opinion about us and the process.

Cesar Cernuda[6] (President of NetApp) confirmed, during the TWC Interview Series, that trust is probably the most important factor for effective communication and making the right calls on crucial decisions. Trustworthiness is the most relevant trait in determining how we look at situations and render our decisions: *"How can I trust that person after they have done such and such a thing?"* or *"They've always been so honest and reliable, why should I not trust them this time?"* Like it or not, our past *judgments* heavily influence our present decisions.

Too often, when we are busy with our daily tasks and challenges, we forget that it is difficult to empower trust and cooperation without clarity and transparency.

When we cultivate an environment where people feel confident and comfortable, they feel they can trust one other.

It then becomes possible to begin a virtuous cycle wherein each team member is willing to share their knowledge, experience, doubts and questions, thereby massively contributing to the team's success.

There is No Success in "I"; Only "WE" Can Succeed

This sentiment may not apply to all sales professionals but, in a broad sense, they typically do believe they can do it all:

"Just give me those leads and step aside!"

"I can prospect. I can send pricing to my clients. I can offer alternative solutions. I can negotiate. I can close deals. I can upsell. I can cross-sell. I can care for my client after the sale"

---

[6] Cesar Cernuda, former president of Microsoft Latin America and corporate vice president of Microsoft, is currently President of NetApp

Wow, that sure is a lot of I's and my's! Does this sound like you or anyone you might know?

While this scenario sure does sound like the work of a Superhero Salesperson, why not put a big 'S' on a Spandex shirt while you're at it? This mindset is not realistic or sustainable in any manner. It would only possibly work for smaller companies with a limited sales staff. It simply couldn't work in larger organisations.

And here is where the problem lies: Sales professionals who believe they can achieve more by working as the *lone wolf* also believe that the more they work this way, the more successful they will be. When someone thinks of themselves as the frontman of a rock band who deserves the spotlight because they bring in all the fame and money, this harks the start of an impending ego problem.

It is a fact that *lone wolves* don't succeed; hence wolves hunt in packs. So why not let nature teach us something about sales?

For a sales team to operate at its peak, it must embrace a team-based culture across all departments and levels. From day one, sales professionals need to put their egos aside and imagine themselves as one piece of a complex jigsaw puzzle. The puzzle simply won't paint a complete picture unless each piece is in its proper place.

There is no doubt that sales is one of the most strategic and, therefore, most expensive departments within an organisation. Returning to the football analogy, no matter how good a striker is, he can never score on his own. He needs the support of his teammates, who all respect each others' positions, follow the team's strategy, and trust one another.

The celebrating and fist-pumping only happens when the goal is scored–or you have closed the sale–and this can only be achieved through constant collaboration between the members, each in their distinct position. This statement may be particularly poignant for sales reps.

Our TWC approach embraces a long-term, team-based culture that eliminates egos and any thoughts of superiority. *Prima donnas* are not permitted in our world, and they shouldn't be tolerated in yours either. If there are concerns, doubts, or reservations about people like this, they should be confronted immediately.

Otherwise, much like a poorly qualified lead that compromises the quality of the sales funnel, prima donnas can compromise team spirit that will eventually interfere with the company's success.

Since we consider all employees (from all departments) to be key contributors to the sales team's success, we should ensure that everyone shares the vision and is aligned with this crucial approach of fostering a team culture.

The Internal Client

We will now highlight the importance of healthy and constructive engagement among colleagues, especially across different teams. We also discuss the importance of "Extended Teams" in greater detail in Chapter 6.

We may all naturally put the external client's needs as a top priority, but we often forget about the rest of the competing priorities when we do this. We get so focused on connecting with clients that everything else gets relegated to second place. Everybody deserves a certain amount of attention; we encourage our readers to notice their colleagues and approach them in a similar manner they would a client. At the very least, we should treat them somewhat like a client, the main difference being that they are *internal* ones.

Regardless of how well we manage to engage a client, we won't be able to leverage this unless we've engaged our own team as well.

When approaching clients, we tend to focus on specific details. We try to understand their pain, their agenda, and the best communication style to connect with them. We understand this need with our clients, so why don't we understand it with our colleagues?

Many colleagues are instrumental to our success, yet we don't seem to recognise the value of their contributions. Perhaps we are trying to steal the spotlight by ignoring their contributions. Is there anyone who can honestly say they have never done this? Is anyone willing to raise their hands? Is anyone feeling just a little bit guilty right now?

Companies have historically underestimated the value of employees' personal dimensions and have recently begun to act conscientiously to keep employees engaged and motivated. Our interconnected world is raising awareness of previously underestimated topics, specifically with regards to mental health issues. We believe this new *climate of awareness* pushes companies to pay closer attention to their employees' well-being.

Empathy, awareness, and emotional intelligence are basic considerations for ensuring that performance lasts for years to come. Truly and deeply caring about our fellow team members makes a world of difference when harnessing everyone's contributions. We encourage everyone to create strong connections and trusted relationships!

A company that struggles with these topics will inevitably raise some red flags among its employees. It would be foolish to plan for any significant future for your company if you can't take care of the people you have around you right here and now.

Complementary departments such as pre-sales, R&D, support, and legal are all pieces of the sales jigsaw puzzle, and we should remember to pay them the same respect and attention as we do our clients.

To do this right, we must understand their professional agenda to support it and help them achieve their goals. It can't just be about us all the time; they must know that we are not there just to get something out of them. It has to be a two-way street at all times.

Team Culture

Once teams have embraced the principles of clarity and transparency and have empowered employees to trust each other fully, we have put in place the most important cornerstone on which to build a high performing and lasting team.

However, having every team member buy into the team's broader culture is not a one-off effort. People are influenced by professional and personal events that can affect their mood and individual priorities. In that respect, it is necessary to engage regularly with the team, to check-in and renew each person's commitment to the team's values.

As **Dan Veitkus** mentioned in his book "*Straight Talk–Your Way to Success*"[7], clarity and transparency are meaningless if your message is not consistent. Anyone who has read the book is likely familiar with the concept of "Leading by example".

---

[7] "Straight Talk - Your way to Success", Dan Veitkus

But how many of us are true practitioners? In his book, Mr Veitkus explains that trust and consistency are essential values for achieving great results. As the inspiring quote from Ralph Waldo Emerson[8] clearly states, "*Trust men and they will be true to you; trust them greatly, and they will show themselves great*".

We invite sales managers to ask themselves: How many times have you undermined the competence of your sales reps because you've questioned their feedback or opinions, even though they have already proven themselves over a long period? If you don't extend trust to others, how can you expect to be trusted? Not only trusted; but also respected? Respect must be earned, and it comes at a very high price. With very few exceptions, it takes time to build and earn.

The very first steps to earning respect are to neutralise the ego, forget about personal agendas, and focus on the greater good: the team's needs and the company's mission.

Wharton School professor **Adam Grant** explained in his book "***Give and Take***" that we dramatically increase our chances of succeeding and accomplishing personal goals as *givers*.

Some of you may have your doubts; after all, don't the most successful people around us appear to be *takers*?

We are confident that if our readers pause for a moment and think about when they were *givers*, they may actually remember how they also experienced personal success in those moments. Being a *giver* and extending care for our internal clients (our colleagues) magnifies the team's overall effort when we need help with clients or important activities. Sadly, "*Do good, and good will come to you*" is an old saying that seems to have been forgotten in our me-first world. By being a *giver* within the team, you are proactively kick-starting cooperation and encouraging people to go the extra mile for you when you need them to.

To end this discussion, we encourage our readers to be *givers*, to neutralise their egos, and make a concerted effort to listen to their peers.

---

[8] Ralph Waldo Emerson (May 25, 1803 – April 27, 1882) was an American essayist, lecturer, philosopher and poet who led the transcendentalist movement of the mid-19th century.

The more we listen, the more we learn, which is what inevitably provides us with more talking points (but only when it's our turn to speak). How much we say is irrelevant if the content does not interest our clients and colleagues. If we don't bring value to the team, it is better to remain quiet and keep thinking until we do.

Like the stoic Greek philosopher, Epictetus states in his famous quote: "*We have two ears and one mouth so that we can listen twice as much as we speak*".

Why Culture Eats Strategy, Process and Operations for Breakfast

A company's culture embodies all the intangibles that make up the fabric of its teams. Even with a brilliant strategy and a best-in-class process, the best sales team can still fail unless it captures the full potential of its people. The company's culture drives its teams forward and ultimately shapes the employees' behaviour, even when no one is looking. It's more than just about leading by example.

People should believe that what you do and what you say are genuine reflections of how you believe - not think - business should be conducted. It's also why social enterprises outpace and outperform their counterparts, because their profit margins aren't a true measure of their success.

For many of these corporations, success is measured by how much good they can do in the world and how many lives they can impact positively.

We believe this is something that everyone can stand behind and should try to strive towards. Our aim is to positively impact as many sales lives as possible with this book.

We invite you to take a serious look at your company culture and reflect on the social norms currently working and those that may be holding your team back from consistently succeeding. It's important to purge the things that no longer serve your team, your company and your clients. Your culture is one of your most valuable assets, only superseded by your people.

When scaling your business, we recommend being mindful of the cultural norms instilled among your team members. Should your business begin to grow rapidly,

35

these norms have the potential to outlive you and become the bedrock by which your employees guide their decisions.

In 1884, **John Henry Patterson** founded NCR; literature on Patterson and his efforts at the company highlight that he was a devoted learner and an advocate for professional development. Five generations of employees and almost 140 years later, Patterson's visionary perspective still drives NCR's ability to weave a culture of lifelong learning and professional development into the company's cultural norms.

It is important to note that social norms and business practices tend to change every decade, especially when employees are given the chance to voice their sentiments on how business should be conducted. Regardless of whether your business is established, or not, we recommend that regular cultural audits are carried out, at least every decade - the sooner the better. By carrying out these audits, companies can better reflect and promote the prevailing attitudes and identities of their employees in the workplace.

When was the last time you asked your sales team how they felt about where they work?

The Employee's Onboarding

A sales team's culture represents the team's collective consciousness and the heartbeat that drives every relationship built at the organisation. Your team may have the best playbook, processes and operations personnel yet fail to build successful chemistry. Culture is more than just a mission but a vision of what your team should aim to accomplish; it is a collectively fashioned ethos for the 40+ hours spent working together and away from our families.

Sales teams will either perform or perish, based on how well they work together. Companies should learn to realise that the time needed to establish an enlightened company culture is not an expense; it is an investment in its future. It's uncanny how culture is probably the highest ROI metric you can ever leverage in an organisation, and yet there isn't a mathematician in the world who can measure it. Ahhh, the wonders of intangibles!

"Often, corporate culture is implied, not expressly defined, and develops organically over time from the cumulative traits of the people the company hires. A company's culture will be reflected in its dress code, business hours, office setup, employee benefits, turnover, hiring decisions, treatment of clients, client satisfaction, and every other aspect of operations." [9]

We would add that the company's culture is also responsible for fostering a sense of belonging, inclusivity, mutual respect, care and equitable treatment for all employees. By successfully creating a dynamic and equitable culture on the team, you create real sales magic.

The company's culture must be widely accepted and upheld by all employees, from senior management down to individual contributors.

We also believe that HR should not be deemed solely responsible for fostering the company culture. Instead, we encourage you to think of it as a shared responsibility. Culture is at the centre of all successful teams. It makes the difference between an average sales team and a consistently top-performing, well-oiled sales machine. As author and interviewee **Mike Figliuolo** put it, "Culture is how we show up every day. We are role models and display our behaviours, good or bad."

The paradigm shift from an "I" to a "We" focused sales team will require a solid foundation and a codified, clearly structured and communicated system of corporate beliefs and best practices. We invite you to think about the following questions with us:

- When employees are newly onboarded, how much time does your leadership team invest in explaining core values and the cultural identity of the company and sales team?

- How much of that information is available for new employees to read and decipher on their own?

- How much time does your company spend thinking about the employee handbook in relation to the sales team specifically?

---

[9]   Investopedia

How Employee Handbooks and Sales Manuals Support Culture

Employee handbooks do more than just safeguard the business from workplace discrimination claims and misconduct. These documents provide new and existing employees with an overview of the identities and attitudes of the people for whom they are working for. In a we-focused sales environment, sales leaders should consider the type of message employees walk away with after reading these handbooks. It is important to note that they also offer sales leaders an amazing opportunity to connect with their employees and express their values and expectations for the sales department.

Being intentional about the message upfront is an investment in the department's long-term chemistry and social norms.

What does your sales manual say about how you expect the sales department to operate?

Some companies have only a general employee handbook, while others invest in dedicated sales handbooks focused on the nuances of the revenue employees. It's like having another sales leader the team can refer to at times of uncertainty.

Investing in your manual is an investment in your resources and your ability to work alongside your team on high-value activities and prized client relationships.

In our experience throughout our sales careers, the following are topics frequently referred to in employee handbooks, and suggestions for what to consider when structuring the team's sales success manual:

1. THE COMPANY'S EXPECTATIONS AND KPI[10]/OKR[11] REQUIREMENTS FOR THE SALES TEAM

This section is vital and sets the tempo for the team's output. The management team can use data on current client relationships to triangulate levels of activities and conversion rates the team will need to achieve their quota. This is an exceptional way to extract achievable and realistic goals for the members of each revenue team. The company's expectations extend beyond the team's required activities.

---

[10] Key Performance Indicator (KPI)
[11] Objectives & Key Results (OKR's)

One can cultivate a positive and welcoming sales culture by defining clear expectations for the behaviours you would like employees to model. This section is a great place to shift the dialogue away from the typical "I"-focused lone wolf mentality to one of mutual collaboration and a principled "We" focused sales methodology.

We invite sales leaders to use this as an opportunity to provide employees with a preview of what the meritocracy system may look like within the organisation. The preview can include information on what accountability looks like from the business leaders' perspective and the benefits and accolades that may be awarded to the best collaborators.

Collaboration is crucial to the success of top-performing sales teams.

This should be a vital consideration when determining the roles of the sales enablement team, the subject matter expert team, the account executives and the client relationship managers in the pursuit of new clients. Each department has a role to play, but the overall goals for the revenue teams need to align across departments.

To drive the right team behaviour, it is of utmost importance to accurately design the right sales compensation plan.

2. Mindset, Attitude, Empathy and Sales Emotional Intelligence/ Quotient (EQ)

Although we have come to know sales as a noble profession and the salespeople, succinctly put by Victor Antonio, as *"Walking profit centres within an organisation",* [12] not everyone thinks this way. The first actual sale a sales professional ever makes is the one of building trust.

Much like Rome, trust cannot be built in a day. There are, however, tools that we can leverage to create pathways and bridges that help streamline this part of the client's journey.

These tools are the mindset, attitude and empathy we lead with during every client interaction. The soft skills of the trade are perhaps the most important and non-negotiable skills we should encourage our sales staff to develop.

---

[12] Interview with Victor Antonio

While undoubtedly important, a positive and smiling disposition will only take you so far when trying to build trust.

Every company has a different take on these attributes. Though empathy and emotional intelligence (EQ) are a spectrum, it's how we approach these behaviours and attitudes we expect from employees that will enable us to shape handling client interactions.

Now is the perfect opportunity to describe the qualities to look for in revenue employees. As stated by the great motivational speaker **Les Brown**, many times:

"Look not upon a person for who they are today, instead, look upon the person for who they have the potential to become, and they will rise to the occasion!"

3. A Product Glossary and Industry-Specific Jargon

Whether you have a subject matter expert team or not, all revenue staff need to understand your solutions and the industry-specific verbiage and nuances. We like to think of these as your baseline instruments for storytelling. Without them, the story falls flat, making it challenging to convey to your clients what outcomes they are working towards with your team.

No matter how differentiated your products are, the salesperson must always be teaching and the client must be willing to learn. Let us think back to when we were students and asked our teachers questions about the concepts we hadn't learned yet. At the time, we were expected to learn history, math, and other subjects without every truly understanding their benefits.

However, it's this process that led us to our place in the world (even for the folks who just fell into the profession). As students, we always expected teachers to have all the answers, but at times even the very best teachers didn't. Instead, they relied on empirical evidence and subject matter experts to help us find the answers on our own. Why should sales discussions be any different for clients?

4. A Client Journey Guide, Breaking Down the Ideal Client Profiles and Client Acquisition and Retention Strategies

It's no secret how the best-in-class companies gain the lion's share of their market. They invest heavily in getting to know their clients, their clients' industries, their clients' pain points and challenges, their clients' clients and the unsolved or overlooked issues within their marketplace.

They have marketing teams, industry experts, external consultants, researchers and academics alike, helping them navigate their clients' unique operating environments.

They conduct client interviews, surveys, and targeted campaigns to define and modify the client journey. Using these data strategies, companies can generate testimonials, client guides and collateral to help shape the dialogue and experience with clients throughout the purchasing process.

In our experience, a lot of this data is sourced from the marketing department, client relationship teams and client success staff. They are the ones on the frontlines capturing each client's unique experience to assist in developing talk tracks and targeted questions that help the top and middle of the funnel employees drive new client acquisitions.

If you are a start-up or middle-market firm, you don't need unlimited resources to conduct client interviews and surveys. Nevertheless, it is an invaluable investment to make for the long-term success of your business. The better your sales staff understand the journey, the better equipped they are to walk shoulder to shoulder with your clients through the buying process.

5. A Product Matrix with Real Use Cases of the Products or Services for the Company's Different End Markets

Most companies deploy a formal training programme to skill up their sales staff on solutions and industry applications. Some companies will even go so far as having account executives start in project management roles or shadow sales engineers to gain as much product-specific knowledge as possible.

Whether or not it's a complex solution, your sales manual should have a section dedicated to product-specific information and application standards to ensure that employees have a reference guide for when their knowledge falls short of the client's questions.

If your solution is specific to one industry, we encourage you to think of the cross-functional selling and adjacent market opportunities your solutions can deliver.

Product outlines become an essential part of the first six months on the job in companies with several industry applications. This section should not be developed without the guidance or, at a bare minimum, the perspectives of sales engineers, subject matter experts, and the people who interact the most with clients.

6. Value Proposition, Storytelling Frameworks and Talk Tracks

The landscape of sales hiring is constantly changing, and companies are beginning to focus heavily on the soft skills they observe in candidates. One such example of that is of storytelling, which is a highly prized skill that the very best in the sales community has down to a science. We do mean literally *down to a science*!

With the advent of data visualisation tools and data dashboards, sales professionals are also becoming expert data storytellers. Data storytelling combines soft skills with a principled approach rooted in credible and objective data to help present truly compelling value propositions to clients. By capturing the best sell by stories and walking through the various value propositions of your solutions, you are creating more than just talk tracks; you are creating client outcomes before your sales team even picks up the phone.

In addition to all the different data visualisation tools, the sales community can also choose from numerous sales enablement tools.

These tools enable sales teams to record calls, presentations and client interactions that can be shared with colleagues at different levels of experience. Whether you're using these tools or doing things the old-fashioned way, codifying talk tracks and the various elements of the client's journey into workable scripts and email templates, help junior staff and industry transplants to hit the ground running.

The goal is to have the team eventually move away from scripts to find their own *storytelling* voice and *sales identity*. However, this takes time and requires a lot of trial and error. These talk tracks help minimise the standards of deviation and yield similar outcomes for everyone on the team.

Incidentally, storytelling is also a team sport. Your sales engineers and account managers will have a completely different view of the client's story based on their unique client interactions.

7. QUESTIONING FRAMEWORKS

Questioning is one of the quintessential skills of top-performing sales professionals. By capturing the questioning techniques deployed by your top-performing sales reps, the rest of the team can better understand the types of questions that drive relationships forward. Not all questions are built the same, and the value and effort you put into this exercise are what you can expect to get out of it.

Exceptional questioning can be developed in a collaborative environment where the team celebrates curiosity and creativity. This section of the manual provides an opportunity to weave a sense of wonder into the sales process during the discovery phase of your client interactions. Though this is not a tangible thing you can illustrate, you can introduce it by writing down what it looks like on the phone with clients.

8. COLD-CALLING AND PROSPECTING METHODOLOGIES–TEMPLATES, PRESENTATIONS, EXAMPLES AND ADVICE

Cold-calling and prospecting are perhaps the most challenging parts of the sales process. The top of the funnel is often met with a barrage of rejection and negativity. All this negativity can lead to insecurity, call reluctance and impostor syndrome for even the most seasoned reps. With the advent of Sales Development Representative (SDR) roles, many of a company's top funnel activities are handled by tenacious junior reps with an insatiable appetite to break through.

In order to break through, we've seen everything from video messaging and personalised corporate gifts to handwritten notes. Some companies continue to invest in the numbers game; others adopt a smile-and-dial philosophy. Both methods yield conversions. Although we can talk for hours about the pros and cons and the ideal prospecting methods, this is about your company deciding what works best to tackle the most difficult conversations in the sales process.

Combine the creativity of the junior and senior staff to define the most optimal means of prospecting within your industry. It may take bravery and a lot of questioning to decide whether these nuanced and different ways of thinking will actually work. To rule out anything that may not work, you can substantiate the methods by analysing conversion rates and identifying trends for the different methodologies.

For some companies, it may be referrals, testimonials or extensive networking. However you arrive at it, the best method will be built by collaborating as a team.

9. Objection Handling and Negotiation Frameworks for Different Buyer Profiles and Scenarios

Preceded only by cold-calling, we would argue that objection handling and negotiations are the second most difficult conversations we have as sales professionals. These conversations often require the aid of subject matter experts, seasoned negotiators and executive sponsors. In his earlier years as a junior sales professional, one of our authors remembers how he had thought that the later stages of a client relationship were about who was going to win and how much recognition they would receive for the sale.

They have now come to realise that this couldn't have been further from the truth. Though compensation and recognition are huge motivators and a great way to entice sales professionals to move mountains, we believe that even Atlas could have used some help to carry the weight of the world.

These factors are also minor considerations when building honest and collaborative relationships with your clients. Ultimately, we believe that if you are out to chase the money, you'll find it, but if you are out to become the best you can be, you can't use your clients as stepping stones.

It would help if you considered your clients your allies, and the best way to handle a negotiation or an unprecedented objection is to come at these from a place of mutual respect. It takes time, but you will eventually reach a level of accountability and selflessness that your clients can perceive.

We believe that the world's best problem solvers surround themselves with a community of like-minded and equally passionate people. These people provide the critical perspective needed to find solutions that matter, the ones that drive human innovation.

To solve those million-dollar problems, you need a team of million-dollar problem solvers with the capacity to match the intensity of different buyer personas and negotiation styles.

Whether you are working with an analytical buyer, results-driven buyer, a frugal spender or an emotionally invested buyer, your team should aim to have someone at the table who speaks their "language"; preferably a team member able to put themselves in the buyer's shoes. This is not meant to mirror or manipulate, but instead, we believe it is the pathway to understanding.

One of our authors has experienced firsthand that you can have multiple people walk into a room, partake in the same collective conversation, and all walk out of the room with a completely different opinion and understanding of what was said. To have a team full of diverse perspectives at the negotiation table is to fully invest in your team's ability to deliver high-quality answers to your clients' most challenging and troubling questions.

Some of the most valuable professional development training they received involved being in a room with colleagues, walking through negotiations and client escalations that they couldn't figure out on their own. Conversations were carried out in a conference room, where everyone agreed that no idea would be considered too junior or too foolish to work.

This helped them achieve consensus on the next steps and ensured that their ideas would never come at the expense of the relationship with the client. They then proceeded to provide the recommended mutual goals to present at the following client meeting.

10. Time Management, Prioritisation and Virtual Communication

Time management is a crucial skill we must all learn at some point in our careers. Time is the most highly prized commodity for professional sales, trumped only by the trust capital we must build with our clients. When thinking about time management, we often think about it in terms of our own time.

However, we encourage our readers to consider the team's collective time management and how quickly we can mobilise our internal resources and communications for client escalations and negotiations by providing a guide and general best practice for handling these situations. This, coupled with a framework for prioritising our endless to-do lists, is essential for getting things done. The Eisenhower Matrix[13] is a phenomenal tool to assist your team in delegating and prioritising their most time-sensitive activities.

With businesses now operating more on virtual platforms, communication tools are crucial for maintaining the stability and connectedness we share within the organisation. By including escalation frameworks and a guide to available communication tools, we believe you can streamline your team's ability to communicate to maximise the team's time when working on time-sensitive client engagements.

Scheduling aids, corporate messaging platforms, project management tools, and data visualisation programs are phenomenal ways to make your teams more agile and provide a clear and effective way of communicating.

11. CONTINUOUS LEARNING AND PROFESSIONAL DEVELOPMENT

Many companies will have required reading for new employees. We believe that exceptional companies should also aim to have year-round recommended reading. This promotes continuous learning and professional development as essential to every top-performing sales teams' culture.

Some companies have an internal intranet, or utilise tools like SharePoint, to create a centralised hub for professional development and continuous learning.

As sales leaders, one can shape the minds of the people you work with by simply recommending books that had an impact on your own sales career. Book clubs are a phenomenal resource and offer team members the opportunity to lead and facilitate group discussions that promote learning and development.

Sales leaders can provide guidelines and initial suggestions to help promote a culture of intentional and continuous learning. The learning should also not be limited to books but incorporate additional resources like podcasts, blogs, motivational speakers, conferences, and any media source that helps promote a continuous learning and growth mindset.

(Please refer to our recommended reading list in the back of the book.)

---

[13] Video tutorial about the Eisenhower Matrix: https://www.eisenhower.me/eisenhower-matrix/

How These Elements Relate to the Company Culture

The company's technical sales manual is more than just a compendium of sales knowledge; it's the company's sales story and identity, as told by the very best salespeople within the organisation.

It's a resource in which sales leaders extract and encapsulate the most important lessons and perspectives for the next group of salespeople joining the organisation. It also includes the norms and expected calibre of work.

The team's culture is no different and can be found in these stories and client case studies.

When our co-author Eddie Baez first started his sales career, like many of us, he spent a lot of time poring over the technical manual. He was a first-generation college graduate, and no one in his immediate circle of family or friends had worked in the B2B sales community. This, coupled with the fact that he didn't know what sales literature to consume, made the learning curve very steep.

The sales technical manuals of both the organisations he worked for became irreplaceable resources for him. He remembers spending hours reading and re-reading the stories of colleagues securing the most important deals and relationships with clients.

Every time he walked out of the door to meet with clients, or before picking up the phone, Eddie spent time rehearsing the talk tracks and client case studies in his head to improve his chances of earning the trust of his clients.

This anecdote highlights the importance of initial sales training and the sales manuals for anyone walking into an organisation for the first time. Given that so many people fall into sales with so few lifelines to help them level up, it is important to invest in solid training and develop robust sales manuals upfront.

Make sure you have a robust sales manual in your company. If you don't, write a good one and make it a team effort, of course.

Mentorship

Mentorship also played a significant role in Eddie's professional development. Eddie sought out mentors and guides on LinkedIn and through networking events to make sense of what he was learning before developing relationships with the salespeople in his organisation.

Mentorship programmes are a phenomenal way to help new salespeople reduce the ramp-up times in their first few weeks at an organisation. Mentors can help teach incumbents in the field to learn the skills in a safe space. Mentors are, essentially, monitoring and protecting the new salesperson from the first day by offering a lifeline before the salesperson has any conversations with clients.

We invite our readers to spend as much time as possible reading case studies from sales professionals and leaders across their organisation and different countries. Reading the collective thoughts and opinions of the best people within your organisation and worldwide provides a broad perspective of the world of sales.

It's like having coffee with these people with the opportunity to ask them about the most glaring challenges you face with your own development. You may learn that each office/department within your organisation has its own micro-culture when reading the manuals.

Salespeople from different regions may have a similar approach to sales but with distinct and extremely effective techniques for their respective regions. Different methods and viewpoints afford you additional perspectives and unique outlooks to some of your own challenges.

These regional viewpoints can be your learning sandbox and help you solve challenges that extend beyond your depth of knowledge, providing an invaluable perspective as you learn how others problem-solve, both domestically and abroad.

We believe that the most common denominator is a client's challenges; however, the resolutions tend to be as unique and varied as the regions from which they derive.

By standing on the shoulders of these international giants, you can become the Swiss Army knife of sales problem-solving. As a side benefit, you may also learn about the different cultures within your company and how they interact with clients.

This approach is likely to be more robust and practical than sourcing solutions from Google or a popular sales book. The technical sales manual is one of the biggest and most important investments an employer can make in a salesperson. It can help the salesperson navigate their place within the company's culture.

Meritocracy

Through our professional experience and that of people within our network, we have noted that one of the core values adopted by successful companies is that of meritocracy.

Meritocracy is *"a system, organisation, or society in which people are chosen and moved into positions of success, power, and influence on the basis of their demonstrated abilities and merit."*

Meritocracy ensures an equitable and fair playing field for individual contributors and sales leaders alike. In our experience, we have seen companies instill this value through clearly defined career paths, tangible metrics to achieve different earning thresholds, and intangible qualities, for example, earning potential and work ethic needed to progress in your career.

This transparency, coupled with ongoing dialogue during mid-year and annual reviews, provides a clear path for individual contributors and managers to better plan for the goals they hope to achieve. There are pitfalls with meritocracy that we want to address to ensure that the approach is truly fair and equitable.

Academically speaking, the key distinction between a meritocracy and a democracy, is that in a democracy there is decision by consensus. Unfortunately, in a meritocracy not everyone has a vote. As **Jim Whitehurst** from Red Hat states, *"While everyone does have a voice, some are listened to more than others."*

Though one of the benefits of meritocracy is that it breeds an environment of competition by driving participants to be the best and make the best contributions, we need to consider that not everyone shares the same intrinsic motivators.

For some sales professionals, being the best account executive or account manager is what they strive for and what they consider to be their major contribution to the team. It is important to note that for those motivated by these considerations, there must be fair and equitable treatment to avoid having one person become the voice or face of the team.

A great friend once told me that there can be no prima donnas for a team to be successful. To avoid this and continue to push everyone towards making meaningful contributions, we invite teams to consider introducing friendly competitions and promoting collaborative projects.

Meritocracy demands active listening to the ideas and considerations of the team at every level of the organisation. Sometimes the truth will hurt, but we encourage your team not to lose sight of the bigger picture.

The people within your sales organisation have a lot to lose when things are not going well, and they should not be demoralized or ostracized for being brave enough to share their concerns.

The team should feel sufficiently empowered to take the lead and speak up when things are not going well and celebrate their colleagues' individual wins and great ideas. This approach acts as a secondary feedback loop, like the ones we build with our clients.

At times the feedback helps us confirm market assumptions and potentially net new opportunities, thereby enabling the organisation to scale and cross-functionally sell to existing patrons.

Diversity, Equity, Inclusion (DE&I) and Belonging

The Ford Foundation for Social Justice defines DE&I as follows:

Diversity is the representation of all our varied identities and differences (race, ethnicity, gender, disability, sexual orientation, gender identity, national origin, tribe, caste, socio-economic status, thinking and communication styles, etc.), collectively and as individuals. Equity seeks to ensure fair treatment, equality of opportunity, and fairness in access to information and resources for all. We believe this is only possible in an environment built on respect and dignity. Inclusion builds a culture of belonging by actively inviting the contribution and participation of all people.[14]

---

[14] The Ford Foundation

We believe that consistently top-performing teams make more sales by proactively recruiting people with diverse backgrounds, education, perspectives and abilities. Moreover, we think that DE&I adds to the richness of the team. The more diverse the team, the more balanced, open-minded and innovative the team will be.

Diverse workforces have been researched. The findings are conclusive: diverse teams cultivate higher rates of innovation, tend to be more creative, have better decision-making capabilities and yield higher levels of profitability than their homogenous counterparts.

A study carried out by the Harvard Business Review found that companies with two-dimensional diversity (2-D) constantly outperformed competitors in innovation and bringing new ideas to market.

> *"Employees at these companies are 45% likelier to report that their firm's market share grew over the previous year and 70% likelier to report that the firm captured a new market."*[15]

Unconscious biases during the interview phase result in businesses losing out on talent every day because managers' perceptions impede their judgment when assessing candidates.

> *Unconscious biases are social stereotypes about certain groups of people that individuals form outside their own conscious awareness. Everyone holds unconscious beliefs about various social and identity groups, and these biases stem from one's tendency to organise social worlds by categorising. Unconscious bias is far more prevalent than conscious prejudice and often incompatible with one's conscious values. Certain scenarios can activate unconscious attitudes and beliefs. For example, biases may be more prevalent when multi-tasking or working under time pressure.* [16]

We believe that sales leaders should receive mandatory anti-bias and anti-discrimination interview training to promote fair hiring practices to find diverse top tier talent. No two candidates will ever be the same.

---

[15] How Diversity Can Drive Innovation by Sylvia Ann Hewlett, Melinda Marshall, and Laura Sherbin

[16] What is unconscious bias?–University of California

By training employees to look for unique perspectives, potential contributions and cultural fit throughout the hiring process, they will be empowered to find the people you need and not just the people you think you want.

The DEI&B (Diversity, Equity, Inclusion and Belonging) conversation and training should be ongoing for sales leaders within an organisation, in addition to any anti-bias and anti-discrimination interview training certifications.

Consistent executive sponsorship and alignment to the DEI&B goals of the business are essential to the belief and trust your sales team places in leadership.

It's not enough to be trained on hiring people and how to avoid unconscious bias. The sales leadership team should also come up with a plan to ensure that diverse candidates can succeed and have enough runway to grow and develop. This infrastructure is crucial and is for the common benefit of both the sales leadership team and the company.

We believe you can generate truly inspiring work experiences by having groups like ERG[17] (Employee Resource Groups) hosting company-wide events to celebrate and promote diversity and setting aside time to get to know your employee's backgrounds and beliefs.

As a supplement to this employee-focused initiative, we recommend that sales leaders consider hosting frequent DEI&B discussions, conducting workforce analyses to review the diversity of the sales floor, and taking stock of the current recruiting methodologies. There are thousands of vacant sales roles in every major metropolitan city because there are simply too few schools and universities teaching sales as a formal occupation and not enough companies promoting the profession to the communities they impact.

The talent is out there, and though it may seem tedious to procure, more and more organisations are competing to bring diverse talent to their clients. As such, we encourage sales leaders to audit their community and academic outreach and the amount of time they spend impacting these communities and conveying the numerous benefits of professional sales.

---

[17] https://www.catalyst.org–Employee Resource Groups

The profession has been misunderstood for long enough. It is time to take a stand and start rebranding sales as the noble profession it is. However, it will take all of us. It is a shared responsibility for the collective wellbeing of our sales floors everywhere.

We also encourage teams to conduct salary analyses to ensure that merit-based and equitable pay practices are in place and create objective criteria for the corporate governance selection process. There are numerous studies on the disparity of pay between different demographics and its impact on morale, empowerment and autonomy in the workplace.

To retain employees and ensure long-term employee satisfaction, you must create and evaluate clearly defined career paths with objective criteria, multiple paths and intentional longevity. Provide employees with ample choice and a real say in their career options by making the ceiling very high with attainable goals and numerous career path options.

Lastly, we believe that sales leadership teams should reflect the diversity of your sales floor. Diversity, at the highest level, breeds innovation, trust and unity between sales leaders and individual contributors. It shows that the company truly cares and that, like many democratic governments, employees' voices, stories and ideas are given fair representation behind closed doors.

The Profound Impact of an Employee Resource Group

When our co-author Eddie was first tasked with creating an Employee Resource Group (ERG), he started by reaching out to colleagues at the National Sales Network (NSN) in New York City for advice. NSN is the largest and most diverse sales-specific networking organisation in the US. The board members were quick to lend a hand and provide Eddie with guidance. One conversation led to several with similar organisations and companies to find and combine resources and best practices to support the ERG launch.

The HR department at Eddie's company also reached out to their networks and conducted internal research to compile a list of resources for employees of colour.

Through this discovery process, the organisation decided to host a company-wide meeting to discuss how they could best support their employees of colour and minority groups within their organisation.

To foster a collaborative environment and avoid censorship or creating a forum for public debate, they focused on the theme of support and guidance for colleagues as the backdrop for constructive discussion. They also reached out to people within the organisation who were passionate about diversity and inclusion to help guide the discussions.

The CEO sent a company-wide address promoting the ERG to ensure that colleagues felt supported at every level. Several SVP's, VPs and senior management also raised their hands in support of the cause by providing executive sponsorship.

The call was a success, and several people shared powerful stories about their backgrounds and the challenges they have overcome in their lives.

The call helped to provide context and understanding, and the company felt more connected at every level. This was the springboard for the next step, which was the formulation of the group.

Following the call, additional meetings were held with the initial group of participants to create a charter for the ERG, including a mission and vision statement.

The charter captured all the unique perspectives and resources within the group and extended to both current and future employees of the organisation. A board and a steering committee were also set up to support the various functions of the group.

The ERG's two primary objectives were:

- to provide opportunities for internal events and collaborative projects that celebrated diversity and inclusion in the office; and

- to provide support for community outreach efforts that celebrated and supported diversity and inclusion in our backyard.

These efforts turned into book clubs, movie nights, and constructive discussions with employees from all over the company. ERG groups are extremely important and add immense value to any organisation. However, they need the collective support of employees, allies, HR staff, middle-management and senior leadership to be truly effective.

It was a rewarding experience and took the collective efforts of several external organisations and networking colleagues to breathe life into the programme.

For more tips, resources and information on building an ERG, please reference the ***top1.fm DailySalesTips*** Podcast Episode 505. [18]

Promoting Culture

Promoting the company culture and getting to know your team are crucial to enhancing the chemistry and consistency of sales performance. Company-sponsored events and outings, volunteer opportunities, community outreach programmes and other similar events help to promote and unify a sales team through shared experiences. These endeavours provide time and space away from the workplace to get to know colleagues and their stories. We need to promote positive outcomes with colleagues as we do with our clients; our colleagues are no different, and their stories and goals for the future should be considered just as important as those of our clients.

Many of us spend more time with our colleagues than we do with our own families and clients. With this in mind, we encourage both sales leaders and individual contributors to spend more time getting to know the people they work with and build political and social capital across the company's functions and support groups.

These endeavours are possible in both large organisations and startups. However, it is up to the individual to make a conscious effort to own this part of their development. It should be their responsibility to seek out mentors, guides, friends, support and anyone else who can help contribute to the team's success within the organisation. This, in turn, will yield long-lasting professional relationships and a more connected workforce. The most meaningful professional relationships we've formed have happened through shared experiences at work and conferences.

Midyear and holiday parties are great ways to get to know colleagues and celebrate the team's collective achievements. Some of the most meaningful friendships of our careers started at these types of events, and it was because we were able to break away from the requirements of work that we could truly listen and absorb our colleagues' stories. Work, however, is not the only place you can build these friendships.

---

[18] Sales Tip 505: Resources for Allies – Eddie Baez

In cities like New York, one of the most densely populated metropolitan cities globally, there is no shortage of opportunities to meet new people and find professional development events. Using platforms like Meetup and LinkedIn groups, you can build an external community of like-minded sales professionals who are just as invested in their careers as you are.

These events highlight the number of opportunities that exist globally to network and learn. These resources even helped one of our authors create a business case for their management team to venture out to the biggest sales conferences in exchange for a transfer of insights and knowledge to the rest of their team.

The management team got the necessary approval to attend these conferences and soon realised how enriching these events are. They met people from around the world, and shared experiences and wisdom and saw, firsthand, the many unique ways of approaching sales, and they dissected the cultural similarities that bonded them.

The team learned that professional sales is a science just as much as it is an art. The way the story gets told is the only thing that makes it unique. The events gave us opportunities to meet some of our sales heroes and authors who had had the biggest impacts on their careers. Three of our co-authors first met at one such major sales conference. Who could have guessed that it would eventually lead to this TWC book writing project! Shared experiences can be powerful and life-changing, both in and out of an organisation, but it is up to the sales professionals to venture out and experience it for themselves.

Shared Experiences and Professional Development

Some of us have been lucky enough to work for companies that invest heavily in creating thorough and well-documented sales training programmes.

One such company that Eddie Baez worked at was a large enterprise with the resources to provide its employees with an off-site sales training boot camp. The boot camp lasted several days and included a sales playbook that breaks down all the stages of the sales cycle and offers glimpses into best practices that employees are using.

Being offsite and away from the family, Eddie could study the playbook with few distractions, which proved an extremely effective approach to learning. In our opinion, these experiences are so powerful because of the diverse experiences in the room and executive sponsorship from sales leaders.

Within this particular organisation, training sessions were typically run by regional and national sales leaders. This approach highlighted the unique perspectives of the different sales teams.

At the boot camp, employees had direct access to senior leaders and people they may only have seen in their directories. Employees were afforded opportunities to ask questions in a safe space in front of people with more experience and a better handle of the sales process.

Trainers assigned homework and in-class group projects with employees from three different offices. Employees were also required to work on projects beyond the sales cycle, but of which they had personal experience.

Junior reps were given the opportunity to have senior professionals walk them through later stage conversations and help them better understand the outcomes for which they need to strive. One of the most interesting takeaways from the boot camp was how differently each office approached similar concepts and client interactions.

In the end, everyone arrived at the same outcomes using the same concepts in the organisation's playbook, which highlights the notion that every salesperson has a 'sales identity' that distinguishes them based on their unique strengths, backgrounds, and regional perspectives. However, the technical skills tend to be universal for everyone.

As sales leaders, it may be challenging to manage different sales identities and individual motivations. The boot camps taught us that exceptional sales leaders coach and amplify their team's individual strengths, reinforce the fundamentals and work through weak areas together to strengthen trust within the team and normalise asking for help.

This approach must not be confused with singling people out or highlighting weaknesses in a group environment. The shared discussions must be constructive and aim to allow the group to review their collective concerns by whiteboarding the different challenges the team may be experiencing.

The challenges across the teams participating in the boot camp, as you can imagine, were not unique. Highlighting this in a safe space helps the team realise that they may all have similar knowledge gaps.

Once the team has a shortlist of the gaps, you can then brainstorm how to overcome them by evaluating the techniques implemented by the different offices to overcome these unique issues and their level of experience.

After several days of whiteboarding, collaborating and learning, the boot camp ended with an exit project. The employees had to apply the concepts they had learned to walk through the different stages of the sales cycle and deliver a successful sales pitch using mock call scenarios and client interactions.

In Eddie's experience, the project was one of the most difficult things he had ever completed in his professional career. It forced him to go to places in his development he had not yet been and provided him with a stage to apply and mimic techniques used by 'the best in the room'. These exercises would later enable him to conduct more value-driven conversations with his clients.

The boot camp was like a capstone project to determine how successful the team would be after the boot camp. No one intended to fail, and losing face in front of the senior sales leaders was not an option.

Eddie remembers that despite the stress and anxiety of presenting to such a broad and respected audience, it was probably one of the most invaluable and formative experiences he could have received early on in his career. He was hungry and determined to make a name for himself, and his ego and confidence were through the roof. He spent the entire night ahead of the big day preparing for every possible scenario and objection the management team could throw his way.

He rehearsed the timing of his pitches, prepared talk tracks for all the different objections he reviewed in class, and committed it all to memory. The next day, he aced the project and received some of the highest marks in the class. However, this doesn't always translate to the real world, and we should bear this in mind when we begin our sales journey. The only thing that translates universally is the need to be prepared, focused on the task at hand and deliver amazing client experiences whenever possible.

Hitting the Field and Working With Real Clients

Let's fast forward a couple of months to Eddie's first AE role. He was going door-to-door, visiting between 40-60 businesses a day, trying to sell an integrated platform to the hospitality industry.

The work was gruelling and, despite all the preparation and countless hours spent rehearsing pitches and talk tracks, he had a tough go of it. It took him months before he came close to selling his first unit, and even then, the deal started to fall apart because of the leasing arrangements. He was travelling a lonely path steeped with disappointment and frustration.

His ego got its first-ever reality check; his confidence took a knock. His self-talk was all over the place, and he kept thinking to himself: "What happened to all my training?"

He talked through the different scenarios with senior colleagues, unpacked all his wins, read every sales book he could find, and nothing was working. It was unnerving, but his team gave him their unwavering support and guidance despite everything going wrong.

Luckily for him, he had some of the most amazing and talented channel partners of any struggling sales rep. While on ride-alongs with his channel partners, he had more than one person point out that the territory he was assigned to didn't meet all the criteria for finding the ideal client profile.

From this fact, coupled with the financial statements of a few local businesses that he reviewed, he was able to conclude that the territory had minimal opportunity for consistent growth and client viability.

After a few weeks and a project management and help-desk role later, he earned an opportunity to work on the inside sales team as a junior rep. The management team felt that he was an ideal candidate for the position based on his sales background, project management and help-desk experience.

As soon as he started in the role, he felt like a fish in water! He immediately began making sales within the first few days on the job, and he acquired a passion for the phone. Every day, the world was his oyster, and with a portfolio of 1,200 clients and a steady stream of inbound and outbound opportunities to work off, he was living the dream.

He sat next to two senior reps with 40 years combined experience who coached him every day. Given the small size of the team, he was like a sponge soaking up everything they were willing to teach. There was no waiting to get a question answered, and if a client needed something that was above their authorisation level, he was able to streamline requests directly to his specialists.

He also worked very closely with the field tech and help-desk teams. He gained subject matter expertise, which was invaluable to his clients. In this junior role, he was responsible for taking care of all the transactional sales opportunities enabling his senior colleagues to focus on major account growth opportunities.

For months he was handling more transactions than the office had ever had. He was then given the opportunity to work on a consumables campaign he hadn't before prioritised as a business. It was no surprise then that with the new set up in place, he ranked 3rd nationally on the consumables campaign while simultaneously achieving his individual quota.

Every day, he checked his ego at the door and then asked himself what it would take to sell more than the day before. Even though he was competitive, he understood his role and that everything he did was for the benefit of the department. The team would lunch together, joke and enjoyed every single day.

If a team member was having a bad day, there was no going through it alone. The team always knew what to say to get everyone back on track. It was at this organisation he first fell in love with sales, but it wasn't until he decided to further his growth at a different organisation that his real sales education began.

A Different Company, a New Found Culture

Though the new firm was relatively smaller in size, it offered Eddie a different opportunity to grow. After being introduced to the product and the company's sales process during a 6-week training program, where employees focused on vertical and product specific training across 14 verticals, he received general and technical sales manuals written by the CSO (Chief Sales Officer) himself.

The CSO was very passionate about sales. He co-authored a 300+ page technical sales manual with the most tenured and successful sales professionals at the organisation, which covered everything from sales etiquette, mindset, technical skills and talk tracks. For anyone who loves to read and has never had a formal sales class outside of their professional career, this manual is the holy grail of sales knowledge.

The manual is reminiscent of John Henry Patterson's sales manuals back in the 1900s, not because it is antiquated, but because it successfully covers every topic imaginable regarding sales.

Even if you've never sold anything before, this is the blueprint for selling in a B2B environment. The manual also captures all the talk tracks, questioning models, client journey guides and negotiation skills used by the top 1% of contributors.

The training was led by the most tenured employees instead of the sales leaders. In doing so, they prioritised those with the most product knowledge and application for each training topic. This training approach gave junior staff the opportunity to listen to the verbiage and distinct methods used by their colleagues daily when on the phone. If the technical sales manual is the bible in this scenario, then the employee-led training is the gospel.

He had access to vertical specialists and account managers, who worked with the largest and most recognisable companies in the world, and he was learning how they approached different relationships and client scenarios.

Though not all the training involved homework and quizzes, the employees were expected to conduct at least a handful of mock presentations of the product to their peers and senior leadership team. They also had to shadow revenue staff in both the account management and new business development roles to learn the distinct approaches to the client acquisition process.

This company offered him a completely different experience from where he'd worked before. The company culture at this firm focused heavily on peer-to-peer learning, where everyone in the business was involved in the employee's development. He distinctly remembers the CEO having flown in for a couple of days and he and his colleagues were given the opportunity to sit next to the CEO and conduct calls.

The best part, you ask? The CEO offered pointers and talk tracks from the people back at HQ. At that moment, he learned that no one at this company was too important or too significant to avoid sharing or cultivating the knowledge on the sales floor.

The majority of those working at the company had a thorough knowledge of the product, including its capabilities, and they were hyper-aware of the impact the revenue staff had on the organisation. This is culture-building at its finest.

It doesn't mean that other departments were neglected or treated unfairly; quite the opposite. The production staff were hailed as the heartbeat of the organisation, and the revenue staff supporting functions were also celebrated. We believe that what the company did best was clearly quantify the impact each department had on the bottom line while simultaneously building a sense of belonging and community between the different groups. Despite having over 500 employees, everywhere at this company felt like home.

Effective and Productive Teams: Right Size, Right Motivation

"To win is not important.
To be successful is not even important.
How to plan and prepare is crucial.
When you plan very well and prepare very well,
then success and then winning can come on the way."

Eliud Kipchoge

The preceding chapters stress the importance of a clearly defined company culture as the catalyst for a well-structured sales playbook. When combined with cross-company communication, team culture and personal involvement, you can build an amazing sales process and get your sales team members in tune with one another. A collaborative team is important for success but, to ensure that it can perform at its best, the team must be defined by a metric that isn't discussed much: its size.

The team and the company will encounter several challenges, and it will be their ability to deal with and overcome these that will define them as winners. With the right size sales team, we can sustain its longevity and carry its team culture forward.

It is possible to find a balance with a team: somewhere between being well-stocked with additional resources to close deals and sufficiently agile enough to keep expenses within a reasonable range.

Leonardo DaVinci, arguably one of the brightest minds the world has ever seen, once wisely said, "*Simplicity is the ultimate sophistication*".

63

Simplicity – like the right size – is relative depending on the complexity of the business and its maturity level. If we think about the thousands of smart and ambitious start-ups from the past few years, only a small percentage of these have survived[19] and, due to their limited size, the founders usually made up the entire sales force. Apart from funding constraints, these start-ups have survived through agility, imagination, sheer will, and the ability to adapt.

Agility and adaptability will enable you to respond timeously to the market's perception of your value proposition and marketing message; you can adapt quickly and reduce your response time to changing market conditions. A sales team that is too big for the market or a company whose maturity phase is too dense and overbearing will affect the business' speed, agility and ability to adapt and respond to market conditions.

If your sales mission takes too long – building the pipeline and closing deals – your company may flounder, leaving behind a pile of wasted opportunities and becoming a statistic of yet another failed company.

Adding the Right Pace to the Sizing Challenge

On the other hand, if we are in a mature market with a well-developed business, a limited team may equally fail because of insufficient sales muscle to engage with clients. It will be near impossible to level the playing field with the competition. Scaling up is an art, as is doing it at the right pace to allow the sales team to find the right balance.

Pacing is a well-recognised running strategy considered to be vital to completing marathons. Creating a high-performing sales team is much like the long-distance run that challenges the world's greatest endurance athletes. Just like preparing for a marathon, building a sales team requires months of preparation before hitting the market with your products or services – activities include defining target markets, rules of engagement, territories, team member characteristics, etc. And that is just the preparation phase. The real hard work starts when we leave the starting line to pace ourselves and maintain a constant effort to scale the business, as needed.

---

[19] Several studies show that approximately 90% fail. Around 20% of new businesses fail during the first two years of operating; 45% fail during the first five years; 65% fail during the first ten years.

Runners often say that a marathon is not a 26.2-mile race; it is more of a 6.2-mile race that begins at mile 20. That is the pain-point, physical pain coupled with doubt and mental anguish. At this point, the muscles start screaming, "*Why are you doing this?*". Many runners hit the "wall"[20], and only the best trained can push through.

The challenge of the distance runner isn't so different to the challenges faced by sales teams whose ability to outlast and outrun the competition determines the company's financial returns.

This marathon analogy typifies the dilemmas faced by many management teams when building up a company. Ideally, the sales manager will have a full team that can pursue every potential opportunity, but depending on its maturity phase, the company may not have the resources available to promote the ideal offering. By scaling correctly, the company can adapt its capacity to seize opportunities in line with its growth plan and, most importantly, the potential of the accessible market (market share).

Some companies, moving through the various growth stages, may face an identity crisis: too small for the big markets, requiring deeper wallets, and too big for quicker markets where it would need to be agile.

It is an eternal struggle for management to avoid employee demotivation, frustration or abandonment.

However, scaling-up is particularly important for one department directly responsible for all incoming revenue: the sales department.

Real-world Challenges When Scaling

We present two potential problems associated with improper sizing and scaling from the financial services industry. This industry segment is one of the most aggressive; competitors are ruthless, and decisions are made in mere seconds. Innovation is a huge advantage in such a fast-paced and constantly changing market. If you have a solution/product to sell that can improve the pace or move the market, your business will transition from an innovator to a market leader.

---

20 The wall occurs somewhere around the 20-mile mark and it is the point when a runner's glycogen within the muscles is depleted. This forces the runner to slow down considerably, sometimes to a walk or even stop.

This transition, though, has some side effects. A limited sales force will undergo a period of sales overload that may raise issues for the company in the short- and long-term.

A possible short-term issue is that despite the wins, the size of the sales team may prevent it from engaging fully with the accessible market.

A potential long-term issue is that, despite the wins, a commission-loaded sales rep may not be the right profile if there is a shift from *demand filling* to *demand generation*. This issue is particularly true for well-established larger businesses with an extra layer of complexity: bureaucracy.

Sales Leadership Needed: Direction and Clarity When Scaling up

When a business scales up to a global level, it must stabilise itself within the new territories. The moment will eventually arrive when a sales rep must conduct an essential activity usually despised: territory organisation.

Reorganising a territory to deepen the company's penetration – or expand its footprint – will go through the same sales representatives who overachieved their quotas in the first place. It inevitably means taking business (earning potential) away from those who built the sales machine, which may result in frustration and potential conflicts.

A short-sighted sales representative may miss the fact that a company must scale up to survive, which requires a more focused view on market potential, ultimately affecting the territory size, segmentation and assignment.

Too often, very little attention or consideration is given to portfolio reallocation. The same goes for what a specific sales rep has achieved and contributed to the team so far, which may be risky as it is liable to lead to frustration and demotivation down the road.

Failing to show due care and respect will demotivate the top-performers and possibly push them towards the exit door.

It's happened a thousand times before and is certainly not an unusual occurrence! We must, therefore, ensure that the sales team can enjoy long-lasting success by granting the salespeople an equal balance between challenge, recognition and gratitude.

A common mistake we've often observed when a territory is reallocated is underestimating the potential of an addressable market and blindly going after a more accessible area. Participants become blinded by the usual suspects: the high potential and high worth countries. The value proposition usually does not reach its full potential when this happens.

However, this is not always the case. Not focusing on high potential and high worth countries may result in a misleading territory analysis by ignoring key variables like the current penetration in a specific region or market.

A country with high potential using GDP or population metrics, for example, may be the best one to guarantee the successful expansion of a business. When splitting a territory to assign to different sales representatives, we must resolve the following questions:

1. What is the average sales cycle of our different offerings?

2. Who are the key targets?

3. In which phase is the company (expansion and pace potential)?

The answers to these questions will indicate how effectively to compose a territory, which may not necessarily reflect the most common criteria to match a geographical region. Likewise, the area of responsibility is equally important.

People must be incentivised with the right target market and accounts to get them excited about their work. If the team is assigned a low-potential market or a list of accounts with no balance between the challenges they'll face and the potential success opportunities, the team will become demotivated or even burned-out. Properly defining a territory with the right mix of challenges and earning potential ensures that teams are appropriately incentivised and empowered to close deals.

Focus and Perseverance: Two Key Success Factors

One of our co-authors likes to joke about how his sales team oversold during the 2008-2009 Credit Crunch in the so-called PIGS region (Portugal, Ireland, Greece, Spain), a period and region where it was almost impossible for anyone else to conduct business. Unbelievably, Greece was one of his hot spots. And yet, his secret was no real secret at all. He kept a close watch over his sales reps, gave them support and inspired them during the lulls, and kept them focused on the team's medium- and long-term goals. As Albert Einstein once said: *"In the middle of difficulty lies opportunity."*

In the book *"The Challenger Sale: How to Take Control of the Client Conversation"*[21], co-written by **Matthew Dixon** and **Brent Adamson**, the authors argue that salespeople who continually challenge the status quo and never take "no" for an answer – both with the client and internally – will work relentlessly to overachieve on targets and will succeed. This popular book includes several empirical studies involving the most successful companies and managers, demonstrating how to develop a challenger profile.

Execution: Clarity and Laser-Sharp Focus

Until now, we have mixed in some of the more refined ingredients like the company's maturity level, the right size team, and the value proposition. It is time to add the execution plan, the final touch to drive home our point.

Victor Antonio granted us an interview in our TWC Interview Series. He explained that for a sales team to buy into the execution plan, the following three steps should be clearly covered beforehand:

1. Clear and supportive leadership style and message;

2. Clear definition of territories and/or responsibilities;

3. Clear, stimulating and ideally dynamic compensation plan.

Some of our readers will ask, *"Seriously, is this the great revelation?"* to which we respond with a resounding YES. The three steps seem basic enough on the surface, but they provide a solid foundation upon which to build.

We have compiled a list of personal experiences that prove that these three key aspects are too often underestimated or mishandled, resulting in a sales team plagued by poor attitude, frustration and low performance.

---

21 "The Challenger Sale: How To Take Control of the Client Conversation", Matthew Dixon and Brent Adamson

We live in a time when managers must lead as *servant leaders,* a term coined by Robert K. Greenleaf[22] back in the 1970s. Conducting oneself as a servant leader is not an absolute requirement per se, but it is a worthy leadership practice. Unfortunately, we know of too many examples of managers who are content with dictating.

A manager with a servant leader mindset will push employees beyond the current norm by giving them clear instructions, correcting their mistakes and supporting their judgement calls. This manager will remain focused on helping to develop employees to be the best they can to achieve their objectives. The servant leader manager will add credence to the sales reps; standing by the sales reps and spending time with them in the sales field, as a good commander does with troops on the battlefield. Conversely, the manager who gives orders from a distant and comfortable position, without facing any real challenges, will make the sales team feel unsupported in their time of need.

We have dedicated Part II of this book to leaders and leadership.

For now, we have summarised some of the more typical examples of bad managers:

- The micromanager obsessed with CRM reporting and who doubts what you say but forces you to spend lots of time filling out forms and ticking boxes;

- The political master, who always passes on the company message without ever questioning or at least checking with the team;

- The *scalper* who drains the team's energy, ignoring team preservation and incentivisation: protecting themself in case of bad performance or maximising personal return in case of overperformance.

These examples, unfortunately, are very reflective of many sales managers today, but Victor Antonio's three steps provide a simple yet effective foundation for applying corrective measures.

---

[22] The "servant leadership" concept was created by Robert K. Greenleaf in The Servant as Leader, an essay that he first published in 1970 where he states: "The servant-leader is servant first… It begins with the natural feeling that one wants to serve, to serve first. Then conscious choice brings one to aspire to lead. That person is sharply different from one who is a leader first, perhaps because of the need to assuage an unusual power drive or to acquire material possessions…"

The Compensation/Incentive Plan: Motivator or Frustrator

Confusions, like overlapping accounts or tasks, can be avoided with clear instructions as confusion leads to frustration, and frustration leads to conflict. Confusion can be further exacerbated if there is a lack of clarity over the Compensation or Incentive Plan.

When you touch someone's money, or they think you are touching money they believe is rightfully theirs, you'd better buckle your seatbelt. Salespeople are notoriously money-driven, and many are in sales mainly for that reason. It makes sense to clarify the Compensation Plan for the salespeople, so they know how they will be paid for their work.

Victor Antonio also discussed how static compensation plans get detached from the reality of a company's operations. He suggested adding certain dynamic stimuli to encourage sales representatives to address specific needs, such as launching new product/service or improving client penetration.

There's an option to include a variable compensation plan that will be triggered upon achieving certain milestones. Rewarding the salesperson's wallet will ensure they remain committed. Sadly, the reality is that companies aren't very good at keeping high-performing salespeople motivated, either from a lack of sensitivity or a short-sighted approach.

Assigning an unreasonable quota or dramatically increasing it after a very successful year will demotivate and, eventually alienate any high-achievers. People deserve to be adequately rewarded for their work, and incentive plans should align with the sales execution plan. Companies may take this too lightly and overcomplicate this very delicate process, leading to the loss of some leading salespeople to the competition or other industries.

We propose a few straightforward reminders: keep things simple and practical, size the team according to the company's phase, and encourage servant leaders to act as guides. The next chapter focuses on the importance of acknowledging the need for multiple contributors to the sales process.

It was Henry Ford who once said: "*Coming together is a beginning, staying together is progress, and working together is success*".

The Extended Sales Team: Sales Execution Across the Company

"Alone we can do so little; together we can do so much."

Helen Keller

Sales processes will vary greatly from one organisation to the next. With so many moving parts (people, systems, rules, incentives, client base), the sales world is rife with vastly diverging theories, methods and opinions.

Everyone believes they have the best methodology and tools, best practice, so to speak, to overcome sales challenges and are best-placed to achieve their numbers. The hard reality is that not every sales team does have this so-called "best practice". However, and despite the major differences in sales processes, there are a select few who have truly mastered the art and science of sales.

Amazing sales results are being produced daily, but let's be honest; there have not been any ground-breaking sales discoveries in recent years, leading to revolutionary new processes. Sales teams basically have two options: they can either take a casual approach and meekly hit their numbers or break through their quotas by simply adding a four-letter word to their sales arsenal: HELP.

The highest performing sales organisations have learned that success reveals a common theme, a formula, if you will, that permeates through the team from top to bottom. With so many variables at their disposal, they develop methods to maximise the help of each participant. In this context, we use the term 'participant' interchangeably to refer to individuals or other departments. The individuals may not necessarily be employees on the company's payroll; they may be external consultants or members of external teams. Through underlying strategies and control systems, the highest performing

71

teams figured out how to harness the best talents and abilities of participants–no manipulation or exploitation permitted here, of course.

Sales is not about a group of salespeople looking to answer the burning question of '*How can we sell this product on our own?*'. If they were to try this on their own, their level of effort would greatly outweigh the results. For any sales team to have any chance of selling anything, it must be supported by connected players who provide extremely valuable services outside of the realm and expertise of the salespeople. External teams like marketing, professional services and R&D are all missing puzzle pieces that lend their expertise directly – from pre-sales and sales to closing and after service – to close the loop on the sales cycle. Sadly, these outlying players – who are all valuable contributors in their own right – tend to be forgotten.

The Soccer Team Analogy: Strikers Don't Score Alone

In Chapter 2, we used the analogy of the football team (soccer for our North American readers) for our organisation. The eleven players on the team have one common objective. Just one: Put the ball in the back of the opposition's net. That's it. It's that simple, right? But is it really?

Let's think about this for a minute. The players also need to prevent the other team from doing the same thing, and they must be managed to ensure they follow the coach's strategy and tactics. The right players must be in the right positions, and we can only hope that they have enough stamina to carry them through 90 minutes of match-time. Our coaching staff must run vulnerability studies (physical, mental, tendencies) on the opposing players and coaching staff to psych them out.

What, at first, appeared to be a very simple plan of '*Let's score more goals than those guys!*' has become a deep and intense study of relationships, planning and teamwork. Strikers are often the highest-paid players on the team, drawing attention and fame away from the rest of the team, which can lead to distractions on and off the field. From a management perspective, this is where the team's leaders really earn their salaries.

Football games are low scoring affairs, and one mistake on the field can cost the team their fortune. Unless every actor plays their part with precision in this theatre of sports – it is called The Beautiful Game for a reason – and does so in perfect synchrony with their teammates, success and glory will always elude them.

There may be some sporadic wins here and there, but a team that does not work together as a collaborative unit can never seriously contend for any championship title. Every single player starts the season with one primary objective: To win the Championship. But, by week 8, we already have an idea of who the serious contenders are. These higher ranking teams in the league are planning, preparing, and executing at a higher level than the rest, and one of them will already have grabbed the lead as early as week 1.

Getting back to our sales discussion, all sales representatives – even the most self-serving ones – know that if the company they work for isn't successful in its own right, then the chances of them meeting their sales quota may only exist in their dreams.

Teams of Teams are the True Multipliers in Organisations

Success can only be achieved if we empower the different teams involved to work together to jump-start cooperation across the board.

The strikers – aka salespeople – must collaborate with the rest of the teams in the organisation: those teams that tend to be forgotten like admin and finance, legal, HR, support, operations and IT, R&D, professional services, pre-sales and marketing. This long list of participants must all contribute to the sales process. They must be permitted to do so, for the betterment of the entire organisation, in accordance with the value they bring to the sales process.

Too often, especially in the latter stages of the sales process, salespeople may feel like they are carrying the burden of responsibility to close deals. They may also believe, as a result, that they deserve the praise and credit when they succeed.

If they were to look beyond their egos and acknowledge the support staff who helped remove the 'perceived' pressure from their sales shoulders, they would realise that nothing could be further from the truth. Do you recognise any of your sales colleagues in this scenario who try to emulate football strikers by looking for fame and glory?

There is no need to despair; the world is not filled with heartless salespeople who rely only on their instinct and ego. Top sales performers – like the very best football strikers – actually recognise and acknowledge the importance of the surrounding teams and honestly attribute their success to them.

Adam Grant's book *"Give and Take"* explains that each team member makes a unique contribution in the quest for success, and we should always remember and be grateful for that.

Everyone makes their mark in one way or another. Closing a sale is only possible when there is a great product to be sold, but the support teams need to be ever-present to ensure that existing clients remain precisely where they are, close by and always satisfied.

In Chapter 2, we touched on the idea of the 'internal client', defined as colleagues who deserve the same attention, care and respect we typically reserve for our clients. In this section, we explore why it is beneficial to take care of our internal clients.

Whenever a sales representative begins work on a new opportunity, they may quickly get carried away by the enthusiasm of potential commissions and forget to follow the strategy and process to win the deal.

Executing on the process must include contributors from outside the sales team, whose invaluable support has been confirmed by our TWC interviewees and the 150+ years of collective experience of the TWC co-authors.

Contributions from contributors may surely be helpful, but we must always be mindful of the number of participants and limit these to a manageable number. The probability of success is inversely proportional to the number of colleagues we involve. Thus, the more people involved, the more they feel engaged, and the level of engagement will be greater than just responding to a simple request for help on a specific task. More participants mean more opinions and viewpoints, which can become overwhelming if not managed well. It is important to find the happy medium with how many people you invite to help resolve sales-related issues.

An exercise that lends itself well to exploring cross-team assistance is the sales pitch simulation with 'internal clients'. Getting help from colleagues in other departments, such as qualified R&D or support staff, is helpful if they challenge you on a dry run before you actually present to the client. These colleagues can use their expertise to question you and spot your weaknesses, so you can sharpen your pitch and get ready for any objections ahead of time and before the real pitch.

This type of mutual exchange opens the door to more conversations to better understand the interconnectivity between different departments. By considering all perspectives, the different departments will be more engaged when they are next asked for assistance; a point touched on by our interviewee, Cesar Cernuda.

It is crucial that everyone on the team feels a sense of belonging with these inclusive actions. When people feel like they belong, they willfully share their knowledge, ideas, objections, energy, and effort beyond what you may even have asked.

This exercise is also valid when conducting a post mortem on an opportunity, regardless of whether the deal was won or lost. It affords everyone involved the opportunity to understand thoroughly what was and wasn't done well.

This critical exercise relies on two vital factors:

- That egos get checked at the door: The facts may be hard to accept if a deal was lost because of our shortcomings. We have to face reality whether we like it or not. The brutal and honest truth is the only way to learn from our mistakes and try to better ourselves, but we tend to sugar-coat our own reality to let ourselves off the hook and not be 'too hard on ourselves'. Our interviewee Victor Antonio said, '*Release the ego*' to empower and accelerate your personal growth. We say, '*Let go of your ego; you will do your team one huge favour*'.

- That people get involved: Involve all players who had a direct or indirect role in the sales execution. Oftentimes, management disregards the importance of sharing results with colleagues at the sub-management level unless, of course, the blame train has come to town and the conductor is handing out tickets. How can a team expect to improve if we don't analyse what could or should have been done better?

This second point highlights a problem that happens far too often concerning success and reward management. There have been improvements in recent years, but we are still far from recognising and rewarding the hard work of the different teams and key contributors to completed sales.

Sales professionals may appear to be a self-serving group to the outside world, always shouting '*Commissions! Commissions! Commissions!*' from the rooftops. This may sound unbelievable to some, but successful salespeople actually care about the support staff and recognise their impact on the numbers.

Hitting or surpassing quotas wouldn't happen unless the salesperson is adequately supported. The best salespeople know this and aren't shy to acknowledge it. Our final chapter sets out some suggestions on facilitating and improving communication and recognition across the company.

When a sales manager embraces the compelling spirit of the 'WE' and drives the team to think likewise, an infectiously positive team is born.

This team is primed to take charge and assume a proactive role; it will likely take on a life of its own with the ultimate goal of overachieving on sales quotas. If you're a sales manager and you've been underachieving, take notice: start by embracing the power of 'WE' and allow your team to spread its wings.

Managers take on a dual role; they are coaches too. Our TWC interviewees agree that when managers fail to put the right amount of time and effort into coaching their members, teams are ill-prepared to attain any level of greatness whatsoever. Coaching is not a one-off exercise but a lengthy and consistent process.

A well-prepared manager leads by example and puts in the extra effort to show members how things are done. It is a demanding activity and, sadly, many managers don't stay the course and revert to a default ward-mode role. This defensive and sedentary action eventually leads to disappointing numbers and possible terminations.

If you're experiencing difficulty with managing your own team, please keep reading. We offer many valuable solutions in Part II, where we explore the good, the bad and the ugly sides of coaching, including the effort and the willingness to coach.

Communication and Collaboration Between Teams

Clear Communication Within the Sales Team is a must!

Clear and effective communication is an essential tool for sales teams, but when messages are not passed along through the proper channels, communication may feel uncoordinated (not sent correctly) and non-responsive (not received). As children, we played the game of Telephone. The true message always got lost along the way, which made for some funny childhood memories. This is fine as a child's game but is inexcusable for sophisticated corporations to allow this to persist within different levels of the personnel structure.

You may be reading this and recognise it as a regular occurrence within your company or department. If so, you may have become accustomed to being left out: *"Hmm, I may have missed something last week that is buzzing around the office this week"*. When this happens – which is inexcusable with all the communication tools we have at hand – it is frustrating to know that you have been left out of conversations or strategic discussions, even if it was not intentional.

Effective communication does not discriminate between companies based on size or scope as similar recurring themes can be found across start-ups, SMEs and large corporations.

Regardless of the size, we believe there is a communication hierarchy within the different levels of any organisation. To ensure every employee has access to a unified message, we found the following 7 Essential Hierarchies that lead to exceptional communication:

1. Communication between individual contributors

2. Communication between individual contributors and their managers

3. Communication between individual contributors and their senior management team

4. Communication between managers and senior management

5. Communication between sales engineers (support) and individual contributors

6. Communication between sales engineers (support) and the sales leadership team

7. Collective communication.

1. Communication Between Individual Contributors

Cast your mind back to the sales playbook examples we used earlier. We explored the impact of *Selling with stories* and the collective *Sales story* of your team, as told by individual contributors.

In addition to spending time getting to know each other, we encourage individual contributors to reach out to colleagues to share best practices within their industry too.

The responsibility of disseminating and imparting best practices should not rest solely on the shoulders of the sales leaders. All colleagues can adopt a more collaborative approach by freely sharing knowledge amongst themselves like call scripts or effective client dialogues. We can also use these opportunities to share wins and review the lessons learnt from any lost opportunities. There is more to be gained when viewing an experience (a deal) as a collective rather than through the narrow lens of our individual perspectives, as self-limiting beliefs are what may hold us back from greatness.

"If you want to go fast, go alone. If you want to go far, go together."

-African Proverb[23]

---

[23] Passiton.com

As individual contributors ourselves, we have found that by taking complete ownership of our learning, we quickly improved in our respective roles. Your colleagues on the front line are the best teachers: managing client relationships, new client acquisitions, and client escalation calls. With a common link to a client's contact points, why not share them constantly and openly with one another? If a secret sauce does exist, this is your opportunity to create it together.

We encourage you to keep several lines of communication open with your peers and, more specifically, with those colleagues dealing with client retention and business development to ensure you capture as many perspectives as you can on how to best position your solutions.

2. Communication Between Individual Contributors and Their Managers

Every sales leader has a different approach to managing sales reps. Some are extremely hands-on, others are extremely hands-off, and the rest find a balance somewhere in between. Regardless of your individual management style, we invite you to prioritise open and consistent lines of communication with your reps.

In addition to your annual reviews and mid-year check-ins, we encourage sales leaders to spend time learning about their reps' accounts, including those not yet forecasted. Whether you have junior sales reps or tenured sales professionals, no one is perfect, and things can still get lost in translation. Regularly reviewing how your team handles your accounts is a great way of truly understanding what your pipeline looks like and where the gaps are in the process.

Getting to know your reps and their lives outside of work is equally, if not more, important. If you don't know anything about your reps' lives outside of work, how can you possibly expect to understand what their personal motivators are and what gets them out of bed in the morning?

As sales leaders, we recommend coaching your reps in the areas where you see opportunities for growth. We firmly believe you can build more synergy and trust with your reps if the relationship is built on professional development and growth. We encourage individual contributors to take ownership of their careers, meet with their managers, and communicate their goals, individual missions, and visions of success.

We acknowledge that for a sales rep, this takes vulnerability and a high level of trust. But this can be practised and learned through repetition and constant communication with their sales leaders. There is no rule of thumb or magic number for these meetings. Much like aiming for sales targets, discussions between individual contributors and sales leaders should be focused on results and common objectives for mutual growth on either side. The key is to simply start having these meetings and adjust them along the way.

This method of learning from people in the same role or job is also known as "Peer Learning"[24] and has been described as an effective learning method for university students.

3. Communication Between Individual Contributors and Their Senior Management Team

Executive presence comes from experience, coaching and time to develop, so why not start within your organisation?

We encourage senior leadership to act as mentors and develop their reps, providing ample opportunities to learn what executive identity is. We understand that time is a precious commodity and that the email inbox is its worst enemy, so we cannot realistically expect to set aside countless hours per week for every single rep. We do, however, encourage some level of frequency for 1-on-1 discussions with individual contributors and group discussions.

These discussions are a chance for you to share your own mission and vision for the business and connect with your sales reps in a meaningful way. For many years, we have heard recurring complaints from individual contributors that senior leadership teams are out of touch with what is happening in the marketplace and what their clients are saying.

This is an opportunity to improve! Another message to senior sales leaders: Go ahead and ask questions, discover your team's challenges and find out what your clients are saying about your solutions. It's like a mini executive MBA in real-time, focusing on what is currently working in your company and what is holding you back. The hierarchy of communication is essential; it helps to shape the direction of

---

[24] What is Peer Learning and Why is it Important? https://tomprof.stanford.edu/posting/418

the business, keeps senior leadership informed about the state of affairs, and keeps individual contributors informed of their executive's expectations.

4. Communication Between Managers and Senior Management

We cover "Leadership and Leader" in Part II of this book, where we present communication as one of the 11 Key Traits of Great Leaders, so we will not delve into it too much here.

Great sales teams are either built or destroyed by the capabilities of their leadership. **Mike Weinberg** discussed this quite convincingly in his book "*Sales Management. Simplified*". This book has become the highest-ranking and best-selling pure sales management book on the market, and for good reason.

Mike recently launched his podcast, "*Sales Management. Simplified.*"[25] which began with an inaugural episode entitled "*Sales Leaders, You are the Key*". In this episode, he talks about the "multiplier effect" of sales managers and their power to increase or decrease a team's performance exponentially. Mike felt that the topic was important enough to create a podcast and put a voice to his book in a bid to help organisations fix their sales culture issues.

Poor communication between different levels of sales management often results in disengaged sales leadership, a non-existent sales culture and lagging sales performance. Accountability is a vital aspect of successful teamwork. It is a means of holding everyone – from the CEO down to the front-line sales managers – accountable through a simple system that encourages parties to engage in the process. Effective communication starts with planning calls, implementing systems and reporting on results. Accountability is the principle of showing your numbers to the group and explaining how you propose to meet them. There may be up to four or five levels of formal communications to plan for and execute on accountability.

Communication starts from the very top: the CEO holds monthly C-Level meetings in which he and the CFO ask the Global VP of Sales – also called the Chief Revenue Officer (CRO) – four basic questions:

---

25 Link to Mike Weinberg's Podcast- Inaugural episode: https://mikeweinberg.com/episode1/

1. How is your plan moving along, and what will you close this quarter?

2. What do you have in the pipeline to make your FY numbers?

3. How are gross margins doing on the different revenue streams?

4. What are the key challenges you have identified that could affect your expected numbers, and what are you doing to mitigate them?

The conversations are typically brief and include reviewing a report where the global regions are displayed, and the aggregated key indicators are shared. Ideally, you should immediately be able to spot the regions at, above or below the plan for closed deals and weighted pipeline[26]. If all appears to be on track, the CRO may be asked to provide a progress report on the top deals for the year.

If all does not appear to be on track, the CEO may ask for more information about the underperforming regions to identify the problem and get feedback from the CRO regarding solutions. The CRO will be expected to have some straight answers. Ideally, this type of accountability call will cascade down to front-line sales managers; however, it won't always make it that far as often, sales managers disappoint by not being prepared with enough discipline or rigour.

When everyone is well prepared, these accountability calls are an essential part of a healthy sales culture. It provides everyone with the opportunity to discuss the most important aspect of sales: closed deals and the pipeline. The power of healthy communication is also demonstrated through 1-to-1 coaching and mentoring calls across the different levels of management. Management/leadership team calls should all be planned and prepared with the same amount of discipline as forecast and accountability meetings mentioned before.

One of the problems with leadership team calls is that they often consist of tedious PowerPoint displays, with only a few minutes allowed at the end for Q&A, acting more as a conduit for the one-way flow of information rather than encouraging critical thinking or open discussions.

---

[26] The weighted pipeline uses factors to reflect probabilities for closing deals. There are usually four levels: Pipeline = 10-20%, Upside = 40-50%, Commit = 80-90%, Closed = 100%. Used to forecast revenue for the fiscal year.

Many will lose interest, and very few participants will ever speak up. These are lost opportunities for collaborative exchanges between participants.

A message for all sales managers, regardless of your rank: Make sure you get the most out of your meetings and encourage healthy dialogue. Use open, direct and honest communication as one of the key tools to nurture a strong sales culture in your team.

5. Communication Between Sales Engineers (Support) and Individual Contributors

The collaborators, known as the sales engineers, product specialists, and subject matter experts, are the ace up the sleeves of individual contributors.

These relationships with colleagues from other departments must be invested in and recognised. These colleagues can assist with their expertise and are the ones who fill in the knowledge gaps. We encourage you to spend time with them, learning about their lives outside of work, about their areas of expertise and what makes them so great at their job.

These collaborators may not be selling in the same capacity as you are, but they are as equipped and trusted by your senior management team to fulfil their role. We make the same recommendation to sales operations professionals to set clear expectations for the expertise by helping the sales reps to understand the scope of the expertise to avoid them overselling your capabilities. This, in turn, enables the team to offer the client clearer deliverables.

6. Communication Between Sales Engineers (Support) and the Sales Leadership Team

Sales support staff, also called pre-sales engineers or solution engineers, are usually part of the core sales team. Any sales manager in charge of a group of Account Executives (AEs) should encourage them to run weekly account team meetings to review the previous week's achievements and challenges and key planned activities for the current week.

To create and advance sales opportunities, good sales managers must run short weekly – ideally Monday morning–activation calls where all account teams participate, including the sales support staff. These weekly calls assemble the team to keep it well informed of all the sales actions of all the account teams. These calls should trigger cross-account team collaborations and mutual support on deals with similar challenges, thereby driving up the levels of trust.

Additionally, there should be quarterly account planning meetings in preparation for the Quarterly Business Review meetings with key clients. The AE running these meetings should invite the sales manager and the whole account team, thereby creating a forum for roundtable discussions between sales support people and all the other team members.

There is an additional indirect layer of communication that takes place between sales managers and sales support managers. They hold monthly meetings to discuss and review their interconnecting teams.

Finally, every good front-line sales manager hosts monthly and quarterly sales team meetings for all sales team members. The quarterly meetings are an opportunity to go through the numbers and discuss how plans are being executed. The monthly meetings can be more specific to the operations; the agenda can introduce success cases or training relevant to the entire team.

A Practical Example of a Well-Prepared Monthly Sales Team Meeting

Goals:

- Share the challenges, failures, successes and best practices across cross-functional sales teams.

- Aim for value creation and positive client outcomes.

- Drive profitable growth for our company and maximise compensation for the team and each team member.

We consider this a triple win: Client - Company - Team/Team members.

Duration: 1.5 hours with a 10-minute break after 40 minutes.

The people involved in cross-functional sales teams:

1. Account Executives

2. Solution engineers/sales support people

3. Business consultants

4. Deal desk/pricing people

5. Client after-sales partners

6. Client technical support partners

7. Engagement managers for consulting

8. Finance: optional

9. Legal: optional

10. Marketing: optional

11. Management: optional

12. External partners: on-demand

13. Clients: on-demand.

Agenda: To be defined by the team, in conjunction with the sales manager, one week in advance of each monthly call.

Agenda Draft:

    i. **Welcome and state of business**: FY Revenue and FY Pipeline versus FY Plan to date (3 min–Sales manager);

    ii. **Corporate update**: Strategy/Go-To-Market Organisational changes/Events (2 min–Sales manager);

    iii. TBD 1: Client success case/challenge (20 min);

    iv. TBD 2: Key problem to solve – Team brainstorming and discussion (20 min);

    v. **Q&A** (20 min);

    vi. Agreed actions/decisions (What) and owners (Who) until next meeting (Deadline).

7. Collective Communication

If we consider a team a unit on its own, then collective team meetings must enable and provide the framework for collective team communication.

The key features of an effective team meeting are:

- Set a clear objective and goal for the meeting;

- Provide an agenda and clear timeframes;

- Assure active participation and contributions from all invited attendees through proper assignment of preparatory work;

- Provide a slot on the agenda, so everyone has an opportunity to contribute actively;

- Always make provision for closing Q&A so team members can voice their concerns and doubts;

- Assign someone to take the meeting minutes;

- Share the meeting minutes with all participants on a shared folder;

- Record the meeting, if possible, so those who couldn't attend can watch the recording later, catch up, and share it on their team folder.

Group meetings may be daunting for some, given how large and public the forum can be. However, we believe this to be dependant on the type of content being shared and what the group meetings aim to achieve. In our collective experience, we have seen group meetings work exceptionally well when they provide context, clarity, direction, and praise. These forums should aim to be inclusive, to have your individual contributors, sales leaders, sales support, and anyone else involved in the sales process. This approach will ensure that everyone receives content and has room to ask questions. Due diligence should be done in advance of these meetings to identify your team's biggest wins, highlight the contributors, and show appreciation and give praise in a timely, honest, and equitable manner.

"Talent wins games, but teamwork and intelligence win championships."

Michael Jordan

... And Across all the Company

Open and transparent communication is pertinent across the sales team and the rest of the company. This section focuses on specific tips and tools to help you communicate effectively so your colleagues can succeed at their jobs.

In Chapter 3, you will recall, we recommended the 3rd step of "Rule of Engagements and Processes" as fundamental for cooperation across the different teams. We also considered the 4th step, "Clear and Flawless Communication", one of the pillars of a company.

These two steps are crucial pillars to ensure that everyone performs their duties to the best of their abilities, but the most crucial factor (the magic ingredient) is the human element. The human element is unpredictable and depends on so many variables that, if not handled appropriately – consider the HR departments and their daily issues – the end result may be disastrous for employee engagement and morale.

However, if you can embrace and stimulate the human element in just the right way, it has the potential to be the single most positive differentiator to a company's performance. Engagement, trust, passion and motivation are key drivers that will push the different team members toward proactive engagement with each other.

Our TWC interviewee, **Ms Marta Martinez**, reminded us that an overachiever gets to that level by singularly aspiring to be the best and relentlessly working towards that. Similarly, we should inspire and enable all teams to fully trust each other. How do we achieve this, you ask? By removing the no. 1 enemy of trust: the ego!

If we abandon our egos and accept that we are human and all prone to doubts and weaknesses, we immediately diffuse ourselves as potential threats to others. From there, we can activate a virtuous circle of *givers* willing to help us with problems we are facing, as explained in **Adam Grant's** book "*Give and Take*".

You may think that removing ego may affect a salesperson's performance as a sales rep's life seems to be rather binary: glory and money if successful, or infamy and possible termination if they fail. This may be true for some sales reps. We are not here to judge; some people are just wired that way; they need their ego to be functional. From their perspective, they need that personality trait to stay ahead of others and dominate their space. "*You are as good as your last quarter*" is a pretty common saying, so those who glorify their egos believe that unless they stay true to it, they will diminish their returns.

We don't believe that there is a need to rely heavily on the ego to succeed; we can all succeed by engaging our self-confidence positively and collaboratively and avoiding harming people who may get in our way. Ego will only get you across the street; self-confidence will get you around the world.

Salespeople, like football strikers, often carry the honour – and the burden – of responsibility to transform the hard work of the rest of the team into a goal. They also have the ability – and the responsibility – to activate this virtuous circle along the different phases of the sales cycle. The most obvious phase is once a deal is done. We could probably fill another book just with the comments of frustrated colleagues from different departments who have ever felt ignored by the *ungrateful* salesperson who simply forgot to acknowledge or show gratitude for the hard work done by his peers.

After closing a lucrative deal, how many of you have approached the different teams and colleagues to express gratitude and openly acknowledge their contributions? Show of hands, anyone? Let's be honest; we all know we can do better. Gratitude and appreciation cost us nothing to give; all it requires is some time and sincerity. But, for the person who has contributed to your success, you will have made their day.

Sales managers may also be guilty of being insensitive towards salespeople or colleagues, wrongfully dismissing their need for a show of appreciation, perhaps under the guise of attending to a more pressing matter. *"Hey, good job. I'm busy right now; let's talk later"*. The chances are very high that the manager won't return later to talk or give any other sincere message.

But, if we were to place ourselves firmly in the shoes of the non-salesperson, we could appreciate the power of giving/receiving gratitude and paying respect to people, whether they are expecting it or not. Those people to whom you show your appreciation – the contributors who helped you succeed – will recognise your sincerity and, you can bet your bottom dollar; they will be the same people who come to your rescue when you need their help next time around.

When it comes to closing deals, we tend to put on the blinkers and focus solely on ourselves, rarely asking what our colleagues may need to be able to support us. We can start by asking the clients what they need – an interview would serve well here– and submit a list to our colleagues for a quick assessment and input. This exercise serves a dual purpose:

- It empowers us to better serve the client by proactively challenging their wants and needs; and

- It gives our colleagues, the subject matter experts, the opportunity to share their professional opinions or assessments on issues that need to be resolved.

We will need to step out of our comfort zone to understand what information our colleagues need–it's OK to admit when we don't understand something–and learn from their perspective. The subject matter experts will thank you; their talents and passions are appreciated, praised and rewarded. This is the jab/right-cross/uppercut combination: your colleagues are engaged, your client reaps the benefits, and you come out as a capable professional.

This approach holds true whether deals are won or lost. How many times have we involved the extended teams in post-mortem debrief sessions? Likely, this has never been done, so if the sales engine has broken down, we should really check the oil level to determine what went wrong by engaging everyone. The message is quite clear, get your supporting colleagues involved at all times!

A discussion on communication wouldn't be complete without talking about Client Relationship Management Systems (CRM)'s[27] and their impact on messaging within a company.

A company's compensation plan is a massive differentiator within the sales framework, and a CRM System is the right tool to monitor this. You're probably reading this and thinking, "*Damn CRM! My manager wants me to fill in thousands of fields!*".

For data-driven managers who love them, CRM's generate enough reports to sink a battleship. For sales reps, the overwhelming amount of data may lead to additional requests from the manager for irrelevant and hard-to-find information. There is no doubting the fundamental need for a reliable and dynamic tool to work the funnel and provide visibility to management. Unfortunately, we often notice some *distortions of reality* that frustrate sales representatives when faced with an extra load of bureaucratic and routine work. It takes time away from prospecting and working on deals, and especially valuable face time that could be better spent with clients.

This additional reporting may also lead to closer scrutiny of the sales reps and their results which may have two detrimental consequences: the sales rep interprets this as a lack of trust from management, and being micromanaged will reduce their energy and creativity. However, managers shouldn't apologise for wanting additional reporting; it is their job to have a clear overview of the numbers, including the pipeline status. CRM tools are ideal for managing and organising this information. Managers must also recognise the limitations of these tools and make an effort to stimulate communication and visibility across the different teams and roles and not just rely on the data produced by the CRM tools.

---

[27] Customer Relationship Management Systems store client and prospect contact information, identify sales opportunities, record service issues, and manage marketing campaigns, all in one central location and keep track of the Sales funnel progress along the different established steps.

We've been discussing how to make people feel like they are part of a team. Although communication plays a significant role, compensating people fairly across the company is just as powerful a tool: The Incentive or Bonus Plan. Sales departments have their compensation plans, so why not reward the hard-working men and women from the support teams too? Managers will probably stand up and yell, *"Heresy! Who does that?"* yet it can be done in a way that aligns with the sales compensation plan. Why not?

If incentives and rewards aren't shared across the company, how can we expect the different teams to be equally incentivised to perform? Sales is a team effort and should be rewarded as such. Hey, we believe it so much; we've made it the title of our book!

Key Takeaways

The foundation for a strong and high performing sales teams:

1. There is no success in "I"; only "WE" can succeed.

2. Clearly articulated and shared values, vision and mission.

3. A strong culture of mutual trust has to be built, nurtured, widely accepted, and upheld by all employees from senior management down to individual contributors.

4. Check on team culture regularly while reinforcing it for clarity as a team exercise, not as an isolated management decision.

5. Honest, clear, timely and consistent communication.

6. Annihilate all egos – No "prima donnas" allowed.

7. Under the "We" focused paradigm, everyone on the sales team contributes to the sales process "as a team".

8. Your vision should represent the inspirational picture of what your team's future can hold.

9. Exceptional sales leaders will coach and amplify their team's individual strengths and work past their limitations.

Part II

Leadership and Leader

Malcolm

This book is written for the sales community; it shares a positive message to inspire our readers to go out there and better themselves. The sales profession is a wonderful career for anyone to pursue and, like any other profession, it has its fair share of good and bad days. We must learn to celebrate our wins during the good times and appreciate the value we bring to the world; otherwise, when defeat rears its ugly head, it may stay with us for a very long time.

There are moments in our lives that come about suddenly, leaving emotional scars that have us asking, "*Why me?*" or "*What have I done to deserve this?*". We can't control everything that happens to us, but we can certainly decide how we react to the negative by avoiding the victim mentality. Certain situations are simply out of our control but, through our responses and actions, we can decide to move on from these dire situations; it's what we make of it that determines how we will come out of it.

It is not our intention to start Part II on a negative tone; we merely wish to highlight the reality of today's business environment with an actual case study of someone who did everything right yet still fell foul of a great injustice. Our hero is Malcolm, and this is his story:

Back in 2011, Malcolm faced one of the biggest leadership challenges of his career. Malcolm was based in Paris, where he was a highly successful sales director in a global company focusing on EMEA (Europe, Middle East, Africa). He had just been awarded '*Sales Director of the Year 2010*' at the organisation's Presidents Club retreat in the Bahamas. He had consistently surpassed his quota over the last 14 quarters (3.5 years), and his team had recently landed the biggest deal in the organisation's 20-year history. The numbers for FY2010 were phenomenal and were celebrated company-wide.

Malcolm's country manager, Robert, was immediately promoted to regional sales VP, and everyone on the sales team expected Malcolm to take over Robert's role. However, to everyone's surprise, Robert hired Frank instead, an external candidate.

In his first weeks as the new country manager and Malcolm's new boss, Frank told Malcolm that he didn't see Malcolm as the right person for the sales director role and that he would soon be 'offered' an alternative position as an individual contributor. In other words, the plan was to remove Malcolm from his sales director role and relegate him to an account executive role. Three weeks on the job, and the new country manager was already planning to get rid of the current Sales Director of the Year! Malcolm couldn't believe what he was hearing and rejected this offer. But things only got worse from here.

Frank was insulted by Malcolm's refusal to move into an account executive role. Like a scene out of **Machiavelli's** "*The Prince*", Frank began harassing Malcolm using the 'Divide and Conquer' tactic.

One by one, accounts and account executives were removed from Malcolm's team, but he was still expected to meet and deliver the same quota as before, even with this reduced team. Frank's expectations of 'do more with less' had reached untenable levels. It is thought that Frank was trying to show that Malcolm didn't have what it takes to hit his targets, so who could argue with removing him permanently?

Against all odds, Frank's short-sighted plan backfired as Malcolm, with his reduced team, was still able to beat the odds and deliver on his targets. Despite still achieving his targets over the next few quarters, though, Frank consistently downplayed Malcolm's efforts in his performance reviews, stating: 'Below expectations.' Frank supported his assessments with statements like "*He only made his number because of XYZ deal*" or "*He was lucky because a big deal just fell from the sky.*"

Frank, through deception, was strategically able to turn management and the HR function in his favour. Malcolm's irritation and frustration grew; despite his exceptional performance and beating the odds by consistently achieving his targets, he got no credit whatsoever for his dedication and effort. Malcolm knew he needed to resolve this; his reputation and professionalism were on the line, and he was being cheated out of commissions that were rightfully his. Malcolm turned to his former boss Robert for answers, but all he got was an abrupt "*The numbers are not everything*" response. Malcolm had hoped for support, and all he got was Robert's refusal to get involved.

Over the next year, Malcolm performed to such high levels that Frank couldn't justify firing him and so had to keep him on. At Malcolm's behest, Peter (the Head of HR for EMEA) was flown in from London to resolve the matter and try to settle things down. Malcolm had nowhere else to turn, so he took his chances and bluntly asked Peter, *"Why is Frank doing this? What have I done wrong?"* Peter responded: *"Look at it as if there was a new trainer for the team, and this trainer doesn't like a certain player."* Malcolm responded: *"Well, I can understand that, but then you should just fire me and pay me what you owe me. You also would not ask me to change my role as a trainer to be a player on the bench."*

At this point, the company was falling behind in paying Malcolm his rightful commissions. To drive Malcolm out, management and the HR function continued to harass and undermine him in front of his colleagues.

If Malcolm left the company voluntarily, the organisation wouldn't have to pay him what he was owed; Frank had calculated and schemed his plan to great effect with lies and misleading information.

Welcome to the management and leadership reality of multinational organisations!

After two months of tough negotiations, and with the stress of it all taking a toll on his family, Malcolm finally reached an agreement with the organisation and left. The experience taught him a valuable leadership lesson:

> *Even if you've done everything right, there might still be someone in the organisation who thinks that you didn't, and if this person has power over you, you are better off going somewhere else.*

Despite all the stress and anxiety, Malcolm continued to conduct himself professionally until the very end of his service, including preparing his replacement Mike for the role. At the end of his time, Malcolm wished Mike luck in his new role before moving on to the next chapter of his career.

Malcolm later discovered that Robert, Frank, and Mike had previously worked together at another company under Robert's leadership. Malcolm finally understood Robert's game of replacing him with people he knew would never be a threat to his own career.

They would be obedient and loyal, blindly doing what he asked of them. This is not an isolated incident but endemic when organisations put anti-leaders in charge, driving out the best talents who then leave to flourish elsewhere. This is precisely what Malcolm did. Today, he is a successful vice president of sales at another global software company leading a high-performance sales team and enjoying his new management's full support.

As for Robert, Frank, and Mike, they all eventually left their positions and no longer work for the same organisation.

Lessons Learnt:

1. Don't stay in a place where they don't want you.

2. Read your management's intentions early: Keep your eyes and ears open.

3. Hope is never a good strategy: If bad things happen and you can't do anything about it, act swiftly and move on.

4. In matters of fashion, swim with the current. In matters of principles, stand like a rock.

5. No matter what happens, always stay true to your values and be a professional until the very last day. This is how you will be remembered, and it will help you to stay strong and positive.

Welcome to Part II, where we get into more detailed discussions about Leadership and Leaders.

As the Leader Goes, so Goes the Team: Importance of Great Leadership

Sales executives occupying leadership positions know this cold hard truth: If you can't lead yourself, you can't lead others.

As covered brilliantly by **Stephen R. Covey** in his masterpiece, "*The 7 Habits of Highly Effective People*", true leaders have learned that the ability to control and manage oneself is the road to mastery. Mr Covey separates the 7 Habits into two categories: adopting the primary habits to achieve the "**Private Victory**" and then following up with the second set of habits to achieve the "**Public Victory**." Only people who have first achieved "Private Victory" can aspire to achieve "Public Victory." To better familiarise yourself with these concepts, we highly recommend this valuable book, also available on audio at Audible.com, narrated by Mr Covey himself. The concepts of the 7 Habits, and the two victories, are explained in full detail for the reader/listener.

The "**Private Victory**" – the victory as an individual – implies the mastery of the first three habits:

Habit 1: Be Proactive – We are all accountable for everything we do. By assuming responsibility for our decisions and actions, we should not permit ourselves to make excuses or blame others such as colleagues or partners, entities such as our companies or the government, or events such as the economy or misfortune.

Remember: Take full responsibility for your actions. Always.

Habit 2: Begin with the End in Mind – The only way to know where we are headed is to set goals for ourselves and align the compass for the direction. It is crucial to know where we want to go before we can take that first step.

Habit 3: Put First Things First – Choose the right things to do and execute according to priorities. Time is a nonrenewable resource: we must use it wisely by deciding whether our next action should be staring at the numbers in the CRM system, coaching our people in the field, reviewing the number of calls of our team, or attending every possible client meeting. Reflecting on where our time is spent can reveal non-productive activities.

Plus **Habit 7,** which encompasses all of the other six habits:

Habit 7: Sharpen the Saw – Abraham Lincoln's famous quote *"Give me six hours to chop down a tree, and I will spend the first four sharpening the axe"*. Constantly taking action requires a balance to settle down and invest time for both mental and physical recovery from our efforts.

To achieve "**Public victory**" – victory in society – you need to master habits 4 to 6:

Habit 4: Think Win-Win – Successful living does not need to be a zero-sum game; we will gain trusting followers by adopting a 'win-win' attitude and seeking positive outcomes for all. This will help us become role models to inspire others towards collaborative agreements.

Habit 5: Seek First to Understand, Then to be Understood – 'Public Victory' requires us to actively listen to others and focus less on our own personal viewpoints. As leaders, the simple act of listening and being empathetic towards others ultimately enables us to appreciate and learn from others.

Habit 6: Synergise – Synergy is at the heart of this book. At its core, the whole of our TWC team (our WHY) is greater than the sum of its parts (writers). Our 6-member writing team (we started out as strangers) embodies the title "*Teams Win Championships,*" acknowledging that the team championship (completion of the book) is bigger than the sum of the individual victories of the writers.

Leadership vs Management

How does one define leadership and management? Are they fundamentally different, or are both terms interchangeable?

Organisational researchers spent many fruitless years trying to compare them and eventually concluded that a reliable measurement could be used to distinguish them. It was determined that both could be rated in terms of effectiveness, as dictated by subordinates' responses.

This was based on empirical research that indicated that subordinates were often identified as the critical success factor in leadership and management success. Leadership has been a driver for innovation for thousands of years, and yet effective leadership remains one of the most misunderstood phenomena and comprises one of the most fundamental aspects of the human condition.[28]

While the study talks about "subordinates," we prefer to use *sales team members* in our book. We ignore direct reporting lines and understand that everyone in the sales team is working towards a common goal: "Sell the best possible solutions to the clients based on the available products and services and achieve maximum value for all parties involved."

Jeff Weiner, executive chairman of *LinkedIn*, in one of his posts, distinguishes a leader from a manager this way:

*"A **Manager tells** people what to do. A **Leader inspires** others to do great things."* [29]

While a manager tends to the subordinates according to the quasi-military principle of "Order and Obedience," leaders use caring and persuasion to gain their followers' trust. We are not implying that a manager is like some overbearing general ordering the troops around; we are simply saying that the delivery of the message is as important as the message itself.

---

[28] Kotterman, James. *Leadership Versus Management: What's the Difference?* in "The Journal for Quality and Participation; Summer 2006; 29, 2; ProQuest Central" pg. 13

[29] Businessinsider 2015: https://www.businessinsider.com/ linkedin-ceo-jeff-weiner-on-being-a-great-leader-2015-7

Both leadership and management represent the sum of activities, including communication of any form, carried out by the leader/manager that focuses on achieving or overachieving previously defined goals for a group of people/teams.

Who is the Leader?

As a prelude to discussing sales leadership, a few questions come to mind:

- What is a leader?

- Who is a leader?

- How do we define that role?

- Do we even need a leader?

Let's review this role within the sales team.

The history of the human race has been defined by leadership. At any point in our lives, we are either leading or following. History books are filled with facts and tales recounted with names that we all know and recognise. For every memorialised leader, there are millions of forgotten followers. The future holds no mystery on the topic of leadership.

The past will simply repeat itself with a fresh assortment of leaders taking on these important roles to guide us in the years ahead. The role does not necessarily need to take on a world-changing tone: it can simply be someone heading a family or a group of friends, coaching a sports team, leading a department, owning a company, or managing a sales team. Depending on how well they perform, some will undoubtedly be remembered and have books written about them. How do we want to be remembered?

Leadership is, therefore, something that we must consider, particularly when it comes to leading organisations. In today's multinational organisations, the corporate hierarchy's broad range and scope might lead us to ponder its executive staff's duties.

Who is the Leader in Sales?

If we take a closer look at the sales department, we may ask ourselves, *"Who executes the sales leader role?"*. Since sales are the lifeblood of any company, we can certainly argue that the **Chief Executive Officer** (CEO) has that ultimate responsibility. A company's shareholders will render judgement on the CEOs ability to generate revenue growth and show profits with the C-Level team.

Within the C-Level of large private organisations, we customarily find the **Chief Marketing Officer** (CMO), **Chief Information Officer** (CIO), **Chief Financial Officer** (CFO), **Chief Human Resources Officer** (CHRO), **Chief Operations Officer** (COO), and often a **Chief Revenue Officer** (CRO).

The CRO customarily assumes responsibility for an organisation's sales at the executive level. In today's organisations, the CRO's responsibilities may include sales enablement, product/services sales, and sales operations, to name the most relevant ones. As the highest-ranking executive within the organisation, the CEO has the power to dictate and direct them all.

Jeb Blount, in his foreword to **Mike Weinberg's** best-selling book *"Sales Management. Simplified."*[30], expresses the importance of sales very clearly:

> *"Here's the brutal truth, though, that you must embrace. Regardless of your organizational role, as a leader, if your sales team succeeds, you succeed. If your sales team fails, your company fails, and all employees that work for your company fail. Without sales, without clients, you have no company. Period. End of the story. Sales Leadership is that important."*

Sales and Marketing Stronger Under One Leadership

From our perspective, marketing should be an integral part of the sales function and not seen as separate. We believe that having a **Chief Revenue & Marketing Officer** (CRMO) is the ideal way to ensure that both sales and marketing share the same goal of providing the best service to clients while simultaneously exploring market share.

---

[30] Sales Management. Simplified., *Mike Weinberg*, 2016

As a corporate function, marketing was still an afterthought, even long after the role of sales had been established. And as an academic field, marketing only emerged in the early twentieth century.[31] We present here a Top 10 list of marketing roles responsible for product success[32] and raise the following two questions:

Which one of the following Top 10 roles are not key objectives of sales?

Which of these roles are executed in closer proximity with the client through salespeople and the sales organisation compared to marketing people and the marketing organisation?

1. **Economic Growth**: Economic growth cannot be sustained through marketing alone. If we sell competitive products and services, then any company's growth will be driven by sales with marketing support.

2. **Meets Consumer Needs and Wants**: Who speaks directly with the clients and listens to them more than the account executives and consultants who work on-site? Sales representatives and consultants understand client needs and feed this information back into product management.

3. **Ensures Organisation Survival, Growth, and Reputation**: Your growth and reputation depend on the trust you earn by making and keeping your commitments and delivering at and above client expectations. Who does this? Certainly not marketing.

4. **Widens Market**: Who penetrates new markets and grows market share in existing markets? Sales are once again the clear winners, supported by marketing and other internal support functions.

5. **Adapting the Right Price**: Prices are typically set by the sales department, driven by cost base + margin + market conditions + discount policies.

---

[31] https://en.wikipedia.org/wiki/History_of_marketing
[32] https://www.yourarticlelibrary.com/marketing/role-of-marketing-top-10-important-role-of-marketing-in-making-a-product-successful/32289

6. **Better Product Offerings**: Better products should be designed based on client needs. Who knows the client's needs best, and who maintains the trusted relationship, so they open up and share those needs?

7. **Creates Utility**: A product or service is qualified by the client's perceived value of the product or service. Marketing cannot define this. Design and functionality will dictate this by the production unit of an organisation and its user experience (UX) in collaboration with the R&D teams.

8. **Face Competition**: Most large corporations have a competitive intelligence team typically run either under marketing or sales. The team investigates competitors and documents battlecards for the sales teams to help them face the competition.

9. **Management of Demand**: This is a true marketing function, but even this part is crucial for selling anything. If your product is of poor quality and does not satisfy a specific need in today's transparent, social media-driven world, you can market and promote as much as you want; people just won't buy your products or services.

10. **Discharge Social Responsibilities**: Another true and important marketing communication function. Rising client expectations, government pressures, and environmental degradation have forced companies to adopt higher levels of social awareness. In this sense, social marketing plays an important role. Cause-related marketing is widely used by big corporate houses, for example.

This section highlights that clients will be better served by integrating the sales and marketing functions under a single CRMO role.

A Closer Look at the Sales Function in Large Companies

In larger companies, the sales team expands down from the CRO to an **Executive Vice President** (EVP) of sales for each region, such as **Asia-Pacific** (APAC), the **Americas**, and **Europe, Middle East, and Africa** (EMEA).

A typical global organisation may have a sales function servicing three to five such regions. For each of these regions, the sales team would include **Regional Vice Presidents** responsible for sub-regions, **Area Vice Presidents, Country Managers,** and finally, **Sales Directors**. Sales directors represent the first management level within sales and may be organised according to industries like finance, retail, pharma, and utilities.

Individual contributors are often called **Account Executives (AE)** or sales representatives and usually report to a sales director. A typical AE may also manage a team even if the teammates don't report directly to the AE. This is the "**Account Team**," and the AE is its de facto leader.

It is critical that the account management and AE functions work as a structured team at large business-to-business organisations. The *lone wolf* method simply has no place here.

Other key players on the account team are:

- **Solution Engineers** who contribute technical skills

- **Business Consultants** or **Project Managers** who help prepare account and project plans

- **Product Management** or **R&D Team** provide improved beta versions of products and services

- **Legal Counsel** to provide legal advice on the contracts

- **Financial Planners** to assist with the financial terms and conditions

- **Deal Desk/ Pricing Team** to support with advising on the configuration and optimisation of the terms and conditions of offers for the sales team

- **Marketing Team** to help with account-based marketing and messaging

- **Competitive Intelligence Team** to support with battlecards and rates the competition

- **Partners & Alliances Team** to find the right partner for the team to be in a more powerful position to win bigger deals in the account.

Far from being a complete list, the AE should at least consider these 10 supporting members to be key players within their team. We round out the list with two of the most critical players: the **Client Manager** and the **Sales Manager**! Hence, we have used the term "**Team(s) of Teams**" throughout this book.

AEs who typically take on the role of leading a virtual or remote account team (not everyone is down the hall from our offices) must now also assume responsibility for the added complexity of unforeseen events such as those brought about by the recent COVID-19 pandemic. More than ever before we, as sales managers, must support our AEs and partner managers with coaching, training, empathy, and mentoring.

Indirect Sales: The Alliance and Partnership Manager

Today's sales and services are increasingly sold indirectly. This added layer of complexity is documented in the most recent data from 2019, whereby approximately 65% of Enterprise Software and Hardware (IT Industry) sales came through channel partners. This indicates that indirect sales in the IT industry have already surpassed direct sales. Anyone who has a sales role in this industry will eventually face the challenge or opportunity of working in channel sales.

Jay McBain, Forrester, Principal Analyst, Channel Partnerships & Alliances, in his article "*What I See Coming For The Channel In 2020*",[33] states that:

> "*To sum 2020 up in simple terms, we are seeing a monumental shift in how buyers acquire products and services and how companies are reacting with their go-to-market and routes-to-market strategies. Over 80% of my time is spent in the technology industry, where 64% of all dollars flow indirectly. That is US$2.26 trillion (with a T), if you are keeping score.*"

33 https://go.forrester.com/blogs/ what-i-see-coming-for-the-channel-in-2020/

The COVID-19 pandemic has contributed to the acceleration of B2B sales in eCommerce. We have witnessed the emergence of virtual sales as a revenue powerhouse, and large-scale eCommerce retailers have benefitted from this new sales avenue. Channel businesses will also profit from this acceleration as online sales are simpler to set up, and relationships with external resellers have been simplified.

A partner manager or alliances manager adds another layer within the organisation. This sales role is directly comparable to the AEs role in direct sales.

We anticipate that the regional sales leaders' role will incorporate managing both partner managers and AEs. Leadership and communication skills will need to be developed and adapted accordingly. We also expect that sales leaders and AEs will build new partnerships directly or participate actively in acquiring these to develop the business further.

Sales are of the utmost importance for any organisation, and sales leaders must diligently play their part in this crucial role. While serving an organisation's C-level, the sales leader must also collaborate with sales management, the sales director, and the account executive/partner manager. They are all on the front line: driving sales and facilitating direct contact with clients, partners, and account teams. The front line is where the magic of sales happens.

Defining Sales Success as Achieving Previously Set Sales Goals

The team (leader's/manager's/members') degree of success is defined by the most recent results measured against previously set goals. The effectiveness of a leader/manager's leadership and management can, therefore, be precisely measured. Success is, however, very relative as it depends on the previously set goals. However, goals often ignore underlying conditions and the resources needed for the team to achieve those goals. One of the most important tasks of the sales leadership team, being highly dependent on the CFO and CEO, is setting goals that are both challenging and realistic. Setting annual goals may be an issue if the CEO and CFO are too disconnected from the field while the salespeople are in the trenches.

Salespeople know precisely what is going on with client relations, but they are rarely consulted or listened to, resulting in sales goals being set that are either too high or too low. The complexity of the sales process makes it difficult to explain clearly how sales goals are achieved; it's the process, together with the methods used and the resources, that achieve results and make all the difference.

Do we Need Leaders in Sales?

A sales agreement (or any communication that leads to an agreement) is not purely transactional; there are almost always relational, negotiable, and communicative aspects too. For instance, more than 85% of B2B sales cycles still run via human sales as opposed to the online purchase of goods through Amazon or Alibaba.

At its core, revenues generated by B2B eCommerce portals still begin with a human account team. A report published in June 2020 by DigitalCommerce360.com shows that B2B eCommerce sales in the US surged by 18% in 2019 totalling $1.3 trillion.[34]

So the question remains, *"Do we need leaders in sales?"*.

The answer is a resounding YES when the right people fill the roles: the AE as the account team leader, the partnership manager as the co-leader of the partners sales team, and the sales director who coaches and mentors while holding the AE and partnership manager to account.

This set-up will determine the success of any sales team and organisation.

In his 2016 Forbes article entitled *"**New Research Shows Why Focus On Teams, Not Just Leaders, Is Key To Business Performance**,"*[35] **Josh Bersin** highlights a shift in focus from the individual sales manager to the teams.

The article refers to a study called *"**A study of people challenges in business, Deloitte Human Capital Trends 2016**"* by **Deloitte** in 2016:

> *"The results were striking. Among the 7,000+ companies who responded (in over 130 countries), the #1 issue on leaders minds was 'how to redesign our organisational structure' to meet the demands of the workforce and business climate today.*

---

[34] https://www.digitalcommerce360.com/2020/06/08/
faster-than-retail-b2b-ecommerce-sales-surge-18-in-2019/
[35] https://www.forbes.com/sites/joshbersin/2016/03/03/
why-a-focus-on-teams-not-just-leaders-is-the-secret-to-business-performance/

*The conclusion, after almost a year of study, was that 'today's digital world of work has shaken the foundation of organisational structure, shifting from the traditional functional hierarchy to one Deloitte calls a "**network of teams**."' This new model of work is forcing us to change job roles and job descriptions; rethink careers and internal mobility; emphasise skills and learning as keys to performance; redesign how we set goals and reward people; and change the role of leaders.*

The research, which identifies the top ten human capital trends for 2016, shows that most of the issues facing companies today (employee engagement, culture, time to market, innovation) are tied inextricably to this new way of working. And 92% of the companies Deloitte surveyed cited "redesigning the way we work" as one of their key challenges, making this the #1 trend of the year."'

This study gives merit to the focus in "***Teams Win Championships***" around the need for a paradigm shift for AEs, as leaders of the account team, from an "I" to a "We" mindset. "Interconnected and Integrated Teams of Teams" is a viable term to describe the new paradigm in today's organisations. Despite this shift, the sales team still needs to be managed, and its leaders must learn to effectively lead their teams through a more complex, digital, and remote economic environment.

Call and Need for Servant Team Leadership

Effective sales managers focus on understanding and serving the entire sales team rather than just the AE, the partner & alliances manager, or the direct reports. This may even include teaming up and establishing fruitful collaborations with leaders of other teams outside of the sales department. The sales manager can gain new perspectives and viewpoints and improve relational and communication skills just by demonstrating a willingness to listen.

Leadership is a complex task, and leaders need to recognise that both the vision and perspective within an organisation are shared and understood by everyone.

The key aspects of successful organisations are shown below in the graphic of the pyramid. In this book, we cover most of these factors in the context of sales teams and any other teams with which they may interact.

The core aspects of an organisation, shown at the heart of the pyramid, reveal two layers:

1. **Purpose layer**: Culture–Leadership & Coaching–People.

2. **Direction layer**: Vision & Mission–Strategy–Goals

Enablers/Cornerstones: Communication–Execution & Process–Teamwork

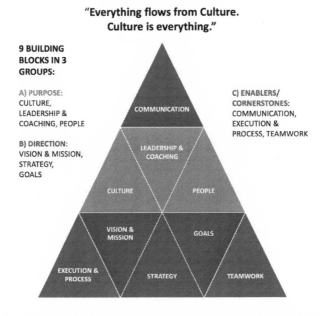

Figure 3: Key Aspects of Successful Organisations

Key Traits of the Right Leader

As job roles and job descriptions have changed, so too have the key traits of successful sales leaders. Sales leaders need to adapt to a diverse, digital, and remote environment while embracing the reality of "**Teams of Teams Organisations**", thereby abandoning the old notion of identifying sales as an isolated discipline or department within the organisation.

"The day you stop learning is the day you stop earning."

At the start of this book project, our writing team of six authors had some group discussions on the topic of leadership qualities and agreed on a set of 11 key traits that we believe are fundamental for any leader in modern leadership. Despite coming from diverse backgrounds, we efficiently agreed on this shortlist. We demonstrated that, regardless of ethnicity or professional background, people generally interact in a similar manner and look for the same things in a leader.

The 11 Key Traits of a Successful Sales Leader in the Current Context are:

1. **Character**: A strong, positive, and optimistic character displaying high levels of self-confidence

2. **Culture**: Understands that the sales culture can make or break the sales team; knows the key aspects of a high-performance sales culture

3. **Coach**: Understands that individual and team coaching and mentoring are key success factors and activities for a leader

4. **Trust**: Trust giver and trust receiver: A role model who creates a safe space and allows team members to experiment

5. **Vulnerable**: Recognises that they don't have to have all the answers and can acknowledge mistakes publicly

6. **Servant**: Understands the importance of servant leadership; thinks "win-win-win" (Client–Team–Individual) and always defends their team and its values/principles

7. **Listener**: Empathetic, humble, compassionate, open to the opinions of others

8. **Learner**: Always learning – A curious mind to improve their own skills

9. **Planner**: Well-organised, good planner, and disciplined

10. **Process-driven**: Understands that a solid sales process with metrics and few KPIs keeps everyone accountable to the team and the team members

11. **Communicator**: Informs and delivers feedback in a clear, honest, and timely manner. Strongly connected to both "3. Coach" and "7. Listener".

Let's take a closer look at these 11 key traits:

Number 1: Character – Strong, Positive, and Optimistic Character Displaying High Levels of Self-Confidence

Anti-leaders possess weak and pessimistic attitudes of distrust towards their subordinates. These types of leaders see team members as inferior subordinates and exhibit low self-confidence. Their weaknesses are often camouflaged behind a façade of fake smiles, eloquent but empty speeches, arrogance, and a big ego. These anti-leaders will often try to impress others with their career accomplishments but will reveal little about how they will lead the team to high performance. These leaders often create good first impressions and use the "Fake it till you make it" approach to manoeuvre themselves into leadership roles, eluding inexperienced HR consultants and moving deftly through *senior* hiring managers.

On the opposite end of the leadership spectrum is the bold, optimistic leader with high self-esteem; they are like a bright light in a dark room. With an engaging personality and self-confidence (not to be confused with egocentrism!), this leader can make difficult decisions and provide guidance that drives teams forward with intent and determination.

Great leaders must also be good people at heart, with strong core values and principles, and a strong character reminiscent of the values found in Thomas Jefferson's famous quote:

"In questions of fashion, swim with the current; in matters of principles, stand like a rock."

The concepts of core values and principles have been around for many millennia, and a great example of these are the eight Ancient Greek core values listed below. Known to be at the forefront of thought and philosophy over 2000 years ago, the list still stands the test of time today. We can even add a ninth, as highlighted by Marcus Tullius Cicero: **Gratitude**.

"Gratitude is not only the greatest of virtues but the parent of all others"

The 8 Ancient Greek Values[36]

1. **Loyalty**: One of the most important values for the Ancient Greeks was loyalty, an obligation owed to both your family and your home.

2. **Hospitality**: In ancient Greece, hospitality included welcoming guests into your home and giving unto strangers, which today is simply considered kindness.

3. **Athleticism**: The Romans advocated the following prayer: "*Mens sana in corpore sana.*" A healthy mind in a healthy body. Take care of your body and mind.[37]

---

[36] The 8 Ancient Greek Values
[37] www.forbes.com/sites/joshbersin/2016/03/03/
why-a-focus-on-teams-not-just-leaders-is-the-secret-to-business-performance/

4. **Teamwork**: Teamwork was one of the eight Ancient Greeks' core values and is the main topic of this book, "*Teams Win Championships*".

5. **Intuition**: Your ability to use your insight to make decisions and solve problems.

6. **Ingenuity**: The ability to use creativity to find your way out of challenges or problems.

7. **Justice**: Justice was also one of the most important tenets of Ancient Greek society. Much like in Hammurabi's code, the Greeks believed that justice was served with equal punishment for a crime.

8. **Respect**: The last and final core value of the Ancient Greeks is respect. In many ways, this directly correlated with their religious beliefs and the Greek gods and goddesses. Family and friends were also an important part of respect. If you did not respect your family and your home, you were frowned upon and cast out of society.

Number 2: Culture – Understands that the Sales Culture Makes or Breaks the Sales Team; Knows the Key Aspects of a High-Performance Sales Culture

The anti-leader ignores culture, usually putting results first. They may use the authoritarian method of applying pressure and controlling the team through fear-mongering, the age-old strategy of "Divide and rule (or conquer)". Instead of creating and developing a powerful team through unity, they do the opposite by keeping the team as divided as possible.

"*Culture eats Strategy for breakfast*" is a quote attributed to Peter Drucker. It means that no matter how strong your strategic plan is, its efficacy will be held back by members of your team if they don't share the same culture.

For fear of developing a capable leader from within the team, anti-leaders will hire weak(er) people who can be manipulated and whose loyalty can be easily "bought" with offers of a better position or salary increases. They surround themselves with 'yes men'. Who has not seen this scenario before? Hands up, anyone?

The people implementing the strategic plan are the same ones who will make all the difference. The right culture is built on shared values, principles, and a vision of achieving a shared goal for the organisation.

The key to making that culture work is that every single member of the organisation must share these. This unity can be achieved and reinforced by allowing the entire team to define and validate the team's culture democratically. By having a voice, each team member will stand behind this culture and will work with positive energy and motivation towards the shared goals. A leader nurturing a high-performance culture will focus on the important things that need to be done (e.g., coaching, training, teaching, planning, preparing, practising) as well as analysis and implementation. The results (data composed of a series of numbers) will be the culmination of all of these actions being done right.

Number 3: Coach – Understands Both Individual and Team Coaching as well as Mentoring as Key Success Factors and Key Activities as a Leader

The anti-leader believes that they don't need coaching. Why should they have to put in the extra effort; they believe their skills and talents are such that no one can teach them anything new of value.

The anti-leader likely doesn't understand the power of coaching and may confuse it with training. Open-ended questions and a willingness to listen to understand deeply are at the core of good and effective coaching. But the anti-leader may think, "*My subordinates are here to do their job, to help me make my numbers, and it's not my job to teach them. We have hired skilled people and what they should do is take the online courses the organisation provides to keep up their skills.*"

A good leader understands that, without the contribution of the team, they are nothing. Team members are deeply respected and are never seen as subordinates. A good leader follows the servant leadership style and understands that good coaching and mentoring are key activities to help the team develop as professionals and people. Under the good leader's leadership, coaching and mentoring will take place at both the team and the individual level with the understanding that this is crucial for the success of every team member and the team as a whole. A good leader also recognises the need for coaching and mentorship to grow to their full potential.

Number 4: Trust – Trust Giver and Trusting: A Role Model Who Creates a Safe Space and Allows for "Trial and Error"

The anti-leader, by definition, ignores trust. The anti-leader does not trust anyone because it would expose them to other people who could use that trust to betray them, or so the anti-leader believes.

To trust is to be vulnerable and exposed. This would make the anti-leader feel uncomfortable, perceiving it as a sign of weakness. The anti-leader will hate this feeling and will do everything to avoid extending trust to their team members.

We have already discussed the importance of trust in Part I, under the title "Trust is a Must", as told by **Marta Martínez** and **César Cernuda**.

This next quote is from **Stephen M.R. Covey**, son of the renowned Stephen R. Covey. As the former CEO of *CoveyLink* and a New York Times bestselling author of the book "*The Speed of Trust*", Stephen M.R Covey is considered a global authority on trust, leadership and culture.

"Trust is the new currency of our interdependent, collaborative world."

Mr Covey claims that credibility is the greatest asset of a leader during times of crisis and disruption. But the greatest power that leaders possess is how they choose to extend their trust to others.

Trust is the one thing that can change everything. In times of crisis, when trust is compromised, the speed at which things are managed and executed decreases dramatically, driving costs up. The inverse of this is also true.

Key aspect: You must first give trust to earn trust. Trust is like planting a seed; you have to water, cultivate, protect and grow it before you can reap the fruit (trust). Trust is, therefore, a process that requires time and patience.

Number 5: Vulnerable – Recognises that They don't have all the Answers and Recognises Mistakes Publicly

The anti-leader essentially thinks of themself as perfect. Any criticism would be deemed a personal attack, and the person who made the "attack" will soon become "persona non grata". Any attempt to criticise the anti-leader will be met with punishment; people may even be fired or intimidated. The message from the anti-leader to the team is clear: "*I am the boss and the only one who rules. You are here to serve me. Period.*"

The leader who is willing to be vulnerable recognises that they are human with human flaws, fears, and emotions. Being vulnerable means also being able to apologise, in public if necessary, if mistakes were made or if someone was judged or mistreated. This requires courage but, if done genuinely, this behaviour will strengthen the bond between the team and its leader with an overall positive impact on mutual trust and the team's performance.

Number 6: Servant – Understands the Importance of Servant-Leadership; Thinks "win-win-win" (Client–Team–Individual) and Always Defends Team Values and Principles

The anti-leader affronts team members and thinks, "*I win – you lose*". The anti-leader is unable to think "win-win" on any level. This leader cannot see that the whole is greater than the sum of its parts. The anti-leader would never stick their neck out for anyone, never expose themself to their own management with demands, or even defend the team's values and principles.

A safe working environment means that team members feel protected by their leader when external sources violate fundamental values, principles and rights. Team members will only trust their leader if the leader can hold firm on their commitments. There is no bigger commitment than defending the team's values, principles and integrity against any attack, no matter the source.

Number 7: Listener – Empathetic, Humble, Compassionate, Open to the Opinions of Others and a Great Listener

The anti-leader is often unable or uninterested in how team members feel. The anti-leader will follow recommendations made by management and selectively listen to peers to gather information that can be used to enhance their own position within the organisation.

117

The anti-leader also loves the sound of their voice, rarely affording others the opportunity to share their thoughts, nor does the anti-leader show any genuine interest in understanding what others have to say.

To really hear what another person is saying, we have to genuinely listen by giving our full attention through our eyes, ears and heart. This act of generosity is also an act of trust and shows a deep respect for the person to whom we are listening.

Having empathy means understanding the feelings of others. Compassion is empathy put into action, helping another person resolve an uncomfortable, dangerous, painful or threatening situation.

Being humble means there is self-awareness in acknowledging that we don't have all the answers and are better served with the support and help of others. With a natural predisposition to respectfully listen to others, we can quickly understand and learn from them.

Strengthening our human relationships is at the core of coaching and begins with asking genuine open-ended questions and pausing long enough to really listen to the student. Great leaders are also great listeners. *"How do you think they got there? By listening to their own voice or by accepting others' viewpoints?"* How would you learn more, by speaking or by listening?

Number 8: Learner – Always be Learning – Curious Mind to Know More and Upskill

The anti-leader believes their education and skill level justifies their dismissal of others' ideas. With their alleged world-class insights into the business world, the anti-leader perceives themself as the only person for the job who can direct others without any additional training for their own self-improvement. *"You all have to 'up your game' to have the privilege of working with me"*. Unfortunately, this narrow-minded approach is prevalent in many business circles, with anti-leaders unwilling to admit to needing training. Ultimately, this narrow-minded approach will filter down to the team members, thereby perpetuating ignorance.

On the other hand, a good leader understands that the world is constantly evolving and that progressive change is all around us, making continual learning necessary to adapt and push their team to new heights.

The good leader also understands that by improving the team's skillset, a series of follow-up studies and analyses can track progress. Learning is a key success factor when planned correctly as resources will be available, as required. High-performance teams also openly share what they learn with their teammates and leaders.

Number 9: Planner – Well-Organised, Good Planner and Disciplined

Anti-leaders surround themselves with amenable subordinates who will support and reinforce their feelings of superiority. The anti-leader will call meetings with no prepared agenda and no intention of establishing objectives, but rather only to impose their will. This time-consuming activity, used to assert the anti-leader's importance, offers little value to the organisation. Little effort will be put into delivering well-designed and clear presentations, and there are not likely to be any follow-up meetings to review the team's progress in line with expectations. '*Preparation? Hah! That's for losers!*'

A good leader knows that a well-designed plan, done well ahead of time, will deliver the best results. This leader gives sufficient notice of scheduled meetings and even involves the team members to establish an effective agenda.

This ensures the team is engaged and the members feel like they are contributing to the planning process, thereby fostering collaboration.

This upfront clarity and transparency will develop into collaboration, planning and organisation, allowing team members to take ownership of the process, paving the way for effective delegation.

Discipline is the practice of understanding that certain tasks must be repeated to follow through on a well-defined process.

Team meetings need a disciplined approach to be effective: Proper planning, sharing the agenda, assigning expectations of each attendee, hosting the meeting, etc. Great leaders understand that they must be role models.

Number 10: Process-Driven–Understands that a Solid Sales Process with Metrics and Few KPI's Make Both Team and Individuals Accountable and that a Solid Process Drives Successful Execution

The anti-leader doesn't typically subscribe to sales processes as they require effort to explain to be understood by the team. These leaders may not be the best salespeople and would fear being exposed in front of the team or the client.

A good leader knows the sales process better than anyone else on the team; they can critically analyse the process and adapt the process to changes driven either from within or outside the organisation. They know that high performance cannot be consistently achieved or measured without a rock-solid sales process and clear and simple KPI's. *"You can't improve what you can't measure."* Fortunately, sales success is easier to measure than you might think:

- Rule number 1: "Make your numbers"

- Rule number 2: "Don't forget rule number 1"

- Rule number 3: "Sell what's on the truck".

All joking aside, though, the sales process starts with a series of preliminary works, each with the goal of creating a pipeline of opportunities. Discovery calls and qualifying meetings set the groundwork to move the sales cycle forward, but you need a starting list of accounts before making these calls. This carefully chosen list creates the territory or target account list.

So, what is the process? What does a good sales process look like?

While we have experimented with a few sales processes, the one we call **The 5P Sales Process,** "**P**lan–**P**repare–**P**ractice–**P**lay–**P**erform", is the one we have trusted and used with much success.

No sales process is EVER perfect, but if you regularly analyse the process with your team and identify its shortcomings, the process can be adapted to maintain the highest levels of effectiveness. Once the good sales leader has a solid process in place and is assured that the team has learned the process and can execute it well, accountability will keep everyone on track to maintain the continuous measurement of sales success.

Accountability calls should be planned well in advance. The sales leader should have these calls at least once a month with the AE, and at least once per quarter with the entire sales team; they should be well-structured, with clear KPI's for the team, the team members, and the leader; and they should be kept short, no more than 15-20 minutes for individual calls/meetings, and 45-60 minutes for the entire team.

This is an example of a typical agenda for a quarterly accountability call for the sales team:

1. Deals closed to date against the quota and the gap to quota

2. Weighted FY pipeline (Commit 80%, Upside 40% and Pipeline 20%)

3. Unweighted rolling 15 months forecasted pipeline (Size: 4 times FY Quota)

4. If it's all good, then "Have a great day and keep it up". Otherwise, look into the individual AE's pipeline and check who is ahead and who is behind, and agree on action points to improve the pipeline for the ones who are behind (you as a leader will know this already because you carried out individual accountability calls beforehand)

5. Key challenges

6. Agreed upon action points.

We recommend the bestselling book, "*Sales Management. Simplified*", written by **Mike Weinberg**, which teaches a solid sales process by offering a practical and proven process framework for the sales manager.

A few of us writing "*Teams Win Championships*" know Mike personally, and we greatly appreciate that he generously offered to write our foreword.

Number 11: Communicator – Informs and Delivers Feedback in a Clear, Honest and Timely Manner. Strongly Connected to Both "3. Coach" and "7. Listener"

John Maxwell noted the difference between communication and connection very well when he said:

> *"Many communicate, few connect."*

This statement suggests that there is definitely a quality aspect to communication. We could say that a mediocre communicator does not create the desired effects of bonding and connecting with people with whom they need to communicate.

Effective communication informs, provides feedback and includes these four key components:

1. Honesty

2. Relevance

3. Clarity

4. Timeliness.

We discuss communication throughout this book and dedicate in this part Chapter 4. "Creating Trust Through Timely, Clear and Honest Communication," to the leader's capacity to earn trust through effective communication.

Servant Leadership Responsibility

The next time you take a walk around your neighbourhood, why not stop and strike up a conversation with some families? After a few pleasantries, casually tell them that you are doing some research for an international project named "*Teams Win Championships*" and ask them this simple question:

'*What do your children want to become when they grow up?*'

Parents will turn to their children, and children will respond with sports celebrity, singer, doctor, or scientist. You will certainly never hear one of these children say: "*I want to become the leader of a high-performance sales team.*" It isn't exactly the kind of thing you hear about anywhere.

But let's think about this for a moment. Doesn't our economic future heavily depend on upcoming stars taking on leadership roles in all kinds of organisations?

We need to prepare these young future leaders now by acknowledging the need to have vision.

While taking on a corporate leadership role certainly comes with personal and financial rewards, it also comes with a vast ocean of obligations and responsibilities that may not be immediately apparent when a candidate first accepts the position.

Certainly, not everyone is geared to handle the responsibilities and obligations of a leader. Still, most of those who do succeed have an innate drive and energy that is closely aligned with an ultimate goal, the endgame.

Defining Purpose, Vision and Mission

Any chess enthusiast will tell you that visualising the endgame will certainly guide your decisions and the strategy for your moves, just as having the vision and foresight of an organisation's long-term goal will guide the team towards their attainable goal. While the leader creates the vision and guides the way, the management team organises and works to get there. As the person with the hands on the steering wheel, leaders will be well-served, surrounding themselves with a team of like-minded, diverse and challenging professionals who all have a team-first mentality to 'rev up the engine'.

As presented in Part I, Chapter 1, an organisation may establish a set of goals that are predetermined by the organisational WHY. This is the genesis of the organisation's purpose and its reason for existing...'*son raison d'être*'. Everything else emanates from this.

The organisation's WHY defines the purpose and meaning behind the organisation's 'reason for existing' and defines the talents and roles needed to achieve the purpose. A leader can do well by the team by establishing a personal WHY that is directly aligned with the organisation's WHY. From the WHY, you can develop the 'WHAT', what we will do to arrive at an action plan for 'HOW will we do it.

For all the parts to fit together, the leader must take on the dual role of leader and servant, a fine balancing act in itself. While taking on leadership and decision-making responsibilities, leaders must also ensure that they are of service to their team by delivering the very best version of themselves. Only then can the leader take on the role of a true leader and provide the team with all the tools and knowledge for their success.

In serving their team, the leader develops a mutual understanding amongst the team members that reduces the organisation's hierarchy. This can be compared to the role of a player-coach. When the leader's actions are perceived as being company-first and personal-second and adopts the old adage of '*you are defined by your actions*', then the groundwork has been laid for trust and cooperation.

Putting First Things First

We have found that acting with a company-first mindset is undoubtedly the correct attitude, but the secret sauce is to precede this with a 'people first' mentality, being of service to the team members first and foremost. Employee engagement is a major catalyst for team building and organisational growth, and an able team leader who prioritises this can do so with the assurance that it is the right thing to do.

The August 2019 Harvard Business Review article entitled *"The Key to Happy Customers? Happy Employees"* by **Andrew Chamberlain** and **Daniel Zhao** drives the point of the 'people first' mentality home. Their research shows that for every 1-star rating increase in employee satisfaction, the resulting customer satisfaction scores improved between 8% and 18% for long-term stock prices.

If serving the employee is a priority for the good of the organisation, then the leader's loyalty and attitude towards the company is a very close second. The two priorities go hand-in-hand; however, we do wish to emphasise that, like motor oil, employees drive the organisation's engine and keep it running smoothly. This recognition of the value of employees will eventually lead to personal growth and, with organisational success, the leader will get others to follow their lead through their conduct and message. Our duty and responsibility are to act in the organisation's best interests and put our personal gains aside.

When there are systems and assignments in place, employee roles can be defined, and individual contributions can be recognised. To get the most out of employees, organisations must uncover unique personalities through commercially available psychometric tests, leading to reduced effort in actual leading. This role can become routine with a supervisory role to manage a team.

Since the human factor is unpredictable, one can always expect interference and disruption. The team's cohesion can be disrupted with a slew of human interactions between members (personality traits, fatigue, stress, jealousy) that can hinder the team's flow.

"In science, when human behaviour enters the equation, things go nonlinear. That's why Physics is easy, and Sociology is hard."

Neil deGrasse Tyson, Astrophysicist

Planning and preparation can reduce future productivity pitfalls, but the leader should always remain vigilant of human factors within the team to prevent the unit from descending into chaos. Group meetings, one-on-one meetings, and open discussions will enable the leader to keep their finger on the team's pulse for the greater good of the organisation.

In a push and pull analogy, one can lead the team by pushing hard for results, but that will likely have a limited positive effect. By constantly pushing and aiming for higher goals and targets, we can expect the team to eventually burn out, lose sight of the targets, or worse, lose interest. A hard-driving boss who never lets up from the 'accelerator' and doesn't follow up with enough appreciation of the team's efforts – the pull – will eventually drive the team to underperform.

However, suppose the leader can demonstrate the value of their abilities, competence and efforts to employees. In that case, employees will understand why things must be done a certain way, thereby reinforcing values. This will facilitate the leader's teachings, and mentoring, who becomes a trustworthy role model employees can look up to. Once trust is established (especially for a new leader on the job), the plan is for employees to continue pushing themselves, setting their own paths. First, you pull them in; then, they will push themselves to follow the leader's example. The mark of a true leader is one who can achieve this alignment and lead a high performing team without the team even realising it is being led, creating a synergy.

As a leader, your team depends on you as much as you depend on them. Repeat that to yourself every day because the team's success starts and ends with you, and your success starts and ends with the team! As the leader, everyone around you will depend on you being at your mental, physical, and emotional best. This has been recounted *ad nauseum* in books, keynotes, and Youtube videos, but 'Always being on' can be exhausting. No one leader can be the answer to all the team's problems or everyone's safety valve.

For any leader to continue to function at their peak, they must rely on the available support structure. There is no shame in admitting when help is needed. Organisations don't need superheroes; they need productive teams. Superheroes aren't jumping off the big screen to save our organisations, so we have to figure it out with our own people and processes.

A leader who sincerely opens up to the team for help on complex matters will make the team members feel respected and valued. They will ideally respond by bonding and gravitating together, which will reinvigorate the trust factor. Part of the leader's responsibility is to persevere through challenges, but without an able and supportive team, the leader may feel the weight of the world on their shoulders. This pressure can be reduced if the leader remains committed to excellence and remains accountable or, better yet, is held accountable by the team members. But why not spread the accountability factor across the whole team and get everyone in on the game?

Teams members are not only our work colleagues. They are also our family, friends, clients, suppliers, coaches, advisors and more, with everyone contributing to the extent that we allow them.

We believe that the 11 Key Traits of a Leader in Chapter 2 can be used with any personal support structure. These Key Traits are not restricted to the boardroom. People come into our lives for various reasons at various times. If we cherish the relationships enough to be willing to keep them close, to listen to them truly, then we owe it to them (and ourselves) to be the best version of ourselves by incorporating the virtues of the Key Traits.

Being a Servant-Leader is not Limited to the Workplace

High-performing leaders often use their talents and abilities for the greater good of society. For example, if you were to become a leader in your local community, it sends a message that you are not a self-serving business person; you are willing to come to the aid of those in need in your local community. By taking part in social programmes or community projects (without financial rewards), you become entrenched in the community by making a difference and contributing to positive outcomes.

Being a leader is not just restricted to the boardroom. Respect, appreciation and fulfilment come after you have demonstrated that you are there to help and prove it through action, no matter where you are. Use your talents to make a difference because those in need will benefit from them and appreciate it.

Human Psychology, Relationships and Communication are Still Enigmas

Many of today's best-selling business books focus on soft skills, with many written by psychology professors and researchers. There is certainly a reason for that. This is an area where we still can't grasp what's right in front of us. Human relationships are still where they were 100 years ago; it has not evolved even though we are surrounded by the latest technology.

This view on human relationships is evident from texts written over a century ago by:

Ralph Waldo Emerson: *"To be yourself in a world that is constantly trying to make you something else is the greatest accomplishment."*,

Orison Swett Marden: *"Don't wait for extraordinary opportunities. Seize common occasions and make them great. Weak men wait for opportunities; strong men make them."*, and

Napoleon Hill: *"Every adversity, every failure, and every heartache, carries with it the seed of an equivalent or greater benefit."*

And they all tell similar tales of unattained greatness for the same reason.

Conscientious and goal-oriented people aim to improve their circumstances, be it their health, finances, mindfulness or other. The world has changed significantly, but the human condition appears to have remained the same. While the world's economies have grown and improved, the lack of diversity and inclusion in our organisations is still prevalent today.

Understanding the Client is a Must for the Servant Leader

From a sales perspective, we must talk about the relationship between salespeople and the client, as they are an integral part of any sales team.

As sales leaders, we are paid to use our expertise to execute our clients' orders. We must, therefore, consider ourselves the CEOs of their "success department". Since we are experts in our field and have capabilities that they don't have, the client also expects us to lead them with our knowledge. Within SME's, business owners tend to be very hands-on, and consider it a duty to serve and lead these clients. Highly specialised teams create an unforgettable experience by simultaneously serving and leading them.

As SME administrators, we have found that you can learn so much more by conducting interactive client interviews and after-sales performance reviews instead of mundane client surveys. Once our clients understand that we aim for win-win discussions, they tend to be more open and honest about what they could have done better for us during the contract. These clients understand that, by supporting us, we can refine our processes that will serve them better for the ultimate win.

To all our readers out there, we can honestly say that, although we love our clients, we do tend to overlook any inefficiencies for fear of insulting them. It doesn't have to be that way, though. By initiating a 2-way conversation to review and agree on improvements and benefits for both, any matter can be raised for discussion through open and informal dialogue.

As expected, our conversations benefitted both parties and, *voilá*, there was the win-win! Our team then committed to following through on what we learned from our client interviews and why they have been so loyal to us. We learnt it, we applied it, and we used it repeatedly. When you gain valuable knowledge and reinvest it back into your sales agenda, you gradually improve the entire process. By doing this annually, we have remained close to our clients and have learned how to serve them best. We dug deep to uncover what we did well, what we didn't do well, what could be improved on, and how we could make the client the real hero of the sales story.

The answers we got to '*How can we collaborate further to handle and solve future anticipated problems?*' are pure gold. By remaining visible (and available) to your clients, even after the sale, you can maintain the status of the trusted advisor and improve your perceived value compared to your competitors. When you can simultaneously lead while serving, you will automatically serve while leading. The distinction is slight, but it's there. Think about it. Is there really any other better way to serve your clients?

It is as important to ensure that things run smoothly after the contract is signed as it is closing the deal. Up to the point of sale, we have merely sold an expectation; however, before the ink has even dried on the contract, we are either building or destroying trust. Trust is built on making commitments (signing the contract) and keeping those commitments (delivering at or above expectations). Trust is built on consistently making and keeping your commitments. Trust can be seen as a bank account: Every time you keep a commitment, you make a deposit, and every time you break a commitment, you make 10 withdrawals. Do yourself a favour and honour your commitments. Keep that trust account positive!

Partners and Suppliers Matter too

Since we are all heavily reliant on our supply chain, a similar comparison can be made with our suppliers.

Like an audit, we can learn what can be done better to improve the supplier relationship and their workflow. Get them to open up and honestly tell you what they could have done better for you and what you could have done better for them, and the conversation will turn into a two-way discussion that benefits both parties. Why not use the same analogy as the client-supplier relationship discussed above? Since you can interview your clients, why not use the same process by encouraging your suppliers to do the same with you? If you change the roles and flip the script, the level of insight you gain may just surprise you. At best, you will both come out winners or, at the very least, you will have a better understanding of how to help each other. Why not give it a try?

Creating Trust Through Timely, Clear and Honest Communication

"Sow Trust and you Reap Trust"

We highlighted trust as one of the leader's key traits in Part I of this book, "Trust is a Must". We also touched briefly on trust in the previous chapter, and you will come across it again in Part III, "Team Members". Trust is that important; it needs to exist, to be sown and nurtured within all teams and organisations. Without trust, relationships fail, and things quickly fall apart.

Trust makes up the fabric of our society. Trust (or lack thereof) dictates most of our daily actions and responses on everything from the routine to the complex, from the personal to the impersonal. We make assumptions all the time based on what we have been taught, what we believe, what we observe and what is part of our lives. We say 'assumption' because, what we perceive as our reality, may not necessarily be the actual situation before us. We believe what we want to believe or what we perceive to be true.

Whenever a negative situation arises in our personal lives that does not involve others, then responsibility and accountability can only fall on us. We can't blame others for any decision we have taken and, by the same token, it is not right for others to sit in judgement of our decisions. However, the discussion changes when a group (or team) is formed, and responsibilities are shared between the members.

The moment two or more people get together, the uncertainty, linked to cooperation and understanding, makes leading a team a little more complicated.

131

"Trust is a function of two things: character and competence.
Character includes your integrity, your motive and your intent
with people. Competence includes your capabilities, your skills,
and your track record. Both are vital."

Steven R. Covey

As business and sales leaders, our team's performance is a direct result of our team's effectiveness and willingness to collaborate as a team. Both internal and external factors contribute to complicating things to varying degrees, but the root of the trust conundrum is to effectively recognise and integrate both the leader's character and competence.

Trust is the backbone of any relationship. The leadership role must be earned through integrity, honesty, and responsibility. A leader who communicates well and often with their team is off to a good start in building team trust.

The Leader's Failure: A Great Opportunity to Earn Trust

We must accept that we will make mistakes and probably repeat them. Real leaders are defined by how they assume ownership of errors and take the opportunity to correct them. We can all agree that when an error is committed and discovered, the automatic human response is to lose confidence in the person responsible. Obviously, the severity of the blunder will dictate the level of confidence lost, regardless of who caused the error in the first place. But if the leader precipitated the error, they must immediately rectify it for the team, climb their way back up, and regain the team members' confidence. Trust takes years to build, seconds to break, and forever to repair.

If we consider that the sales transactions only close when there are trusted relationships between the salesperson and the client, it is clear that losing the trust of our clients due to wrongdoing, either as a company or as salespeople, could have a significant impact on our reputation and devastating consequences for the business.

Trust: A Tale for Small Medium Enterprise (SME) Owners

On Sunday, the 1st of February, 2009, 100 million Americans tuned in to watch Super Bowl XLIII, showcasing the Pittsburgh Steelers and the Arizona Cardinals in a game that would decide the 2008 season's National Football League (NFL) champions.

The game was broadcast in over 30 languages and across 130 countries. For a brief 4-hour period, people around the globe were distracted from their daily lives to witness a thrilling Steelers victory that concluded with Ben Roethlisberger throwing the winning touchdown to Santonio Holmes with only 35 seconds left on the game clock. This was an unforgettable season finale for football fans that will be talked about for years to come.

For one football fan, in particular, this game was the last thing on his mind. Even though he hadn't missed a Super Bowl in over 25 years, he had to pass it up this year. He was sitting alone in his office, preparing for a disaster. He had less than 24 hours left to save his SME company from bankruptcy.

At 9:00 am the following day, banking agents from the 'special accounts' department were scheduled to walk into his office with only one objective: recover the funds from an overextended operating line of credit (LOC).

Finances were a problem, and the secured loan was being recalled. Questionable management decisions and the business's poor performance led to this downfall, and the business owner was left with just two options:

a. desperately try to save his company, or

b. give up and shut it all down.

The agents arrived the next morning, as scheduled. They bullied their way into the company's accounting records, froze all banking activities and took control of all receivables and payables. In less than an hour, they had annulled all payments made over the past two weeks, essentially reversing all recent payments to employees, suppliers and utility companies. Employees immediately found out and stormed into the owner's office demanding to know, "*What happened to our paychecks?!*". Panic ensued. It was time to begin some serious damage control.

While the football world was still abuzz with the previous night's big game, the business owner felt the weight of the world crushing him. He needed to take immediate action if he was to ease everyone's doubts. Within a few hours, the owner personally wired funds into each employee's bank account to make up for the last two payrolls. Desperation led to frustration, frustration led to sorrow, sorrow led to a feeling of defeat.

Over the next few weeks, the bank collected all incoming receivables to cover the LOC. Not a dollar was spent without the bank's consent; only weekly payrolls were accepted, and suppliers were told to wait. With all this going on, the owner hired a trustee to handle all debt-related activities and provide guidance for a debt reduction plan.

The owner had, by now, lost the confidence of all his suppliers. The trustee gave him the brutal truth: the road ahead would be long and steep, and it would be many years before any chartered bank would consider allowing him a new operating LOC.

A debt reduction plan was presented to suppliers, which they accepted, begrudgingly. With the last of the debt collection complete, the bank stripped away the final strands of the LOC, ignored the company's pleas for assistance, and left them to fend for themselves without any funds for suppliers. It would have to be Cash-On-Delivery (COD) for all suppliers from that point on.

Suppliers were contacted once again for a 'second chance' at credit and, no surprise, they all refused. To make matters worse, several employees left the company, fearing this was the end of the road.

"The ship started taking on water, so I might as well jump off now before the whole thing sinks." It was certainly understandable for them to think this way. Confidence was at an all-time low, and it was the bleakest of scenarios.

Re-establishing trust among all business partners and the remaining employees was the first step towards any resumption to normalcy and continuance of its operations. The big question was: How do you rebuild this trust? The owner began with an honest and open dialogue with employees to reassure them that the primary goal was to survive this crisis, continue all operations and avoid any layoffs. Beginning with group meetings, management laid out the situation with complete transparency of the financial issues.

These discussions proved to be embarrassing at best, disheartening at worst. Yet, it was crucial to tell the story as it actually was with no sugarcoating whatsoever. The thought was, "*Get the worst news out now*", and identify which employees will remain on board. Going forward, these are the employees you will want on your team.

Any employee that needed individual time was granted it without hesitation; everyone was on the same page, and no one was left out of the discussion. Indeed this goes without saying, but getting to know your staff and adding in that personal touch are essential team-building blocks.

Most discussions between ownership, management, and staff were carried out at a very basic human level to rebuild trust. Employees inquired about job stability, their future, and the future of the company, very much like a basic case study of Maslow's Hierarchy of Needs. Actual figures and numbers were rarely discussed, not because there was anything to hide; it just wasn't a topic that the employees inquired about.

The second order of business was to reassure all major clients that the operations would not be compromised as long as their accounts payable departments would agree to accelerated payments. Such an outlying team would not customarily be part of any sales-related discussions, and yet they took on the crucial role to allow the supplier-client relationship to continue.

If any were to refuse accelerated payment terms, it could very well constitute the loss of that client. Cash was that tight. Personalised phone calls to all major clients led to all of them accepting the renegotiated payment terms. Oddly, these departments contributed to the ongoing sales process and kept the business afloat. Both client and supplier were now in agreement, and a big reset button had been pressed with a renewed outlook on the relationships.

The lesson to be learned here: even the most unexpected players may participate in the sales process and provide assistance to your sales team.

While the details had not yet been completely figured out, the upcoming days and weeks would set the stage for an eventual turnaround. It was a daunting task, but a slight sense of optimism was in the air, which grew as the days turned into weeks, and the weeks turned into months.

Some assets were sold to raise cash, and a significant cost-cutting process was carried out for the company's new defensive position. Without any operating funds, revenue growth was not on the cards which, under the circumstances, was acceptable. The company quickly learned to manage finances tightly and set appropriate priorities for a future with this re-energised team. Within a year, suppliers began extending credit again in place of COD conditions. Extending credit = extending trust.

Four years on and a new operating LOC was granted by a chartered bank, albeit eight times smaller than before. It wasn't much, but it was something to work with and build upon. You could almost hear Bob Dylan singing, *"When you ain't got nothing, you've got nothing to lose"* from 'Like a Rolling Stone'. An apt theme song for this moment.

Mistakes stemmed from a lack of attention to details which resulted in the mismanagement of the company's finances. The employees believed that the company did not intentionally act irresponsibly based on its history with them.

The managers had historically been honest and very open with the team. It is most likely this key factor that provided much-needed credibility during this anxious time. *"They've taken good care of us for all these years; we should at least give them a chance to make this right."*

We can all learn from this real-life story. When something goes wrong, you should ask yourself:

1. Why did we get here?

2. How will we get out of it?

3. What will we do to prevent this from reoccurring?

The worst-case scenario was, had things turned out badly for this company, the business would have failed and would have had to shut its doors. But isn't there always an opportunity to start over again if you believe in yourself and are willing to put in the effort?

You may not always have the answers in front of you, but as long as you have the will to survive, you will find the energy to recover. The rest just gets figured out along the way. Remember always:

"Believe you can, and you are halfway there!"

Theodore Roosevelt

Belief in Shared Values, Purpose, Principles and Communication

The shared values and belief in an organisation's purpose and principles are the building blocks of the company's foundation to create a future vision. Simply having a written statement on a memo or a mission statement hanging on the wall is lazy and inadequate.

For this to actually work, the leader must firmly believe in the values with an unshakable faith to uphold the values and create a future vision. Only then can the leader project this onto the employees and business partners. When it comes to distributing information within an organisation, everyone should be kept in the loop and be expected to participate. **Jack Welch**, the former CEO of *GE*, called this flow of information *"boundaryless communication"*, which embraced team members and eliminated cliques.

Employees were treated equally concerning access to information.

- The first law of communication is to be a great listener.

- The second law is to ask good questions.

- The third law? Simply go back and re-read the first law.

The "Trust Pyramid"

We can use the difficulties faced by the SME from our earlier story to highlight the definitions taken from **Patrick Lencioni's** book *"The Five Dysfunctions of a Team"*, wherein he defines a "Trust Pyramid:" the basic foundation to building a great team.

A well-built team has five solid requirements:

1. **Trust**

2. **Commitment**

3. **Accept conflict**

4. **Accountability**

5. **Attention to goals and results**.

Coincidentally, these building blocks were encountered by the SME as detailed below:

Trust: The employees in our story already had a level of trust based on past history with management. Although the crisis tore away at that trust, it was slowly re-established when the management team took good care of its staff in their moment of dire need. At the root of this recovery was constant communication at all levels. The more we discuss, the more we learn from one another.

Commitment: Management acted swiftly to manage the employees' wellbeing and fallout around the company finances. Worrisome days and sleepless nights defined the next several months, but the employees rolled up their sleeves and bought into the cause with their full attention since the owner was fully committed too. Like the old adage says, '*lead by example*'. When the leader demonstrated that he applied an intense work ethic to right the wrongs, his employees understood that they also had to 'up their game' if they were to survive as a group. The leader suggested what needed to be done as a joint team to succeed, and all team members were welcome to provide any further insights or recommendations. This joint collaborative effort provided a company-wide level of engagement rarely seen within the building.

Accept conflict: Disruption and instability created scheduling problems between the planning and production departments. There were disagreements on expenses (which the accountants deemed unnecessary). Sales and production teams argued when the sales leader took on more contracts with a production team that was temporarily short-staffed. Diverging opinions eventually led to intense verbal conflicts between the teams. The leader felt a heightened need to 'stay the course' and keep all team members calm and focused. During times of heightened tensions, the leader encouraged more dialogue between the teams to improve communication and understanding as any misstep could set off one department against another.

Accountability: There was a renewed sense of accountability and responsibility throughout the organisation. Oddly, everyone had each other's backs while at the same time suspiciously keeping an eye on each other. This may sound contradictory, but while an organisation is navigating a highly stressful situation to re-establish itself, it may be subject to internal suspicion. This happened on a company-wide level, and no one was left out of this recovery process. The owner realised that the organisation might benefit from an appreciation system. It was possible that staff members were feeling underappreciated, even though no one had said anything to that effect. The leader adopted a more understanding approach by inspiring employees with a message that everyone needs to hear every once in a while, "*I appreciate you, I appreciate your efforts and trust, I believe in you*". This approach created a stronger connection between him and the employees and increased everyone's confidence levels. Only the strictest combination of integrity and complete sincerity will yield positive results; anything less verges on dishonesty and manipulation. Eventually, accountability took care of itself from the early stages of the recovery phase.

Attention to goals and results: There was a renewed sense of the need to measure performance using data, statistics, metrics and results for future guidance. Sales targets and goals were set, and a fresh new mindset took hold. For team members to truly visualise the future, the vision must be presented and communicated as often as possible. The best leaders constantly remind their teams of organisational goals, team goals, and future vision. By clarifying a new set of expectations (or reminding the team of an existing set), the leader creates the idea of goal-setting and provides a destination for the organisation's success. With a new set of expectations, you can press the reset button and help your team visualise your 2.0 organisation, which can further quantify your team's future HR needs.

A crisis is the real test of levels of trust.

A Crisis to Shake up the Global Economy: Threat and Opportunity

"*Never waste a good crisis*". Although attributed to Winston Churchill, it was **Niccolo Machiavelli** who first coined the phrase in his famous book "*The Prince*". The quote was, "*Never waste the opportunity offered by a good crisis.*"

While researching the quote, we came across a brilliant blog post entitled "***How to Never Waste a Good Crisis***", written and published by **Dan Rockwell** in his Blog "*The Leadership Freak*"[38].

He writes:

> *Leaders are developing a healthy case of humility during COVID-19. Frankly, it's a good thing because lousy leadership is rooted in ego.*
>
> *Success followed by admiration tests character.*
>
> *An ancient Jewish proverb puts it this way, "The crucible is for silver, and the furnace is for gold, and a man is tested by his praise."*
>
> *The beauty of disruption is the rediscovery of humility.*
>
> *Disruption exposes the power of humility and the folly of arrogance. Where are the cocky leaders? They can't tout their accomplishments and spout easy answers today. If they're smart, they've shut their arrogant mouths.*
>
> *"Pride makes us artificial, and humility makes us real." Thomas Merton.*

This post was written during the COVID-19 crisis when remote leadership became the new norm. While I write these lines, on the 7th of February 2021, the global pandemic reached record highs compared to the first peak in April 2020, both for Daily New Infections (500,000+) and Daily Deaths (close to 15,000). The greatest success story to come out of the COVID-19 pandemic has got to be the acceleration of society's digital transformation and its prevalence in the world's economy.

---

[38] The Leadership Freak Blog: https://leadershipfreak.
blog/2020/04/15/how-to-never-waste-a-good-crisis/

Teradata, the company that co-authors Andy and Pablo both work for, decided to close most of its global offices, keeping only the largest ones open.

This sudden change to the way in which we work was extended further when it was announced that there would be no return to the remaining offices before April 2021.

How can sales teams and their leaders navigate big crises like the Lehman Brothers in the 2008 financial crisis and today's COVID-19 crisis?

While researching this book, our co-author Eddie Baez interviewed sales leaders Victor Antonio and Mike Figliuolo. Victor Antonio and Mike Figliuolo are examples of how a growth mindset, strong belief, creativity and decision-making, together with bold and fast execution, are key to a leader's ability to navigate challenging times successfully.

In their interviews, both Victor and Mike stated that their traditional sales training and coaching businesses which, before COVID-19, relied heavily on on-site events and offline sales based on face-to-face meetings, simply wouldn't be feasible from April 2020. Both of their companies faced uncertainty.

Victor Antonio is a well-known and in-demand keynote speaker on sales and sales leadership. The onset of COVID-19 resulted in the cancellation of all of his upcoming speaking engagements. Victor realised that this was his opportunity to accelerate his digital coaching activities.

He quickly pivoted towards digital and invested in sophisticated IT equipment. His new digital sales coaching studio was up and running in less than two months. He was able to keep his business running and actually grew it further thanks to the speed of digital sales and coaching.

Victor is now regularly on LinkedIn, giving live coaching sessions to sales professionals around the world. He has succeeded in driving more clients to his 100% online coaching business. He also hosts his podcast *"Sales Influence"* and a Youtube Channel. Both serve as digital multiplicators driving more awareness and clients to his business.

This is clearly a great real-life example of a growth mindset, creativity, and willingness to adapt.

Mike Figliuolo offers more insight into dealing with a crisis. As the owner and CEO of thoughtLEADERS, a professional training coaching business, he was asked by Eddie Baez about the impact of a crisis such as COVID-19 on a sales team. He said that the key thing about a crisis is not what happens to us but how we react to it.

Many competitors in his market space started complaining about the negative impact of the pandemic. They began cost-cutting, reducing their teams, and entering into a negative spiral affecting their businesses. Mike took a different approach. First, he recognised the crisis as a serious threat to his business. Like Victor, he faced the problem head-on and challenged his team: "What are we going to do? What are our options?"

They saw the opportunity to shift to digital online training. They quickly built a new online coaching concept and launched their adapted courses in record time.

In October 2020, Mike's business was only down 9% for the FY 10 months compared to his best year ever (which was 2019). Due to the intrinsic ease of access, the speed of payments, 24/7 availability, and immediate digital content delivery, he is now growing faster than ever before.

"Necessity Begets Ingenuity" – proven, yet again!

To put it bluntly: Crises are great opportunities to prove that a team is really strong, that the culture is strong enough to hold them all together against all odds, and that the team can adapt quickly to the challenges. The same is true for leadership and leaders. The team will quickly turn problems and challenges into opportunities and will not only get through the crisis but will come out the other side stronger than ever before.

Effective and Clear Communication: The "Oil" of the Team's Motor

The team that can lead itself is like gold to a leader because it allows for complete delegation and frees up additional time to focus on strategic, high-value leadership activities. But for this to happen, the leader must create an employee communication circle whereby team members learn to discuss matters amongst themselves, solve problems as a unit, and assume individual leadership, albeit on a smaller scale.

The leader must demonstrate expertise in their profession to gain credence with team members; otherwise, why would anyone follow them? The leader's expertise can be taught and coached regularly and, as with everything else in life, repetition leads to regularity, forming healthy habits.

With the right amount of coaching and teaching, a great leader can provide just enough guidance and leadership to create a self-sustaining machine that enhances the individual qualities of those team members who wish to aspire to greater leadership positions. If the team can take care of itself with members who care for one another, they will first commit to the vision and cause, leading to a dedicated and energetic team.

If done well, more capable employees in the team may compensate for those team members who are less skilled, thereby simplifying the leader's job. The ultimate benefit of this approach is that the team's overall performance is enhanced, resulting in personal rewards and benefits for all.

When a leader has a team member who is willing and able to work with others and understands their role on the team, this is an ideal starting point to building trust among the team members. Leaders must surround themselves with members who truly believe that their loyalty (and well-being) lies with the team's advancement.

"What is good for the team is also good for me."

Although you may not always choose your initial team members, you can still shape the team's make-up for the future. Take, for instance, a newly hired coach coming in to take over an established sports team; fans may say, '*But we have lousy players; how much can he really accomplish with our team?*' For any incoming coach or leader, they have to be given the benefit of the doubt and be granted the opportunity to do what they do. If we all cooperate, we may very well realise the coach's vision for the team. He will look to stock up his newly acquired team with skilled players and make adjustments to his roster.

The sports world is not so different from the corporate world, is it?

"Start where you are. Use what you have. Do what you can."

Arthur Ashe

Provide a Safe Environment – Allow the Team to "Fail forward"

Team members will make mistakes, but as the leader, you must reassure them that you have faith that they can carry out their duties. Team members must be afforded the psychological safety to know that if their decisions lead to errors, they will not be reprimanded; otherwise, no one will ever take on any new responsibilities or create added value for the team. It is certainly reasonable for employees to feel uneasy about acting or speaking out against their boss; there will always be the fear of a reprimand. A reassuring leader, however, will not be handing out pink slips at every mistake which will go a long way towards creating an autonomous team. We learn most from our mistakes, so any loss must be accepted as a learning experience. We don't fail; we learn.

> *"You may learn much more from a game you lose than from a game you win. You will have to lose hundreds of games before becoming a good player."*
> **Chess World Champion, José Raúl Capablanca**

A leader must accept these mistakes and reassure the team members that, while it is unfortunate, it is also understandable and somewhat expected. We have found that constructive criticism is a powerful instrument for improving performance. Employees who receive positive support and guidance will be willing to repay the company far more than any other method. Building up the team as though they are a unit of 'independent contractors' means that each team member will carry out their orders and lead their mini-teams, resulting in widespread engagement.

This is a slow process, and leaders must be willing to sacrifice their time and energy in developing and nurturing their teams.

Good leaders will get the best from their people by following this approach. Great leaders understand this and can work wonders in elevating an average performing team to greater heights. Even when things seem disjointed, anything is attainable with the right training and supervision. We say 'attainable' not 'guaranteed'; it is a process that takes time and patience. The delegation of tasks is crucial to this process; otherwise, there will be an insufficient sharing of duties, resulting in the leader taking on everything. Delegating will afford the leader the 'space to get the ship out of the port'. We will explore this further in Chapter 5 when we discuss the value of the leader's time, the scarcest resource.

The Importance of Coaching and Mentoring

One of the most effective techniques for preparing your team for improved future performance is to coach the members with regularity. A leader will use their strong character to openly and honestly impart knowledge, expertise, and skills.

We recognise that the growth prospects of the SME company from our story relied too heavily on the business owner; the employees were ill-equipped to contribute.

The SME owner did not sufficiently teach or delegate to his employees and was left shouldering the burden of many tasks. Employees became too comfortable in their roles, resulting in a stagnant workforce with minimal challenges.

Without a doubt, this was the biggest hindrance to the company's development and expansion. The business had enormous potential; both for the company in terms of revenue growth, and for the team members in terms of personal growth, yet this potential remained largely untapped. When the business was in crisis, it became a priority to abandon the routine and create a level of tension and discomfort that would see the company through unchartered and choppy waters.

Authors **Bill Eckstrom** and **Sarah Wirth** recently published the book *"The Coaching Effect"* after spending a decade researching the activities, behaviours, and performances of leaders.

A description of the book, found on Goodreads, says it best:

> *After studying more than 100,000 coaching interactions in the workplace, primarily of sales teams, they have been able to determine how coaching affects team outcomes and growth. The authors share three critical performance drivers, along with the four high-growth activities that coaches must execute to build a team that is motivated to achieve at the highest levels.*
>
> *Through both hard data and rich stories, Eckstrom and Wirth demonstrate how leaders can measure and improve their coaching to lead their teams to better results. The Coaching Effect will help leaders at all levels understand the necessity of challenging people out of their comfort zone to create a high-growth organization. Leaders will learn how they can develop trust relationships, drive accountability and leverage growth experiences to propel their team members to the highest levels of success.*

The chapters relating to high growth present straightforward, no-nonsense activities that are well laid out with a simple coaching process that any company leader can use. Committing time, effort and follow-through to these tasks should yield positive results.

A formalised training plan was lacking at the SME company. At the time of writing this, the SME has initiated a process to build a company-wide teaching strategy through training and execution. Though still in the early stages, they are confident that employing the techniques from "The Coaching Effect", including planned and scheduled coaching with solicited feedback, will eventually promote voluntary feedback and growth among the personnel. When that happens, the SME company will be well on its way to achieving internal team collaboration. Coaching is all about communication.

Giving the team the necessary tools to recognise the stages of growth, as detailed in the book, any business can help sustain the learning process and reshape the vision for the company's future.

Communication Takes Time–More Than you Might Think

We can all agree that clear and timely communication is a key aspect of effective leadership, so let's look at how much time this may take.

The table below shows a simple communication planner giving an estimated time (in minutes) for a sales director in a multinational software company with only three direct reports.

Here is a snapshot:

Communication/Event Description	Format	Recurr.	When	Dur. min	Prep time	Post call time	Total time	Total	Total time	Invite Done
Account Executives (AE) Accountability Call: Closed - Pipeline -	Remote: Teams	Monthly	Second Tuesday	15	15	15	45	30	1.350,00	YES
Sales Team Accountability and Business Development Call	Remote: Teams	Monthly	Second Friday	90	90	30	210	10	2.100,00	YES
Quarterly Team "All Hands" Business Review Call	Remote: Teams	Quarterly	First Friday	90	420	30	540	4	2.160,00	NO
Solution Engineer (SE) Manager alignment call	Remote: Teams	Monthly	Second Tuesday	30	15	15	60	10	600,00	YES
Customer For Lifetime Partners (CFLP) alignment call - Italy & Spain	Remote: Teams	Monthly	Second Friday	30	15	15	60	10	600,00	NO
Partner Mananger alignment call - Spain & Italy	Remote: Teams	Monthly	Second Friday	30	15	15	60	10	600,00	NO
Customer Success Manager (CSM) alignment call - Italy & Spain	Remote: Teams	Monthly	Second Friday	30	15	15	60	10	600,00	NO

We have identified 21 lines of activity showing that the sales director needs a total of 750 hours or 94 days of work just for communication alone, i.e., calls, meetings and events.

This already accounts for 43% of the sales director's total available annual work time with only three direct reports. If we stretched this out for a sales director with six direct reports, we soon realise that there is a natural limit for effective team leadership and management, and 6-8 direct reports are more than enough. At this point, the player-coach model would no longer work; there would just not be enough time to do both jobs well!

Doing the Right Things: Understanding What is Important

The trademark of a well-led organisation is one that is reasonably self-directed and self-sufficient without the need for constant involvement by its leaders. As discussed in Chapter 4, the leader is on the right path when the team members proactively and confidently organise tasks amongst themselves by combining their talents to analyse issues, find efficient solutions, and act upon them.

While an autonomous team takes time to develop, it will come about sooner when the team structure is planned and drawn up ahead of time. The leader's role is to create this framework for the personnel.

An organisation taking on business projects will expect a financial return through a combination of finances, time, logistics, and human resources. These project expectations are not new, but unless the leader recognises their own personal value attached to the project's Return-On-Investment (ROI), it will take much longer to get any plan deployed.

Despite being in charge, leaders are human too and getting bogged down in daily mundane tasks will continue unless they recognise this as a costly use of time and extracts themselves from these activities. Handling growth-related essential activities and delegating non-essential tasks to others is a much better use of the leader's time.

Delegate or Die

We can calculate the importance of the leader's input and use those figures to determine what the leader should do, what can be delegated to others, and what can simply be eliminated from the task list. Priorities should be based on what is of prime importance to the organisation, not what is urgent at that time. While a leader can plan for the quarter and the upcoming month, daily and weekly routines establish discipline and habits.

> *"No person will make a great business who wants to do it all himself or get all the credit."*

Dale Carnegie

Planning and Setting Priorities

There are numerous daily productivity planners on the market that recommend establishing three major tasks per day. We may be so inundated with emails, meetings, and requests for our help that we lose sight of who we are, what we were hired to do, and how to achieve our goals.

> *"The key is not to prioritize what's on your schedule, but to schedule your priorities."*

Stephen Covey

> *"Deciding what not to do is as important as deciding what to do."*

Steve Jobs

Time is a scarce resource, and any leader who cannot control their use of it may undermine the team's collective efforts and disappoint them by not attaining the goals. As discussed in Chapter 4, the team's growth is determined by the team's initiative, training and the sharing of responsibilities.

> *"Time is also a unique resource. Of the other major resources, money is actually quite plentiful. We long ago should have learned that it is the demand for capital, rather than the supply thereof, which sets the limit to economic growth and activity. People—the third limiting resource—one can hire, though one can rarely hire enough good people. But one cannot rent, hire, buy, or otherwise obtain more time."*

Peter Drucker

Co-author Andy Jaffke created a tool to set priorities for the four key areas of your life with his "**Top3Planner**"³⁹.

Of the four key areas (quadrants) shown, he demonstrates that Quadrant II (Important and not urgent tasks) is ideal for great leaders. Many leaders will dedicate time and strive for the Change Quadrant by eliminating Quadrants I, III, and IV tasks.

The two essential methods of achieving the Change Quadrant are by saying no and delegating.

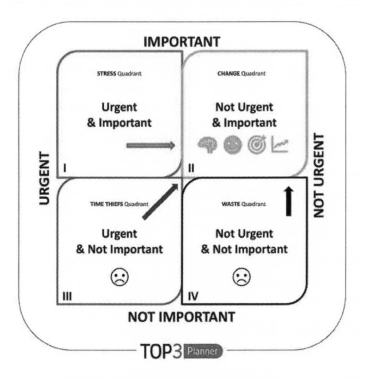

**Figure 4: The Urgent/Not Urgent -
Important/Not important Quadrants**

---

39 http://www.top3planner.com/

Manage your Scarcest Resource Well: Time

A leader can effectively manage their time by being productively selfish about it. The leader needs to have a well-designed plan if they are determined not to be the group's 'safety valve' and free up time. The team members will still progress in the leader's absence by submitting to the leader's pre-established plan. A forward-thinking leader's plan will account for possible crises, such as leave due to health issues or retirement, that enables the business to function even in the leader's absence.

There is an excellent analogy in *"Clockwork"*, a book written by **Mike Michalowicz** for SME business owners. He asks you, as the leader, to dig deep and identify the one major role (a role, not a person) of supreme importance that will 'move the needle' in your business. Once you identify that role, you must protect it at all costs and ensure that nothing ever interferes with it. While Mike Michalowicz wrote this book from an SME owner's perspective, we can apply the approach to all aspects of our lives. Through common sense, self-discipline and self-respect, we can regain control of our time and our lives.

If, as leaders, we cannot set an example by managing ourselves, how can we expect our employees to do so? Why not nominate one or two colleagues to act as your personal internal auditors and have them hold you accountable for your commitments? It may be hard on the ego at first, having a colleague keep track of you, but it will prove that you are fully committed to the team.

Like any company quality control system, the QC manual states:

1. Have written and documented what you will do; then

2. You must do what is written and documented.

Can we apply the same thinking to our daily lives? Are we not more forgiving of ourselves when we are only accountable to ourselves? Of course, we are!

You Can't Improve What you Can't Measure

We give ourselves free passes and procrastinate every chance we get; otherwise, there wouldn't be so many books on time management. Consultants make a living just on this topic alone, and the concept is not beyond our grasp if we are simply willing to put in the effort. Ask a colleague to hold you accountable, measure the outcomes, take control, and aim not to disappoint. It will work wonders.

Our SME owner from Chapter 4, when feeling unproductive, began calculating and measuring his time allocation by collecting data in 30-minute increments to produce a series of in-house metrics. The same was done with employees to relieve the owner of some of the duties eventually.

After some weeks, the SME owner noticed a pattern. The time he had allocated to business development revealed that every hour spent on sales-related activities (prospecting, bidding, research, proposal preparation, contract negotiation, closing) resulted in substantial revenue generation and company growth.

While this obviously made sense, the owner was surprised by just how much of a difference it made. It far exceeded his estimations! He continued collecting data over the next several months, and the numbers remained at their lofty levels. He proceeded to identify and categorise tasks and found that there were 45 distinct tasks, on any given month, that were routinely his to do.

Armed with this new information, the SME owner identified those tasks which could either be eliminated or delegated. He held a round table session with his team to agree on which tasks could be transferred to other colleagues. The team decided to defer some 20 tasks, thereby reducing the leader's tasks by over 40%. Even though the team could have assumed responsibility for these tasks, the company owner had been doing them himself all along.

With an upcoming internal coaching programme, the goal was to reduce the owner's tasks even further down to 15, a total reduction of 67% of the leader's original task list. The time the leader regained from this exercise could be reallocated to the company's major critical task, a complete sales development.

And it all started when the company owner first discovered the power of calculating the Return-On-Time-Invested (R.O.T.I.) for himself, essentially the company's return (margin) generated for every hour he spent on business development. This eye-opening experience made him much more aware of how he used his time; it was as though a bright light had been cast on years of confusion and time mismanagement.

As you read this, we invite you to contact us for more detailed information on the process and thinking behind this. We would be more than happy to explain this further. Both SME's and larger organisations can use the methods we've set out to determine the value and worth of sales team members.

Two questions arise for you, the sales leader: Do you know your own worth? Do you know your manager's value as perceived by your colleagues?

Wharton School professor **Peter Fader** wrote the books "**Customer Centricity**" and "**Customer Centricity Playbook**" which identify and quantify the **Customer Lifetime Value (CLV)** defined as "The customer's value to a supplier over the entire lifetime of the relationship."

We've taken a slightly different approach by reviewing the client/supplier relationship in reverse to calculate, what we call, the **Supplier Lifetime Value**, defined as "the supplier's value to the client." Using a quantified approach to calculate the % of mindshare, we can estimate how much we believe our company is worth to the client. This is done by conducting client interviews with your largest clients and calculating the wallet share through a series of metrics suitable for your organisation; for example, what is your share of your client's annual purchasing volume?

You can generate a whole series of metrics, including calculating the sales coach's value and effectiveness in the team (how much is the leader/coach worth when they are there?).

How about we take it one step further and just call it **Servant Leadership Value (SLV),** the leader's perceived value to the team. This value will either be a net positive or net negative team effect of employee satisfaction, revenue, or wallet share of the clients under the leader's leadership, all done while serving and leading the team, as explained in Chapter 3. Data can easily be captured through employee interviews and questionnaires and reduce the time frame to a year or quarter instead of a 'lifetime'. Once you identify what is essential to your organisation, you can begin incorporating whatever metrics you deem appropriate.

Start by considering these questions:

- What is considered high performance (HP) anyway?

- Is there a generic formula or number that can be used?

- Who determines this in your organisation?

- Is it based on individuals or oriented towards teams?

These are questions that can be answered by self-assessing the needs, the capabilities and the targets for growth. Should you first create the team and define what HP means, or do you target HP personnel beforehand to build your team from the front?

Coach Up or Coach Out, Training & Self-Learning

How can you ensure that a team is constantly and consistently growing? We will use a professional sports team to demonstrate. We can all agree that most of what professional athletes do stems from an exceptionally well-thought-out plan. They don't just show up to games hoping for a win. All the time between their games and competitions is filled with training sessions, nutritional plans, health checks and everything else that promotes teamwork.

For sports teams, planning is the most important activity reserved for the managers/coaches. These are not activities that managers and coaches can delegate to individual players.

Plans are great, but they are worthless unless accompanied by proper preparation, practice and execution (playing the game), and this next chapter introduces the key activities of self-learning, training and coaching.

While self-learning is more focused on the individual, training and coaching are key activities for developing teams and improving performance at a collective level.

Team Training and Coaching

Team training and coaching activities usually happen simultaneously. When setting up a client meeting, the account executive (the de facto team leader), will prepare for and run a client meeting while the sales director assumes the role of trainer and coach.

As a trainer, the sales director will review if the account executive has effectively prepared for the meeting, e.g., setting an agenda and assigning roles to each contributor, to ensure that the client meeting runs smoothly and everyone knows when and how to perform their assigned tasks.

As a coach, the sales director will observe how the meeting is run, taking notes on everyone's participation or non-participation. As a coach, the function of the sales director is to quietly observe the team at work, focusing on what is seen and heard, and considering, "*Was this client meeting good enough to be repeated in front of other clients?*" After the meeting concludes, he will immediately meet with the team for a debriefing session and question them to get feedback about their individual and team performance.

The following are sample post-evaluation questions: "*What went well and what didn't go so well?*", "*What was missing and what was not necessary?*", "*How was the energy in the room: Positive, neutral or negative?*", "*What can we improve for the next meeting?*", "*How efficient were we with time?*".

The point of coaching is not to give (unsolicited) feedback by telling the team members what they did right or wrong, but to ask open-ended questions that will make the team members think about their answers. This method of coaching is much more powerful as it triggers a complex creative mental process.

Feedback involves merely listening to the trainer without actually thinking about the actions. In contrast, open-ended questions require team members to do their own assessments by thinking and formulating responses that go beyond the simple "Yes" or "No" of closed questions like "*Was that the right thing to do?*" or "*Did you check this with the client?*"

In the sales environment, an effective leader must assume three different roles at the individual and team levels, i.e., manager, trainer, and coach/mentor.

Manager: The manager's role is to tell team members and the team what to do, when to do it, and provide the resources and support for them to perform optimally. Support may include external resources and partners, and internal experts, teams and departments. Management will also control and measure both the resources used (Cost of Sales) and the results produced (Revenue and margin).

Trainer: The goal is to simultaneously develop the skills of the individual team members and the team as a unit with materials like books, podcasts, videos, feedback and motivation. For a successful trainer, the focus will be on the "How" of establishing a solid sales process.

It is important to measure each team member's performance across the whole sales cycle to identify strengths and weaknesses and harness the talent and mindset that each brings to the table.

The trainer will analyse the team's performance after each sales cycle and, if necessary, identify any adjustments to be worked into a training plan for continuous improvement.

Peer learning is also a very effective way of improving the skill set of team members. Consider putting three sales teams in the same room to share their best and worst practices. It's incredible to witness how ideas surface and how problems and challenges are analysed and solved in a wider group of peers.

Coach/Mentor: As previously discussed, a key aspect of good coaching and mentoring is using open-ended questions formulated to make people actively think through the processes and activities they participated in and/or their own observations, experiences and emotions.

Coaching addresses the individual's and the team's cognitive and emotional skills while healthy connections between people provide cohesion.

Dysfunctional teams are usually disjointed; the lack of communication between team members may be due to poor emotional connections between some individual team members. At times, the coach needs to act as a therapist and openly bring out these emotions for discussion and resolution if the team members are to move forward as a cohesive unit.

Coach Up or Coach Out

Talent in individuals is not everything. An individual who doesn't fit into the system or simply refuses to accept the rules or processes may be toxic to the team, negatively impacting team members, the team, and the team's performance.

Initially, the coach may attempt to get the individual to recognise that their behaviour is not helpful to the team and that change is needed. If the individual does not correct their behaviour, it may be time to have an exit conversation, expressing that they should pursue other opportunities more suitable for them.

A sales team may do this through monthly 1-on-1 accountability meetings between the sales director and the account executive (AE). The sales director's responsibility is to hold the AE accountable for their performance. By looking at the basics, we can check on two key metrics:

1. **Where are you with your sales quota attainment**? If it's the July review, we should be at or above 50% of the annual quota attainment.

2. **Where are you with your opportunity pipeline**? Review both the current fiscal year (FY) pipeline and the 15 months forecasted pipeline. For the 15 months forecasted pipeline to be healthy, it should be 3-4 times the AE's current FY quota. It also depends on the individual closing ratio of the AE and the history behind the numbers.

AEs could be under quota at any given time of the FY due to seasonal impacts on their business. For instance, in enterprise software sales, Q4 is usually the strongest closing quarter, mainly due to procurement departments knowing that the last quarter provides a good opportunity for getting extra discounts.

The pipeline, both the current and the 15 months forecasted, is the key metric that defines the AE's efforts. AEs who have developed solid long-term pipelines have these three things in common:

1. The AE understands that to reap; they must first sow;

2. The AE understands that without a long-term focus, they run the risk of relying on only a handful of short-term deals; and

3. The AE constantly works with their team and talks to clients and prospects; they follow the process and use the resources to develop new opportunities.

If both the current FY and 15 months forecasted pipelines are below target, it is time to question the AE's agenda and activities.

Let's assume our FY is from the 1st of January to the 31st of December, and we are doing the July accountability call. The AE has reached 60% FY quota, but for the remaining 40%, he has coverage with 60% of opportunities. The AE is relying on only two potential deals to close out the year: one deal accounts for 40% of the FY quota, and the other deal for 20% of the FY quota. Both potential deals are planned for Q4 with a closing date of the 31st of December, and both deals are in the forecast category "**Upside**".

These are the probabilities based on the four forecast categories:

- **Pipeline: 20%** – Request for proposal received from a client or prospect and the value of the deal is known;

- **Upside: 40%** – Formal proposal and scope well defined, pricing clear, deal advanced, and we are on the shortlist;

- **Committed: 80%** – Usually a verbal commitment to close on a given date;

- **Closed: 100%** – Deal is signed. Additionally, the 15 months forecasted pipeline shows five opportunities covering only 2x the current FY quota, with all of them in the forecast category "**Pipeline**".

As a sales director, this situation raises a red flag for me. Here are some typical questions I would have for the AE in the July accountability call:

1. What is your closing plan for the two opportunities in Q4?

2. What are you doing to advance the closing date to November and prevent the deals from slipping into next year?

3. What have you done during the last month to move both deals forward?

4. What have you done with your team to create new opportunities in other accounts for the next FY?

5. Which existing opportunities have you moved forward in the sales cycle?

We are looking into the AE's activities, and while some people may see this as micromanaging, I consider this to be effective accountability management. I always tell my AEs:

> *Treat your clients and your territory like it was your own company, and always remember that as an employee, you will always get paid at the end of the month. Entrepreneurs don't always have it so easy when they have to chase payments. So if you want to increase your revenue with extra commissions, you have to develop your business. You have to meet with your clients, identify new opportunities, move these opportunities forward and make sure you close them. That's entirely up to you, and as long as you show me that you are managing and nurturing a healthy pipeline, our accountability calls finish after 10 minutes, and you are good to go.*

I use an elementary but highly effective Excel spreadsheet to prepare, run and report back to my AEs. My accountability calls focus on two key elements: what has worked and what needs to be improved on, which usually accounts for three to four items. The AE and I then agree on action points to be carried out for the next month.

Below is an example of one of my accountability call reports.

Roger Federer	04/11/2020				
	Targets ($k)	Closed TD	Gap to Go	% Gap	X-Factor
FY Quotas & Closed	$ 418.00	$ 487.00	$ -69.00	-17%	1.17
Pipeline Target 5Q	$ 1,672.00	$ 2,268.00	$ 96.00	-36%	5.43
Last Acc Review (Date)	05/10/2020	Total Quota Achievement FY2020	117%		

Notes: New Opportunities created since the last review.

Existing opportunities moved forward in the Sales Cycle.

1. Very positive: 5Q pipeline (5.43x FYQuota)

2. Very positive: At 117% quota achievement

3. Very positive: Key deal 1 (Closed) and Key deal 2 (Closing)

4. Very positive: FY2021 planning well advanced (Key Account 1, Key Account 2, Key Accounts 3 and 4)

Actions:

1. Schedule Q4 QBR's: Key Account 3 (After closing a key deal), Key Account 4 (Dept. A)

2. Close Key deal 2 either through partner A or partner B

3. Close Key deal 3 (Analytics Ops)–Close before Dec 15th!

4. Deliver final FY2021 budgets for Key Acc 3 and 4 (Key deals planned for FY2021

5. Agree on key projects and budgets FY2021 with Key Acc 5 (Key stakeholders)

Rating: Green = All Account & GOST (Goals, Objectives, Strategies, Tasks) Plans, Salesforce Opportunities regularly maintained and up to date, Pipeline Coverage sufficient to beat Quota

Rating Definitions:

Red = *Significant work to do on Account Plans, Salesforce Hygiene and Pipeline Coverage.*

Amber = *Gaps in completeness of Account Plans and/or Salesforce Hygiene and/or Pipeline Coverage.*

Green = *All Account & GOST Plans, Salesforce Opportunities Opps regularly maintained and up to date, Pipeline Coverage sufficient to beat Quota*

This short report is copied and pasted into an email template and sent to the AE just after the accountability call.

Here is another example:

Rafa Nadal	05/10/2020				
	Targets ($k)	Closed TD	Gap	% Gap to Go	X-Factor
Quotas & Closed	$ 553.20	$ 29.00	$524.20	95%	
Pipeline Target 5Q	$ 2,212.80	$ 758.00	$ 1,545.20	-70%	6.79
Last Acc Review (Date)	05/10/2020	**Total Quota Achievement FY2020**		5%	

Notes: New Opportunities created since the last review

Existing opportunities moved forward in the Sales Cycle

1. Very positive:Strong 5Q Pipeline (6.79x FY Quota)

2. Positive: Key Account 1 requested formal offer for MS Azure migration

3. Caution: FY2020 quota achievement at risk

Actions:

1. Key Account 1: Close key deal; Expand MS agreement (3 years)

2. Key Account 2: Close key deal; Upgrade + MS Extension

3. Schedule QBR with Key Account 1 Management (Stakeholder): Expand and move out of the IT department/ develop a plan with Industry Consultants

Rating: Green = All Account & GOST Plans, SF Opps regularly maintained and up to date, Pipeline Coverage sufficient to beat Quota

Rating Definitions:

Red = *Significant work to do on Account Plans, Salesforce Hygiene and Pipeline Coverage.*

Amber = *Gaps in completeness of Account Plans and/or Salesforce Hygiene and/or Pipeline Coverage.*

Green = *All Account & GOST Plans, Salesforce Opportunities Opps regularly maintained and up to date, Pipeline Coverage sufficient to beat Quota*

While the first AE, Federer's, current FY results are not great (COVID-19 has heavily impacted several of his retailing accounts), he did make a significant effort to build a solid pipeline for FY 2021. He also has two key deals sitting in Q4 that could bring him close to 90% of his quota achievement. What would you do if this AE couldn't achieve his FY2020 quota?

In our second example, the data from AE Rafa's accountability call report indicates a potential deficiency in his closing and negotiation skills. These are deficiencies that Rafa may overcome with training and coaching opportunities.

At Teradata, we used two metrics to measure quota achievement during the FY2020: Annual Recurring Revenue Growth (ARR-G) and Non-Recurring Revenue (NRR). ARR-G accounted for 70% of the FY quota, whereas NRR accounted for 30%. In the example tables above, we used only one metric: the ARR-G. Please note that if you use two or more metrics, you can simply add these to the Excel spreadsheet.

When is the Right Time to Let an AE go?

When evaluating an AE, you should consider having a final exit call and letting them go if, after three to five accountability calls, they consistently fail to set out their plans to hit targets or show improvements on key metrics. This AE is clearly not suited to the role, and it would be a disservice to both your department and the AE for them to remain in the AE position; their talents may be better suited in a different role.

Tip for the Sales Director: You may already have started the recruitment process after the second accountability call with your underperforming AE and looked into alternative AEs previously qualified by talent acquisition. It is critical for effective sales leadership that you always have a virtual 'bench' (going back to our sports analogies) of strong AE candidates in case of the following:

1. A top AE leaves because they want to move on to better offers;

2. You have to replace people who are not the right fit or who aren't performing; or

3. You promote one of your best AEs into a leadership position.

Our work is based mainly on "Open headcount", so many of us won't have the luxury of a virtual "bench" of ideal candidates and will only start looking for another AE after exit steps have already begun. To better manage the stress of this reactive approach, we tend to plan for a 3-6 month delay for recruiting and onboarding. A proactive HR process also provides stability for the sales teams.

Team Coaching and Team Accountability

While writing this book, we conducted a great interview with **Prof. David Clutterbuck**, author of the book "*Coaching the Team at Work–The Ultimate Guide to Team Coaching*".

We are proud to share his views on team coaching taken from the introduction to his book:

Team coaching is a significant part of the remedy for team performance shortfalls. It harnesses a combination of intelligence and curiosity to help teams think through what they are doing and why, how they will integrate individual skill sets and how they will innovate.

It also helps the team ask questions that will stimulate the intellectual dialogue necessary for addressing performance issues effectively.

Team coaching also fosters a higher quality of communication, both within the team and between the team and external stakeholders in its activities, ensuring that the dialogue is both intellectual and emotional in character and content.

Team coaching further promotes the social dialogue that builds rapport, stimulates understanding of self and other team members, and develops the skills to avoid negative conflict and enhance positive conflict within the team.

Yet team coaching is only partly about performance. It is also about capability – the ability of the team to perform in the future by growing and adapting to changes in its environment. Concentrating only on performance now creates short-term perspectives that endanger performance in the future.

A classic symptom of short-term thinking lies in the many corporate scandals that have hit some of the world's largest and (at least formerly) respected organizations – for example, the emissions misreporting at Volkswagen and the LIBOR fraudulent trading amongst large financial institutions.[40]

Team accountability and team coaching activities/meetings for sales teams are much more challenging to manage and execute than individual accountability calls.

Goals and Compensation

Setting the right sales goals and creating a solid, simple and fair **Sales Compensation Plan** (SCP) is arguably the most challenging task for any organisation whose growth and survival depends on sales.

Let's work on an exercise to explore this further.

---

40 Coaching the Team at Work–The Ultimate Guide to Team Coaching" Prof. David Clutterbuck

Let's assume that the company has set the same sales goals for Team A and Team B: $1M of signed net new business for the Fiscal Year 2021 (FY2021), and both have five accounts. On the surface, the targets seem identical. However, two of Team B's accounts announced that they would not be renewing their upcoming contracts for Q2 2021.

The company has a compensation plan that does not differentiate between AEs. They are all paid based on the same metrics: 100% quota achievement means 100% variable compensation, and 100%+ quota achievement means 200% variable compensation (double for each dollar of additional revenue). This 2x accelerator ends at an achievement of 175% of the annual quota and goes back to 100% for every dollar beyond 176% annual quota achievement.

This situation with Team A and Team B now raises some questions:

- How do we factor the change in Team B's situation into the goals?

- Should we ignore the change in Team B's situation and keep the goals the same?

- What do we do about the compensation rules?"

At the end of FY2021, Team A achieved 125% of the quota. Team B lost two clients (= 40% of its client base) but still achieved 90% of the quota. Which team performed better? Team B played with a handicap and ended the year disappointingly on a dollar rated basis. When we consider that they achieved a 90% quota based on 60% of their clients, they actually fared better than Team A with a 150% rating, and yet only Team A will be rewarded.

The company's leadership should follow up with a modified structure to account for this type of unforeseen event and create a level playing field for all teams. This is the reality in today's sales world, though, and sadly, there has been little attempt to correct the imbalance. While there is no quick fix solution to this scenario, inflexible sales compensation plans can break the best sales teams.

Who to Compensate on the Sales Team

Who do we compensate, and how much?"

We still live in a sales world of "The winner takes it (almost) all" where AEs are awarded 90%+ of the compensation if a deal is won. Other team members responsible for closing the deal are either directly ignored or receive a symbolic congratulatory note. They may be named as part of the "Winning Team" but will rarely get anything other than a pat on the back and a *"Great job, keep up the great work!"*.

Sales Team Goals, Team Recognition, Team Rewards and Team Compensation

As sales leaders, we identify teams goals as opposed to the individual goals of each AE.

To rectify the compensation imbalance, the sales leader must first address the fact that the sales team's goals are nothing more than the sum of the AE's individual goals, minus a correction factor. Consider the following:

Suppose a sales director with a sales quota of $5.4M manages a team of six AEs, each with a $1M FY sales quota, thereby yielding a quota 10% less than the six AEs combined. As the team goal of $5.4M is the overall responsibility of the sales director, each AE is only required to focus on their individual $1M FY quota and accelerator, which kicks in when 100% of the quota is achieved. Under a typical sales compensation plan, the AE would, for example, get paid double commission on every dollar closed above the set target of $1M up to 200% ($2M) achievement.

The second issue the sales leader needs to address is the lack of team rewards. As long as we compensate AEs and sales directors based on the sum of each AE's achievements, there is no incentive for the team to make an effort.

The more you align all team members' compensation with the same sales goals, the more likely the collaboration and the higher the interest of each team member. Everyone will benefit from team results, all working towards the "greater good" which is bigger than the sum of its parts.

The third issue to consider is the many other individuals, outside of the AE teams, who also contribute to the sales process. How is their contribution compensated? In many organisations, these other individuals may not report to the sales director as they fall under other departments. They are likely measured and compensated based on totally different goals and metrics.

This is also true at Teradata. While our solution engineers are well aligned with our sales goals (most specifically the ARR-G metric), others do not share these goals and are compensated on work objectives unrelated to sales. These goals are often called MBO goals – Management By Objectives goals.

The result of organisations not addressing these issues is that we will never see great sales teams stay together for long. They will continue to work in a disconnected and sub-optimal manner, driven by individual rather than team goals. There is nothing substantial enough to motivate them to stick together and work towards a common goal.

In the "*Daily Sales Tips*"[41] podcast episode number 760 entitled "*4 Fundamentals to Setting Your Sales Team up for Success*", **Zeeshan Hafeez**, Chief Revenue Officer at *VeeMed*, shares the four fundamentals for building high-performance sales teams.

1. **Compensation**: Create a system with uncapped commissions that allows salespeople to make money that reflects their contribution to the organisation. Money matters in sales. By capping their top performers' commissions, companies run the risk of facing a win-lose or win–don't win anymore situation.

2. **Rewards**: Introduce additional rewards, aside from compensation, to keep salespeople engaged and motivated; reward them, for example, for displaying the proper behaviour or for hitting targets as a team. This will motivate the entire team to go to even greater lengths to achieve future success.

3. **Recognition**: Salespeople need to be recognised for their achievements. There is power in identifying people who have contributed throughout the entire sales cycle, both for small wins and big wins. During the early stages, it may just be a matter of calling out the early meetings, celebrating

---

41 The "Daily Sales Tips" podcast is hosted by Scott Ingram: https://top1.fm/DailySalesTips/all-sales-tips/

the early smaller opportunities that enter the pipeline, and the deals that get closed. From there, you can build momentum, get people excited, and create more positivity, which all acts as a catalyst for high performance.

4. **Fast career growth**: Zeeshan claims to run a system that provides for unlimited career growth at an accelerated rate, the potential for high performers to promote and advance their career at a rapid pace. He states that many top performers leave companies like Google and Microsoft because they get levelled to a point where they can't really grow fast enough.

While we agree with the first three points, we are wary of the fourth. It is one thing to be an extraordinary contributor in sales, but this does not automatically qualify that person for a sales management position. These are different disciplines, and a whole new skill set must first be developed and proven.

It takes patience to learn and develop the new skills one needs to fill a sales manager role competently, and not everyone with an impressive sales reputation would enjoy the demands of the management position. The transition cannot happen overnight; we have seen many people shatter their self-confidence and destroy themselves when promoted too soon into "the highest levels of their own perceived value". Many of these individuals were happy to move back to their previous roles where they were more successful, where their role felt more natural and more within their comfort level.

Always Be Learning

A key characteristic of a successful leader is being open to continuous learning. Being a role model for life-long learning inspires team members to do the same. Great leaders can also inspire their team by explaining and demonstrating the benefits of continuous learning.

While reading books is one thing most successful leaders have in common, new learning methods have emerged, such as blogs, social media, video and podcasts. There are literally hundreds of sales-related podcasts available, but only a few are dedicated to sales leadership. Hence, we recommend "*The Sales Management. Simplified. Podcast*",[42] recently launched by **Mike Weinberg**, author of the bestselling book with the same title "*Sales Management. Simplified*".

---

42 https://mikeweinberg.com/podcast/

Key Features of Remote Leadership

Earlier in the book, we presented how the COVID-19 crisis changed the business landscape, forcing companies to adapt to survive. The 2020 GDP declined for most countries, and the economic repercussions are likely to be felt well into 2021 and beyond. Millions of jobs have been and will still be lost. A prolonged economic crisis will undoubtedly challenge the political and economic leaders of the most powerful nations and organisations in the world. Social distancing and working remotely have become the new norm, creating a shift in the way we interact. So what challenges do organisation leaders face in this new norm with new digital and remote rules?

So What Are the Key Features of Good, Remote Leadership?

The **"11 Key Traits of a Good Leader"**, presented in Chapter 2, are just as relevant with remote relationships as they are with face-to-face ones; however, we would like to draw your attention to the following, additional aspects to consider:

1. **Technical equipment**: Audio, video and interactive presentation techniques;

2. **Communication**: Not as effective in the virtual arena as with face-to-face or in-person team meetings;

3. **Attention span and concentration**: Capacity of attendees of remote calls to concentrate and effectively collaborate;

4. **Situational context**: Working from home may introduce new and possibly additional distractions that can cause psychological stress. This requires high levels of empathy and the willingness to understand how

people are feeling. Body language is not as easily decipherable through a computer screen as in an on-site face-to-face or team meeting.

Let's face it: The opportunities for in-person "micro meetings" have largely disappeared. Having a coffee with your colleagues for a "*Do you have a minute?*" conversation just doesn't happen anymore.

These brief face-to-face interactions are important. They are a means of affirming yourself and others in what you are involved with, what you are working on, and a way of solving problems. They help to create trust, nurture and maintain human relationships and keep an emotional balance between the team members.

Andy has been working from his home office (actually, his living room turned into an office) since March 2020. When writing this, it's already approaching a whole year since he last had any face-to-face interactions with his manager or his clients. Now is an opportune time to review and analyse the impact of remote working: what has worked, what hasn't worked, and what can be improved. He recounts his experiences below.

At the start of the pandemic, we were all overwhelmed by the confusion and uncertainty. We dealt with it by having frequent one-on-one phone conversations with team members to understand how COVID-19 and remote working affected them. Our biggest concern was the collective health and well-being of our colleagues and their families, both physically and psychologically. We called each other weekly with a recurring theme of understanding and togetherness: "*How are we doing?*" "*What are we experiencing?*" "*What is challenging for everyone's families?*".

The last week of March 2020 and the first weeks of April were especially tough. Several people in our circle of friends in Spain–mostly parents of our friends in nursing homes–died of COVID-19. The CIO of one of our clients also died. We experienced eight casualties over a span of two weeks, which was heartbreaking to our inner circle.

In May 2020, we started hosting a Monday morning weekly warm-up call for the whole team. These 20-minute calls allowed each account executive to share key achievements and key challenges from the past week and set action points for the upcoming week. These calls proved to be an effective means of keeping track of the business and commenting on important issues, events, or changes we may face. Now in February 2021, we are still having these calls.

Technical Equipment and Applications: Upgraded audio and video equipment have become essential. If we want to recreate the person-to-person experience in the best way possible, we must be conscious of how we present ourselves online. Many people (C-Suite executives included) are still using built-in microphones and low-resolution cameras from laptops; a small investment would go a long way for the user experience with clients and colleagues.

Voice/Audio: In his podcasts, Scott Ingram uses a dynamic microphone, and he recommends them to his interview guests. You can purchase a decent headset with an external microphone for a little under $20.

"A dynamic microphone will reject a lot of background noise, and you don't have to worry about your space as much. It's designed to pick up just the sounds that are spoken into it."

Regarding applications, Zoom, Microsoft Teams, Webex and Skype have certainly been the most popular for conducting and hosting different communication forums during the pandemic. These applications all work well and can facilitate private and public chat, and virtual backgrounds for a more professional look. Zoom and Webex are suitable for hosting larger audiences as all attendees are visible onscreen.

The share function enables screen-sharing for when we want to interact with our call audience. We recommend you test the complete functionality of the share function beforehand. When sharing a video, do a test run of the video and the sound to ensure they are supported by your audience's devices (desktop vs application).

There are great free applications available. We support **Mentimeter**[43], an application that enables you to set up attractive surveys that your audience can participate in from their phones. Results are displayed instantly as delightful animations.

Communication: We have dedicated an entire chapter of this book to communication. It is one of the most essential leadership skills and a key factor to consider in the remote relationship model. Communication is vital for effective in-person and face-to-face leadership. Leaders must consider a number of things if remote communication, for example, via phone or computer, is to be effective.

---

[43] Mentimeter: www.mentimeter.com

John Maxwell's famous quote: "*Many communicate, few connect*", implies that we, as leaders, must encourage and stimulate connections with and between our team members. Communication is the path to human connection; therefore, delivering and receiving messages must be done right. Connecting two people remotely is more challenging as there is no physical connection to reinforce and nurture a deeper mental connection.

Here are our takes on the key aspects of remote leadership regarding communication:

1. Empathise

a. Show your team empathy for this new way of communicating: "*You are not alone!*"

b. Regularly ask how everyone is coping with the remote situation, how is it affecting them and how you can help them.

2. Before every call

a. Keep the calls short or include 10-15 minute breaks if they run over 45 minutes. Prepare your content well in advance and test everything to avoid problems.

3. During the call

a. Engage with everyone on the call and get them to participate.

b. Ask everyone to switch on their cameras; eye contact is preferable.

c. Record all team calls so they can be watched by members who may have missed them.

4. After the call

a. Send meeting minutes and share them on a central server together with a recording of the call. Everyone can then review and understand what was discussed and what the next agreed steps are.

5. Stay in touch

a. Use the chat/messenger function of your video call platform to stay in touch and show that you are there to help and support your team, not to micromanage. We use Microsoft Teams, for example.

b. Consider using WhatsApp from your phone to message individuals and the team if something is urgent.

c. Use your phone and frequently make brief calls to your team members to touch base, check-in and see how they are doing.

6. Video

a. Start using video messaging as an alternative to emails or team calls. It conveys so much more, and people can watch the videos when they have time.

b. Keep videos short and to the point. Adding a few slides can be helpful to communicate your message better.

c. Prepare a brief script, and try to be clear and concise with your messages, using a clear tone of voice and pausing after every sentence.

d. Always end the video with a call-to-action and feedback from everyone.

e. Speak slower to make sure you are well understood.

f. Ensure your lighting is adequate.

g. We use tools like **Vidyard**[44] and **Vimeo**[45] **Record**. Both offer free versions that you can experiment with and offer Google Chrome extensions so you can start recording directly from your browser with just a few clicks.

We cannot ignore the problem of reduced attention spans. An article written about a 2015 Microsoft Canada study published in TIME[46] revealed that people's average attention span went down from 12 seconds in 2000 to 8 seconds in 2015. We now have a shorter attention span than a goldfish, which is estimated to be around 9 seconds. On the positive side, the report states that our ability to multitask has greatly improved in the mobile age. The same study prompted another article, "*The Eight-Second Attention Span*", written by **Timothy Egan** and published by the New York Times.[47]

You must consider your audience's attention span for your online calls and consider these tips:

- Keep them as short as possible

- Use great visuals and little text per slide to communicate clearly

- Remember that in a remote context, less is always more and better.

We must be considerate of everyone's situations as we no longer share the same office spaces or meeting rooms. Everyone's living conditions (room sizes, access, background noise, distractions) are unique, which can make remote meetings more complicated. We must be willing to accommodate our attendees regardless of their living space.

It is vital to establish clear meeting expectations and goals, prepare agendas, get everyone to join the call early, and ensure everyone actively participates in the call. If you highlight the benefits to them, you increase your chances of keeping everyone motivated and focused on the subject at hand.

---

[44] Vidyard: www.vidyard.com

[45] Vimeo Record: www.vimeo.com

[46] Time: https://time.com/3858309/attention-spans-goldfish/

[47] NYT: https://www.nytimes.com/2016/01/22/opinion/the-eight-second-attention-span.html

We have found that rotating the host's role among attendees increases the awareness of what it takes to prepare and run these meetings. Attendees will appreciate the level of effort required once they have run a meeting themselves. This approach also encourages people to step out of their comfort zones and overcome any fears they may have of presenting. It is imperative not to pass judgement if someone's first performance is poor; rather, thank them for making an effort and attempting this. It's all about you, as a leader, creating a safe space where your people can experience and learn failing forward.

Key Takeaways

1. Unless the leader displays and exhibits positive leadership, the sales team will be unproductive at best.

2. Being a leader comes with huge responsibility: Serve your team first, then build it up to provide your company with sustainable results.

3. Sales leadership–Done well, will yield exponential growth; done poorly, will see sales come to a screeching halt.

4. Positive leadership is more important than attentive management.

5. First, create a positive sales culture; second, design a great sales strategy.

6. As a leader, listen and observe more than you speak.

7. When you address your team as a leader, do it with honesty, clarity and in a timely manner.

8. A fair compensation and reward system can make or break a great sales team.

9. Team coaching is a sales leader's most important activity: it provides guidance to excel and prevents performance shortfalls.

10. To assure sustainability in performance, the sales team leader needs the best possible players on the team who are willing to learn more.

11. A robust process will enable the sales team to see the vision of success.

Part III

Team Members: Hiring, Nurturing, Coaching and Renewal

Team Members

Before we kick things off with the third and final part of this book, we wish to extend our warmest thanks to all of you who have invested your time and money purchasing this book. Your decision to support our "*Teams Win Championships*" writing project will bring about a meaningful contribution to some well-deserving charitable organisations.

We, the co-authors, can assure you that this entire experience has been truly gratifying from a writing and learning perspective, generating educational discussions and sharing a wealth of ideas. We certainly hope that Parts I and II have provided you with insight and guidance on your path to building and leading better sales teams.

We now welcome you to the third part of this book, dedicated to the hard-working women and men out there in the sales world. By grinding away day after day, these leaders develop and nurture their own sales teams with the goal of 'being better tomorrow than we were today'.

On the surface, sales may appear to be a straightforward process; but, below the surface are many moving parts, any one of which may lead to inefficiencies, especially when you combine direct sales teams with extended partners.

The results of combining extended partners with the direct sales team, without having adequate processes in place, may include underperforming sales leaders and a negative impact on the organisation's revenue.

However, when there's a measured approach to combining the contributions of extended partners with those of the direct sales team, wonderful things happen for the collective good of everyone involved.

Let us celebrate these people and begin our discussion of *Extended Sales Teams*.

The Extended Sales Team: Who is Who and Who Contributes What?

As discussed in Parts I and II, the organisation's sales are heavily reliant on the effectiveness of the organisational team. Each person within the organisation contributes to its overall success; therefore, there needs to be a company-wide alignment of the organisation's culture regardless of the product line or service or whether someone's position is directly related to sales or not. The precursor to promoting the organisation's culture is a mutual understanding and agreement amongst all team members of the organisation's shared values, spread out across the entire organisation.

In this chapter, we identify the people (and look to leverage them to a greater degree) involved in three distinct stages of the sales process:

1. Pre-sales

2. Closing the sales

3. Post-sales.

Different departments exist to support the sales process, and these may differ slightly from organisation to organisation, depending on the nature of the organisation and the industry.

The following are more common job titles we have come across in the software industry and which may also apply to your specific business:

- Marketing managers;

- Client success managers;

- Industry specialists;

- Sales engineers;

- Product managers;

- Consulting services managers;

- Client experience managers;

- Partner managers; and

- Finance operations managers.

Let's review these positions to see how they interact amongst themselves and contribute to your sales team's performance.

Marketing Managers – Marketing is Your Ally

Sales teams do not generally recognise the value of marketing and do not take advantage of its full potential. According to **Michael Brenner,** a best-selling author, keynote speaker, and CEO of *Marketing Insider*, "*60% of content created in the marketing department was never used*".

Sales teams can undoubtedly turn this around and learn to utilise enterprise marketing. This will, of course, depend on a variety of factors like company size, nature of the business, and the organisational structure.

In Part II, we mention the value of marketing and integrating the marketing organisation with global sales leadership. Only when there is synergy between these two can the full potential of sales and marketing be leveraged to benefit both the clients and the business.

A dedicated marketing team in a small organisation usually means that marketing will contribute substantially to the revenue numbers. Marketing can generate qualified leads and guide the lead-nurturing journey for a specific account, such as in Account-Based Marketing (ABM).

For example, in an attempt to enter the fashion industry, a third-party data company wished to present their product to the top company in the market. This third-party data company's marketing manager used a combination of LinkedIn campaigns and email newsletters to share insights that might be of interest to the prospect's Chief Data Officer (CDO). They targeted one specific employee from the CDO's team with an email, who clicked the link and filled out the trial request form. This is a simple example of how the gap between prospecting and contact was bridged because a member of the CDO's team recognised value in the prospect.

In larger organisations, marketing managers do not typically work on one specific opportunity, participate in client meetings, or participate in sales team meetings for ABM. Instead, marketing leaders and managers generally work on broader awareness like:

- **Inbound marketing:** creating content to generate interest with clients and prospects through websites, blog posts, videos, webinars, white papers, case studies, and analyst reports.

- **Outbound marketing:** using LinkedIn, other social media campaigns, and newsletters to connect.

- **Powerpoint Support:** preparing presentations for leadership, products, presales, conferences, presentations, and proposals.

- **Marketing Events:** organising events to showcase new product portfolio releases and presenting to various clients, prospects and partners.

The following example highlights how the misdirection between marketing and sales in a small software provider led to missed opportunities in 2019.

The organisation was struggling to leverage digital marketing properly and wasn't achieving its growth targets. There were apparent issues of accountability in the missed opportunities. The marketing department generated several Sales Qualified Leads (SQL) per week from a series of campaigns: clients/prospects showed interest in a Forrester analyst report, clients were directed to the company's website, or they could try out the product. These marketing leads were not aligned with the sales team's objectives, who only followed up on these leads up to a week later, by which time the "wow" effect had dissipated, resulting in lost opportunities. The sales teams claimed the leads were low quality, but the reality is that these leads called for an immediate response. When things like this happen, the blame game starts.

So, how can marketing activities in your organisation be used to maximum effect? One way is by signing up to a Service Level Agreement (SLA) between sales and marketing wherein the two disciplines agree on the quality and quantity of leads. In terms of quality, sales need to define a qualified lead: Is it a lead that enables one conversation? Is it a registration form filled out by a prospect? In terms of quantity, the number would be based on the typical conversion rate the sales team achieves with those types of leads.

Marketing and sales can be allies only if there is this agreement between the teams. Marketing needs to communicate freely with sales to understand what they need to follow through and finish what marketing has started. Conversely, the sales teams need to be aligned with the organisation's global marketing plans so the teams can work in unison and maximise the marketing-generated content to generate substantial benefits in the latter stages of the sales funnel.

Client Success Managers–Business Development Associates

Sales managers can improve their team's numbers with the addition of an associate, a business developer or a client success manager, specifically assigned and dedicated to the team or a few sales teams. Not all teams have the luxury of such an associate, so when they are available, they should be appropriately leveraged by taking part in sales team meetings and client conversations. In our experience, excluding a dedicated associate from client visibility or participating in high leverage situations are wasted opportunities.

Sales leaders and teams will increase their success by sharing their vision, mission, culture and goals with all their associates, including them at the early stages, and giving them opportunities to make valuable contributions. These associates should receive similar recognition and incentives to the rest of the team if the team's quota is achieved, with the sales executive receiving a specific percentage of the variable income. Similar incentives may include an accelerated career path towards becoming a sales manager; associates will likely do all they can for the team.

An associate's contribution would be most effective to the team when there are coinciding activities that need to be split up and worked on. Associates can assist with the following duties: ownership of Request for Information/Proposals (RFI/RFP), presales workshops, attending conferences, extending networking inside a client's organisation, and increasing the level of engagement of a specific stakeholder. They can also handle specific sales documentation like proposals, responses to client questions, and presales presentations so the rest of the team can focus on other tasks.

The old saying "being at the right place at the right time" certainly sounds like a lucky turn of events, yet there are times when you have to create your own luck. Here is a story of an associate who saw an opportunity and seized it:

A number of years ago, one of our firm's client success managers attended a partner's conference where an important prospect was to give a keynote address. The client success manager researched the prospect's profile beforehand and took a seat in the front row of the conference where the speakers would be seated. The prospect and the associate had never met before. However, before the event, our sales manager had already set up a meeting with the prospect's company for later in the week. The associate used this information to break the ice and introduce himself to the prospect. Whilst exchanging pleasantries, the associate and prospect found they had things in common like their experience, knowledge and a passion for their industry.

They shared their thoughts on the conference and had productive conversations about needs and challenges, which eventually led to discovery questions. A few days later, at the very meeting the sales manager had previously arranged, the sales team presented a proposal tailored specifically to the prospect's needs, based on the conversation between the associate and prospect. This was key to winning the prospect's trust and led to many years of recurring revenue. The sales manager's approach to the meeting was resourceful and strategic, specifically targeted to the needs of the prospect's business.

Industry Experts–Industry Expertise Generates Trust

When revenue relies on positioning complex products within very specific industries, it is essential to bring additional expertise to client conversations. This may only be a temporary need throughout the entire sales cycle, but this kind of expert advice can be invaluable in the right place.

Expert support can take different forms: industrial experts can contribute from their global centres, consult from vertical organisations, or participate from virtual teams. This cross-functional role provides value with documented business cases, presentations, or demos, to name just a few. They can also attend business events specific to their speciality and promote a sense of awareness for clients, such as introducing them to the latest trends.

Industry Virtual Teams are commonplace with today's enterprises. Their value-add includes:

- **Share:** Client presentations, best practices, industry white papers, common trends and case studies with client stories.

- **Access:** Sales teams can benefit from internal publications such as script notes and sales pitches. Sales teams can access Subject Matter Experts (SMEs) on demand for specific events and access the latest news and industry trends.

- **Collaborate:** With a global approach, your team can partner with virtual teams and your clients.

In addition to making valuable contributions to your team, by interacting with other sales teams, Industry Virtual Teams can further extend their expertise to benefit the entire organisation. Presenting an expert to the client adds credence to the sales team's relationship with the client and promotes sales opportunities.

Consider this example:

During the final stages of a data and analytics project in 2018, certain automated analytics processes were already generating returns on the original investment for an established client looking to replicate another company's success in a different area:

fraud prevention. By seeking out and finding a financial crimes industry expert for the regional virtual team, a pre-sales workshop was added whereby the Industry Expert simultaneously gathered information from the client. After we jointly presented an anti-fraud solution, the client quickly recognised the value and signed off on a contract extension.

In upcoming sections, we will discuss the trust factor and its importance both within and beyond the sales teams and reveal how the client can be an added extension to the sales team.

Who are these other Industry Experts who can add value to the sales team?

Sales Engineers – Because You are not the Expert

There comes a time when we have to recognise that we don't know everything and that seeking help is the best option. Engineers are not particularly noted for their soft skills like managing people or empathising with clients, but they do possess traits that are valuable to the sales cycle. By delegating technical activities to our engineers and specialised technicians, we can harness the required hard skills of the experts. Relationships with pre-sales members require a certain balance of so-called hard and soft skills. When pre-sales members, like engineers and specialised technicians, are added to specific sales teams, they can contribute to tactical and strategic solutions under the sales managers' guidance.

Sales engineers can be a valuable resource; when clients have any technical questions, sales engineers can give more elaborate details and act as a valuable link between the product's configuration and possible customisation/integration with the client's needs. They can contribute by dedicating time to these technical conversations, leading technical workshops, showing proofs of concepts or other similar non-paid activities to the client.

Product Managers – Bring Market into your Conversations

N.H. McElroy, former president of *Procter & Gamble* and the U.S. Secretary of Defense from 1957 to 1959, published a famous 3-page company memo in 1931 called "***Brand Teams***", setting out the principles of modern product management.[48]

---

[48] **Martin Eriksson**. The History and Evolution of Product Management https://www. mindtheproduct.com/history-evolution-product-management/

He defined product managers as "brand men" and assigned them full responsibility for the brands–from business development review to planning sales calls, advertising and discussions with sales managers. We have extracted the following from the memo: "*in short… brand men should take from the shoulders of the sales managers a very heavy share of individual responsibility… leaving the sales heads in a much freer position to administer the sales policies.*"

The product manager's responsibilities were defined almost a century ago; to relieve the sales managers' work. Product managers and their teams conducted field studies to determine if the strategy yielded the expected results and suggested corrective actions to the salesmen in charge.

Product personnel's contributions have remained largely unchanged. Product managers are still responsible for individual products; they can be seen as smaller scale CEOs, able to establish inbound and outbound strategies around their products.

Inbound Product Management refers to creating an internal product strategy: gathering client information, identifying competitive intelligence and market trends to realise the product vision and mission. This team works with R&D, marketing and research teams to gather information; however, the most relevant data comes from the sales stakeholders and clients. Product managers have been known to get excited about feedback on their products which can be internal, from R&D, competitive sales, marketing and services teams, or external, from partners, consultants and clients. Sales teams hold the key to client accounts. Therefore, the inbound flow of information is highly dependent on the sales and product relations and where product managers revert to sales teams for client feedback.

Outbound Product Management refers to the Go-to-Market activities: establishing the value proposition, messaging in the field, and determining when a product is ready for release. Here, the product management department collaborates with Go-to-Market operations, industry consultants, professional services and sales representatives. This collaboration ensures that positioning and strategies around the products are aligned with the marketing and sales teams and the organisation's other Go-to-Market plans. Product managers enable sales teams to scale their approach by providing specific information on the latest products or release dates from competitors.

Outbound activities appear to be most relevant to sales teams. So, how can we optimise these interactions?

Sales teams might request that the team be extended to include a product manager for different situations, for example:

1. A product may be ready for early release before pre-sales engineering and sales managers have been enabled. The technical expertise will, therefore, come from the product management, engineering, and R&D departments.

2. A client may own the previous version of a product and be impressed by the added features of the latest release. Product management may be called in to liaise with the client in a pre-sales activity like a product demo.

The following is an example of a success story:

An established client, of more than ten years, owned one of our company's core products, our Data Warehouse Solutions. Our sales team held meetings with them every quarter. These Quarterly Business Reviews (QBR) revealed that the client was considering a strategic new initiative based on new advanced analytics applied to their various business departments.

The sales manager, fearful of losing this key account to competitive products, was troubled to find out that their advanced analytics program was not yet ready for release. When you ask the question: "Is it ready now?", and the response is: "Soon, it's coming very soon", it doesn't fill you with much confidence!

The sales manager immediately called an internal meeting with the product manager of the soon-to-be-released product. He explained to the product manager that there was a real possibility of losing out on a valuable opportunity. They decided to include the product manager on the client call, where the product manager enthusiastically presented his new product's value proposition to determine if it would fit in with the client's plans. The call resulted in the client trialling the Beta version of the product. It also led to an agreement on the release date, the start of an early adopter programme for the client, and a partnership for enhancing some priority features for this client. Everyone came out a winner: the client recognised the ROI benefit, the sales team increased their team's revenue stream, and the product manager tweaked his brand-new product based on a valued client's needs.

Regular meetings with clients, like Quarterly Business Reviews, allow clients to present their challenges and problems. When discussions are centred around current and future plans, the time is ripe for upselling.

Teams linked to pre-sales, sales and other Go-to-Markets are already engaged when there is a mature product line. Product managers simply need to engage the organisation's Go-to-Market strategies. With a mature product line, the sales teams should not expect an expert always to be available to them; neither is this necessary for products that are already recognised industry-wide.

Consulting Services Managers – Together with Product Sales

Consulting directors, client services managers, and other such roles related to services (e.g. service account managers, delivery leads, and managers) each generate business revenue, primarily when they are linked to product delivery, integration or maintenance. These additional players each have a crucial role to play in maintaining client satisfaction, both with the products and the overall sales experience. Including sales managers, pre-sales and other service professionals in your sales team can bring significant value and optimise the entire client experience.

The service roles may be more client-facing than the sales teams as they are usually involved in pre-sales and on delivery. These roles will not continually be part of the team, but their involvement can be valuable. They may, at times, 'wear the hat' of the salesperson in looking at all possible revenue opportunities. At other times they may 'wear the hat' of delivery assurance having to slow a client down on requests that may be beyond the scope of work. They may even contribute to sales opportunities while attending pre-sales meetings and providing client success stories and experiences.

Client Experience Managers – Support your Clients' Queries

Working our way through the organisation, we can see many places where the extended sales team can greatly influence a sale. Specific support services might be part of the overall sales deal. A sales client service representative can be included in client conversations, temporarily extending the sales team to include support services, if required, thereby customising services with the option of offering different standardised levels of support.

Your sales team must have a holistic view of the client and the different teams' touchpoints. The client service team will own the after-sales relationship with the client, helping with queries and complaints. The client experience can go either way: client satisfaction is typically a result of a great sales experience with the client service and support team. Conversely, a client who experiences poor client service may be less inclined to re-purchase for reasons unbeknownst to the salesperson.

These hidden 'gotchas' are part of the sales process, even after-sales. Sales teams might use Customer Relationship Management (CRM) tools or, at the very least, should be recording the relevant client-related activities. Including client service touchpoints in these tools will give the sales team a 360-degree view of client interactions, from pre-sales to post-sales. By reviewing these interactions before having a conversation with your clients will provide more context with your client.

There may be instances where this is a challenge, especially as companies grow larger and departments, processes, and communication become more siloed. It will be necessary for the sales teams and client service teams to align their roles to ensure that everyone has insight into these interactions, regardless of whether they are negative or positive.

Partner Managers – Managing the Channel as Part of the Team

In certain instances, external partners may take on a more significant role, primarily when selling products through vendors instead of an internal sales team. It is essential to include partners in the organisation's sales strategy when revenues are generated through a combination of sales and partner channels. The partners' contributions to your team and organisation will depend on the type of partner. Partners can be defined as:

1. **Resellers:** Product and partnership teams are responsible for resellers' success and, as such, will establish the reseller's strategy. These partners may only focus on your organisation's products or have multiple products from multiple organisations to resell. Due to their influence and relationships within the market, these resellers may create opportunities for other accounts, so maintaining close contact with them can result in a win-win situation.

2. **Integrators**: Relying on external consulting organisations enables scalability in the Go-to-Market approach and ensures that clients receive the support they need to use or integrate your solution. Prominent technology vendors use the common strategy of combining proprietary consulting with external consulting. While having a somewhat key role within the sales team, it is important to include these partners in client conversations right from the outset of discussions.

3. **Analysts, Independent Software Vendors (ISV's) and Independent Hardware Vendors:** Relying on these partners is specific to the high tech sector. They could be invaluable in establishing trust as, through their expertise, they can offer the end client better solutions to more complex problems.

You should be aware of any existing strategic alliances your organisation may already have with resellers and integrators. Review the client success stories where these collaborations have worked in the past, learn the outcomes and lessons learnt from working together, and replicate and enhance them for better results.

Finance Operations Managers

We purposely left the discussion of this role to the end as this department is not a client-facing role. They are not direct contributors to the pre-sales funnel, nor do they participate in any sales conversations or procurement negotiations. They are the last link in the chain. They spend most of their time reviewing operations, invoicing and collecting payments, and recognising revenue with the assignment of sales teams' recognition quotes. These finance operations, however, do directly impact the sales teams.

Any delays or mistakes in reviewing and recognising the numbers could lead to the collapse of the whole chain. As finance operations play such a critical role in the sales process, it makes sense for the sales team to include them regularly in team genesis meetings, team celebration meetings, and team reviews. This inclusivity will lead to closer relationships with a clear understanding of the team's vision, mission, values, and way of working.

Channel Business: Managing Indirect Partners and Sales Teams

As already mentioned in the previous chapter, many companies rely heavily or entirely on a distribution network that may include channel partners where you have much less influence on how they engage with clients.

Successfully managing an indirect sales channel creates tremendous opportunities for leveraging additional resources. A partner support manager can manage many opportunities with partner organisations, as opposed to one-on-one. This scenario works very well for companies like Cisco.

Smaller companies may face several challenges in leveraging these additional resources. There may be challenges around being reliant on very large distribution partners, or you, as the salesperson or partner manager, might have to 'sell twice'.

The question is, how do you do this sales coordination and joint business development with channel partners most effectively? We had an epiphany: the industry in which we were selling took a big hit, and many of the people we were dealing with were no longer in their positions. It led us to question: Do we go directly to the client, or do we engage with partners and try to rebuild those relationships?

We decided to go directly to the client again. This has been challenging; currently, we cannot meet with clients physically and don't really have the luxury of time to build up those relationships again as this would overextend the sales cycle.

The question then becomes: How do we get to partner management with the tools that we have? We believe there is scope for a future book focusing specifically on partner management as an extension of the sales team. Some companies are doing very well under this model, and others are not. Companies like Cisco and Microsoft are using the partner management model to great effect, but they do have many large, global accounts that they sell to directly. Many people may go directly to the partner of companies like Microsoft to purchase hardware products but may be more inclined to purchase software and other such intangible goods directly off Microsoft's website. This may be different for hardware companies like Cisco that sells physical items only and are thus heavily reliant on partner distribution.

So, how do you nurture an extended sales team? How do you gauge client sentiment with an extended sales team that lets you know what is happening with your clients? From our own experience, we have found that with these indirect channels, if we can bring a lead from a lead generation standpoint and bring opportunities, we can really get their attention. Sales partners see the benefits of working with us when we deliver information to them in a timely fashion.

We have spent many hours coaching partner sales teams and been on four legged sales calls, acting as their sales engineer, which is crucial to drive explosive sales and get partners 'firing on all cylinders'. You typically do what you would for your own sales team; you are now just doing it with an extended sales team.

There are ample opportunities for smaller companies to partner with larger companies with existing client bases in existing distribution. One reason for a smaller company to partner with those larger companies is to take advantage of the larger company's reach into existing industries, new regions, or both.

The challenge is for the company to properly manage the channel to maximise the sales potential of what is going through other salespeople. There are many books and articles written on best practices for managing channel partners. We thought we would try to give you a list and some insights into what has and has not worked in the past, focusing on smaller companies selling into larger companies through established sales channels.

A critical requirement of selling a new solution to a channel partner client is to have reference clients so that both the channel sales team and the end client understand the value of the solution. It is imprudent to skip this step; we have seen where teams thought they could engage the end client with a new solution, but the reality is, you end up having to sell twice with long sales cycles for both Business to Business (B2B) sales scenarios.

Another critical requirement of selling a new solution is to have a champion in the channel partner organisation, typically the owner or a senior member of the company, who can help or make decisions when required. This is normal for most sales rules, and the key to this channel partner engagement is to remember that you are, in essence, selling twice, as you are selling to engage the channel partner too. You have to develop a specific plan around remuneration, support, and ways to feedback on new product requirements (e.g., if there are things missing from the product or solution). That champion in the channel partner organisation can make the process easier for you. Without the champion, you may never get the traction in that channel partner organisation that you need to achieve critical mass.

The following is a sample checklist of items for successfully engaging with a channel partner:

1. **Compensation:** You need a partner compensation model to start with; they need to know what is in it for them. While not entirely money-driven, the sales process, the channel partner organisation, and channel partner sales team members will undoubtedly be motivated by remuneration that increases. Typically, rates may range from 30 to 50% of the product value sold through a channel partner. These rates must be borne in mind when determining the cost of goods to ensure a sufficient margin to support what the channel partner needs to engage with your product.

   It's important to discuss any challenges or potential challenges with the channel partner. For example, selling software as a service is a challenging area in the sales models as it is recurring revenue. This is something to decide with your channel to determine if you could do something over the lifetime of the recurring revenue model; is it something you pay the channel upfront and manage the partner over time? Having a suitable compensation model that incentivises the channel to sell can propel your sales exponentially, far beyond what you could do directly.

2. **Onboarding and Coaching:** You need to have an adequate plan in place for onboarding and coaching the channel partner and the channel partner's sales team. The assumption here is that this is a B2B channel and that the sales team will be engaged with the client.

   Part of onboarding and training the channel partner is to give them the tools that will enable them to understand the product and your process. This may include sales presentations and other such information that the channel partner can brand or co-brand. You may have to significantly subsidise an initial system or solution if there is ambiguity from the client about what will sell.

Some of the best solutions we have seen for partner enablement are having dedicated portals for the partner sales team to get the latest materials and knowledge-based repositories to ensure that their team is up to speed with new product developments.

Coaching channel partners is critical for the longer-term success of the channel and may include similar activities to coaching your own immediate sales team. The key difference is that your channel partner does not directly report to you, and you have to influence their activities indirectly.

The initial challenge is getting buy-in from the client channel, which helps them identify the correct client attributes for them to sell your product to their client base. Ongoing coaching uses the company and channel partner's successes to foster future successes, requiring ongoing engagement with the channel partner sponsor and the actual channel sales team actively selling your product. Having regular check-in meetings and ensuring that the channel partners are as successful as possible with your product is part of the ongoing coaching process.

3. **Measure:** Metrics and performance management, part of ongoing coaching, are crucial to ensuring that the channel partner is motivated to get behind your product or service.

Metrics such as when an opportunity comes into the funnel and when it closes can help determine whether you can assist the channel partner throughout the sales process. This is sales funnel 101 but makes it more difficult given the additional layer of abstraction from the end client to you.

Overall, these measures are a leading indicator of whether or not the channel is working for you. If not, you have to decide whether to keep the channel partner on or not.

Something that newer, smaller companies need to remember is that you need to make the sale as easy as possible for the channel partner. Give them any support they need, like four legged sales calls, and ensuring that any product deficiencies are quickly rectified. Desh Deshpande would say that you have to get the sales done early, 'by hook or by crook', until the traditional sales process is engaged.

When dealing with the channel, you typically only have a small sub-section of the channel within their sales team who actually engages with you, and the metrics make those people stand out. Ensure that you handle those particular individuals with kid gloves because they can make you much more successful within the channel. One would even suggest trying to get to know them personally, from a team management and coaching perspective, to establish a level of confidence in each other.

We have seen and worked with extensive channels where, realistically, only 20% of the sales organisation was really engaged with what we were doing. That's not a bad thing: it can help you focus your success criteria and metrics on a smaller sub-team and make coaching much easier and more focused.

Marketing Support: You need to provide the channel with ways to create demand, such as marketing and channel support activities. This marketing component of channel management should not be overlooked as this can really engage the channel sales team. The challenge of demand generation is how to create the demand to purchase your products amongst clients within the specific industry or geography of your channel partner, depending on how you set things up.

There are many approaches – for example, case studies to show what has worked in the past. Success breeds success when trying to sell a product or service. If 9 out of 10 large clients in the industry have purchased your solution, it's an easy sell to get to other parts of that industry. This will not typically be the case, so it is a question of targeting the right clients through the channel partner.

Don't forget that your direct sales efforts can include handing off an active opportunity to the channel partner. This approach is designed to motivate a channel partner as they see that you are bringing tremendous value to the partnership by stimulating their success which will resonate with the whole channel partner sales team.

The Hidden Sales Team Member: The Client–Sponsors, Influencers and References

If we could hire someone to educate our prospects on the benefits of our products, we would not need to look any further than our very own clients. Our most loyal clients are also our most ardent sponsors and supporters. By referring prospects to our most satisfied clients, we could draw on our history with these 'sales reps' to add to our credibility.

As one of the oldest methods for introducing and presenting someone, the word-of-mouth technique is perfectly suited to sales and marketing. And what better vehicle for this than by using our most loyal clients! By leveraging this relationship to exclaim our virtues to every available prospect, we can quickly and efficiently be recognised at no extra cost whatsoever.

Leveraging others to tell our story validates the organisation and encourages others to join in too. A powerful tool in the sales arsenal as using these referrals as much as possible can result in new relationships. One big question arises, though: How can we successfully use these referrals?

There are a number of ways to get a client in front of a prospect, but before doing so, we need to ensure that we have chosen the right client to convey our intended message. We can't expect a client to take on a salesperson's role, so there should be a nominal amount of training beforehand. While this is not mandatory, your success rate will likely increase if the sponsor-client understands your organisation's vision.

Let's take a closer look at this.

197

Identifying the Correct Sponsors

We would gladly accept any help that our clients can offer us, but we can't expect them to possess the skills that our own sales reps have developed over some years. By focusing on some soft management skills, like integrity, communication, and reliability, for starters, a client may become an effective advocate for our products. While integrity and reliability can be quickly taught and monitored, communication skills may require a little more work. After some training, proper communication skills may add credibility to your products and smooth out the entire sales process.

If you want your clients to act as promoters for your products, you must instruct them first to understand the market and then become experts of your products. The goal is to entice new prospects to listen to stories about positive client outcomes.

Bear in mind that today's client was once a prospect and possibly had several options available to them. Whatever efforts you previously put in to turn that person into a client obviously worked. By researching and evaluating all available alternatives, prospects will ultimately decide whether or not to proceed with purchasing your product. This decision will depend on the specifics of your product, your organisation, the overall experience, and the approval of others. Prospects will seek endorsements from peers to reinforce the notion that their decision to become a client is the right one.

The client you select to become a promoter of your products must have a certain level of influence within their organisation and industry. They should also meet certain quality requirements such as good levels of sales/management skills, product/service knowledge, business expertise, an understanding of the benefits of your product/service, and a good level of influence in the industry.

If your client can access the upper hierarchy within an organisation, it could significantly impact your product's recognition. For instance, due to the increased importance of digital transformation and data usage over the last few years, we have seen that Chief Data/Digital Officer (CDO) roles have grown rapidly. Despite being competitors, we've witnessed CDOs from financial institutions and Telco providers developing relationships with one another while attending similar conferences and networking events. By freely sharing their knowledge during these networking conversations, they are creating a platform for any popular product. This could be your product.

When selecting sponsors, there are several questions we must think about:

- Will the sponsor recommend the products we have in mind?

- Has the sponsor used the products to the desired extent?

- Does the sponsor understand the expected ROI from the prospects' perspective?

- Is the sponsor well-known within the prospect's community?

- Can the sponsor influence others both internally and externally from their organisation?"

This sure is a lot to consider, but half the battle is won with a well laid-out plan and adequate preparation. To feel comfortable with the sponsor's influential range, you can either rely on your past relationship over the years or research their career and skill set. When considering all of the required attributes, the sponsor you select may not necessarily be the largest client in terms of influence or organisational size, but they must be willing to and be interested in acting as a valuable sponsor. You can ascertain this by observing the client in action, for example, talking to others, making presentations or speaking at an event.

Likely, your first shortlist of potential (and available) sponsors will not have the level of knowledge or expertise you expect. But if we think they can become good sponsors who possess the rest of the necessary skills, you can simply focus on teaching them the skills they lack or at least speed up the process to get them in front of other clients or prospects.

Teaching your Clients to Sell

Your organisation is probably already investing in 'enablement resources' for clients to use your products or services. To maximise the benefits, you can provide the client with a services catalogue; they can be referred to watch specific videos or attend instructor-led workshops and tutorials.

Reflecting on what we can teach and where we can focus, it would be best to dedicate less time and effort to improving soft skills as, we believe, the learning curve is steeper for these. The same applies to the level of influence the client has; this depends mainly on career achievements (credibility) and networking efforts (exposure).

To determine the level of training the client may need, we use the analogy of the layers of an onion; when the 'layers of the onion' are peeled back, what we want to be left with are the knowledge/expertise of the products and the unique benefits people will gain from using them.

In the book "*The Challenger Sale*", the authors **Matthew Dixon** and **Brent Adamson** write about a company's sales team using a grounded approach with clients: "*Take control of the sales conversation by tailoring the message to specific clients' needs and objectives.*" This sounds reasonable, so why not ask our sponsors to do the same for us?

Sales teams dedicate much time and energy to creating new perspectives and insights for commercial messaging, so why not focus these efforts on the unique benefits that set us apart from the rest? We can learn how we've solved our clients' problems by conducting thorough interviews and, if done right, the marketing message should practically write itself.

When your sponsor dictates the wording of the marketing message, the market will quickly identify with the terminology and overall message. With a slight nudge in the right direction, we can guide them to take on the 'Challenger Salesperson' role by getting them to share their reasons for purchasing.

The messaging will be familiar to your sponsor but new to your prospect. Once the sale is made, this prospect not only becomes a client, but a potential future sponsor too. If you do the math around using clients as sponsors, you will realise that building up your client sponsorship base is a powerful addition to your sales arsenal.

"Don't wait around for your prospect to get in touch with you. Keep thinking of fresh reasons you can get in front of them, bringing them more ideas, insights, and information to help them achieve their desired business outcomes."[49]

---

[49] **Jill Konrath** . *SNAP Selling: Speed Up Sales and Win More Business with Today's Frazzled Customers*

Make the Sponsor Sale Happen

In the later stages of the sales process (prospect's time to decide), we will eventually need to think about introducing them to one of our clients' experiences. Setting up the introduction and getting the conversation started takes time to prepare. We've listed some options that have worked for us. These are not the only options available, but we will focus on the few that your team can directly influence, for the sake of brevity.

Peer-to-Peer Conversations

A well-known form of business conversation is peer-to-peer, whereby one of your clients will speak to another client or prospect, usually without you being in attendance. We have seen many successful peer-to-peer conversations, specifically during opening conversations and closing sales opportunities. These conversations can occur by phone, video conference, or in-person and can focus on a multitude of topics, like case studies and solutions. It is important that you review the conversation topics beforehand to ensure that the prospect is clear on your offering.

These conversations should also offer the sponsor client tangible benefits for dedicating their time to this endeavour. Your organisation may introduce a credit compensation package, like converting credits for travel and expenses to company events.

When the sponsor client leads the conversation with a prospect, it is sufficient for it to be an interactive session without a rigid agenda. The prospect might be interested in specific talking points, so it's vital that the meeting remain flexible to accommodate talking about particular topics the prospect deems important. This flexible meeting format is fitting because it is your role to guide the prospect to a solution anyway.

Business Events

Whether these are company, partner or industry events, they are excellent opportunities to introduce clients to prospects and get them talking about their initiatives. If the event is not held by your company, you can accompany your clients, attend sessions together, and initiate conversations during coffee breaks. If the event is run by your company, you are in a very strong position as the master gatekeeper for the duration of the event. Your networking skills are invaluable at these events.

We recently completed a successful project with a financial institution launching a digital marketing initiative at scale. Some members of the financial institution were attending one of our organisation's sales events. During the event, we could schedule a one-to-one conversation between a new client and a prospect also in attendance. We introduced them and left the room. Our new client ran the conversation from a buyer's perspective for the first half of the meeting; she spoke about their reasons for choosing our proposal and the risks associated with the alternatives.

The prospect related their current strategy, which turned out to be quite similar to that of our client. The conversation then turned to our client's challenges during the integration period and how our solutions resolved these challenges. The prospect thanked us for this informative meeting and gave our sales team the contact information for their key stakeholders. This one encounter led to a new opportunity that our account team patiently pursued over the next six months. It eventually led to a sale.

Early Adopters Programme

When it's time to introduce a new version of your products to the market, you have the option of launching an introductory programme to a discretionary list of clients who are willing to try it out. By limiting the number of candidates to a select few who already have experience with your products, you can draw on their insights and honesty. They will be more tolerant of minor defects and will provide feedback to your team for improvements, where needed, before the product release date to a wider audience.

Companies with an 'innovators and early adopters' mindset will likely be interested in supporting research and product development. And the 'early adopters' will enjoy being the first to experience the new product or features, feeling like they have contributed to the product's future success.

Better yet, it makes for great marketing content that they helped Company XYZ with their development, especially if the product garners widespread acclaim.

In 2019, our company launched new software as an accelerator complementing our organisation's Data and Analytics core solution with Model Risk Management. The new software required some integration into the clients' infrastructures. We decided to launch the program and offer integration to a limited number of early adopters, free of charge. One of these early adopters was a financial services firm seeking to comply with new European regulations. They provided some valuable feedback and encouraged other clients to become early adopters themselves. The product received enough fanfare and recognition that our management authorised a plan to expand it even further and make it more relevant within the company's overall core product.

The Collective Mindset: Teams of Teams

We might think of the sales team as an independent system of individuals with its own goals, mission and values; however, when it links to other teams, this can, to an extent, influence the sales team system and its performance.

This chapter will illustrate these links to other teams and their influence on the sales team to enable you to understand and recognise their existence and importance. We'll provide examples of these other teams external to the sales team and show how they influence the sales team's performance.

One of the flaws with research on teams and most team coaching practices is that it tends to concentrate only on what happens within the team, especially those factors that influence high or low performance. However, the sales team does not operate in a vacuum, and its connections with other teams are highly relevant to its potential to perform and evolve. **Rensis Likert's** (1961) initial research into the concept of linking pins within the corporate hierarchy focused on the team leader's role. More recent studies have widened the research to include a dynamic that involves the team as a whole. A study by **McComb et al.** (2005), for example, finds that the quality of the links depends on multiple factors, including:

- team size

- the abilities of the team members

- support from higher levels of management, resources and continuity of team leadership.

Hawkins (2011) explored the concept of a team as an evolving system within systems in the context of team coaching. He focused on interactions between the team and its stakeholders, like understanding what is expected and negotiating for resources. [50]

Communications between Teams

Communication between different teams may often be taken for granted or underestimated. Teams, by definition, have different missions, tasks and priorities; hence, their composition is often very different in terms of skill sets, professional profiles and academic backgrounds. By implication, communication and interactions across teams must consider such–often cultural–aspects and fine-tune communication protocols and style accordingly.

When different teams interact and exchange communications, people assume that communication is clear and that their counterparts clearly understand them. The truth is that that rarely happens, or at least the understanding and the speaker's intent are not exactly aligned.

A classic example is when sales engage a prospect and, after the initial pitch, the team holds a deep dive session to gather specific details about the product or service to be provided. When this stage is completed, the phase of creating 'technical profiles' can begin. Most of you will already have experience of the difficulties involved in getting a clear understanding of what the client wants, an agreement of what should be proposed, and what should be shown to the client. These difficulties are usually based on several factors that many players often overlook.

Sales, for example, start from a privileged position: they have been directly engaged with the prospect, most likely several times, collecting information, knowledge, and impressions. However, on the other hand, technicians get involved at a later stage. They lack the visibility and clarity of sales; they have to make judgements and rely on the information the sales executives provide.

---

[50] **Clutterbuck, David**. Coaching the Team at Work 2: The Definitive Guide to Team Coaching. John Murray Press. Kindle Edition.

Salespeople and technicians may have very different academic and experiential backgrounds; salespeople are typically more empathetic, whereas technicians are typically more analytical. These differences may affect the flow of information, how it is delivered and how it is understood. The level of detail a technician needs may be substantially different from what was initially provided.

We should also consider the different teams' *forma mentis*, or the form of mind, which may further complicate interactions. Typically, the sales department comprises communicative, flexible profiles who are not overly keen on processes. In contrast, the technical department is conventionally made up of more disciplined and process-oriented people who expect, nay demand, clear and ideally structured communication.

Differences in backgrounds also affect communication, a very important aspect in the teams' interactions, facilitating or undermining discussions, depending on how successful the teams' cooperation is.

These differences and consequences can span both direct and indirect communications, each with its own pros and cons that can impact efficiency and effectiveness across teams.

Direct communication can be clear and effective but can also be hurtful to sensitive people–the truth, although undeniable, can be harmful and hard to process. Alternatively, although it avoids hurting the most sensitive individuals, indirect communication styles can lead to ambiguity and a longer cycle to get to a common understanding.

There is no single or exact way to communicate. Still, it is important to consider what communication style our counterparts prefer and their background to ensure that we approach them most appropriately.

Considerate communication will facilitate cooperation and productive interactions that are seamless and frictionless. Failing to achieve this may result in communication breakdowns, misunderstandings and misalignments, which inevitably will delay and undermine the process and create poor team dynamics.

We conclude this section with a final piece of crucial advice, as per Habit 5 of **Stephen R. Covey's** book, "*7 Habits of Highly Effective People*", which states: "*Seek first to understand, then to be understood.*"[51] It advocates listening to the other person intently to understand what they are saying and only speak once you truly understand the other person. The best way of achieving this is by asking probing questions like "*Did I understand that you said…*" or "*I understood that what you wanted to express/say was…*"

In addition to considerations of background and preferred communication styles, it is important to consider the team members' cultures when engaging in cross and intra-team communications.

Cultural Diversity between Teams

Cultural diversity is an important aspect of today's business world, considering the global nature of the world in which we live. And it's not just larger companies that are affected; it is any company with business dealings across borders or employing a diverse workforce.

Cultural sensitivity and awareness are of huge importance. They must be given all due consideration as any underestimation or mismanagement could have serious consequences, including driving team performance down.

When we travel to different countries, we are very aware and respectful of the different traditions, rules of social engagement, and communication that we respect. However, when we are at work, we may forget and revert to communicating in our usual way because we are in a familiar environment.

We must never lose sight that teams comprise individuals: professionals with their unique skills and academic background, and people with their own values, personal priorities, and cultures.

The teams of teams are at the heart of all communication within a company. This fact is not given due consideration in the flow of communication and interactions of every sales process, with particular reference to clients and the partners.

---

[51] The 7 Habits of Highly Effective People, Stephen R. Covey

Clients' Teams

Clients are crucial to the sales cycle. Too often, the client is seen solely as the target of the sales process instead of being part of it. In fact, the client should be considered the epicentre of any sales effort. The client should be viewed as another team in the sales process – and a very important team – to interact with and integrate into the sales process.

Just as we coordinate the activities between the different teams within the sales cycle, we should address the 'client team' background and characteristics properly and adapt our communication accordingly, including style and expected protocols.

Switching our perspective of clients from merely being objects of our process to being an integral part of it is no minor feat and presents several challenges. These include transparency, engagement levels and commitment, which need to be assessed and guaranteed on both sides. Once this is achieved, the relationship really makes a giant leap towards a real partnership and long-term relationship everybody should aspire to build for the business's long-term success. Mutual trust, so important for reaching agreement, is quickly established after that.

Partners' Team

To facilitate the ambitious goal set out above, consideration must be given to the role of the partner. Regardless of the stage or nature of the business, the importance of a good partner to accelerate growth and sustain a healthy business is undeniable.

Depending on the business type and size, the partner's role may vary in terms of influence, capability, and business impact. If due consideration is given to the partner's role, it can positively impact the business.

When considering the client team regarding the sales cycle activities, most of the company will fail to integrate and manage the partner team properly.

Acknowledging the presence of a partner within the cycle is just the beginning of a wider exercise. We need to understand clearly the role of the partner and our role, as part of a collaborative team. We must always be thinking about the triple win: the client, our partner, and us.

To fully optimise sales engagements and shared responsibilities, the goals must be agreed upon so that all are actively contributing to the sales opportunity success for our client's benefit.

Apart from facilitating the deal win, the partner team management should generate a virtuous cycle to replicate the successful sales cycle repeatedly.

This can only be achieved with clear rules of engagement, and well-defined and shared processes, to ensure seamless interactions and complete alignment with the partner team at every step. It is also fundamental that we establish a clear and effective communication protocol with the partner, similar to what we do with our own teams.

This will build trust and clarity and promote that everyone is fully engaged in the work of the other to serve the ultimate goal: to facilitate and accelerate the sales process to positively impact the client's business and contribute to their success.

Trusted Relationships with Team Members and Clients: Make and Keep Commitments

In Part I of this book, we covered the birth of a team and a series of common-sense founding principles to encourage unity. A team needs a starting point, and transparency and inspiration are good places to encourage communication and trust among people. This chapter will focus on taking that notion one step further by nurturing trust across all team members to be ingrained in the team culture. When a team expands and connects with other teams, it becomes vital to reinforce healthy communication and relationships. The importance of this cannot be ignored.

"Trust is the most essential ingredient in effective communication. It's the foundational principle that holds all relationships,"

says **Stephen M. Covey**[52], bestselling author, when defining trust as the "glue of life". If we apply this principle to an established sales team, the glue bonds the team together from the strongest (leader) to the weakest link within the team.

Creating a Culture of Trust with Commitment and Accountability

Trust is the bridge that connects people from various places: your team, other departments within your organisation, your partners, and your clients. You will encounter multiple cultural and/or personal differences as your team scales, but as long as the core values are emphasised and shared, leaders can expect to cultivate trust to its fullest.

---

[52] Stephen M. Covey, son of Stephen R. Covey, author of "The Speed of Trust" (https://www.speedoftrust.com)

Our TWC authors conducted interviews with some exceptional sales professionals and recognised global leaders not directly related to sales. While compiling the interview talking points, questions around 'trust, teams, and strong cultures' were at the top of the list. The top two questions were: *'How do you build a strong culture of mutual trust and a sense of belonging for a team?'* and *'How do you cultivate employee buy-in?'*. Even though these experienced and successful professionals came from different backgrounds, they all shared something vital in common: they had all created and led successful teams for decades in their respective fields. The common theme that emerged from every single interview we conducted was the unwavering commitment and accountability of their team members to cultivate a culture of mutual trust:

"Creating or re-establishing the trust in team interactions starts with the commitment and accountability of our actions in the team."

Santiago Campuzano, the Senior Director EMEA Hyperscalers Alliance at Citrix, believes that to sow the seeds for a strong culture and mutual trust, you must first sell yourself to your team. By demonstrating to the team who you really are and how you can contribute to the team, you will create a platform that allows others to do likewise. This first step in relationship-building leads to openness and faith. When you build a personal brand around yourself and sell this to the rest of the group, you can guide the team in creating followship. The old adage of 'a leader leads by example' lights the path for all group members to reach the finish line together through commitment and accountability.

Commitment is the act of '*voluntarily taking on and fulfilling obligations*'. In relation to a team, commitment can be as simple as finishing some planned tasks by an agreed date. And accountability is "*the willingness and interest to assume responsibility for one's actions and work*".[53]

Commitment and accountability are codependent, like two roommates who cannot live without one another. By following through on a commitment, you demonstrate your character and willingness to do whatever it takes for the team. The commitment you make in today's meeting needs to be completed by the next meeting; otherwise, the team will doubt you next time around.

For commitment to remain an integral part of the culture, we can apply positive psychology[54], focused on the individual well-being of team members. The following reflects the nuanced application of 'psychological safety':

- **Organise your Team:** Plan team activities based on available resources. Organise yourself and enable others likewise. Use a framework and progress reports to track the number of activities the team members can perform. Start simple by limiting the different sales actions of team members for each week and have one sales plan per client or per team.

- **Transparency:** Track commitments and make the data accessible to all. As covered in Chapter 2, micromanagement will hinder the trust factor. Guide the team to commit and report their advancement. **Scott Ingram**, the host of the "*Sales Success Stories*" and the "*Daily Sales Tips*" podcasts, said this of micromanagement:

  Most people react negatively to being micromanaged. To me, that is because micromanagement means lack of trust: I don't trust you to do the things that you say you're going to do, so I'm going to look over your shoulder and hold you accountable.

---

[53] Commitment and Accountability definitions extracted from
Jamie Wood. *Commitment Plus Accountability - Formula for Unstoppable Success*
[54] **Heather Craig** . 10 Ways To Build Trust in a Relationship
https://positivepsychology.com/build-trust/

- **Honour the Commitments**: Team members must do their best to keep the promises they make or at least have the 3courage to admit when they will not meet a deadline. There is always a learning curve when a new team is formed, or a new team member joins. Missed commitments need to be attended to carefully, acknowledging the impacts of these misses with transparency and honesty. Use past experience and common sense when assuming responsibility for future commitments. Every missed commitment is an opportunity to learn and grow both for the individual and the team.

- **Open Participation for Team Decisions and Actions**: It is important to create a safe space that allows for trust by giving feedback respectfully, showing a willingness to trust others, and applying active listening. **Scott Ingram** explains further: "*Creating an environment that is open and encourages people to step forward and say 'Maybe I don't have this. I could use some help whether that's from the leader or from others on the team.'*"

- **Honesty at Every Level:** Shows that team members do what they believe is right, according to their and the team's values. It's about being upfront about making mistakes and missing commitments.

- **Helping each Other with Kindness**: Healthy relationships require spontaneous acts of benevolence. As Scott Ingram says: "*you have to give trust to gain trust*". You need to be open-minded to accept help and return the favour by showing kindness.

Our TWC book writing project (carried out by six co-authors spanning three countries) was a success because we held weekly organisational calls during the writing phase. Like clockwork, every Saturday at 10:00 EST / 16:00 CET, our writers joined a Zoom call to review the actions taken in the past week and plan for the upcoming week. Every team needs a leader and Andy Jaffke, with a natural gift to lead, assumed that role. Under his leadership, we applied positive psychology to manage our weekly individual commitments, highlight issues that might be affecting these commitments, and assist any writer who may have fallen behind schedule. Everything was done positively with encouragement and praise for everyone's efforts.

When positive psychology patterns and common sense are applied, there should be a clear way to hold every team member accountable and understand the teams' capacity. The team's culture will initially be based on existing trust between members, but when commitment and accountability are included, the team can move forward towards achieving its goals.

> *"Trust is like love. Both parties have to feel it before it really exists."*

This was a statement made by **Simon Sinek**, a bestselling business author. Mr Sinek introduces trust and compares it to love. Both trust and love need to be nurtured and worked on every day to make them stronger. So, other than committing and being accountable as a team member, how else can we keep cultivating trust and making it stronger?

Cultivating Trust to Hold the Circle of Trust

In the 2000 American comedy film, "Meet the Parents", starring Ben Stiller and Robert DeNiro, DeNiro's character introduces the concept of 'the circle of trust' when he meets his son-in-law for the first time who is subsequently expelled from the circle of trust. "Once you're out of the circle, you're out, you're not coming back," says DeNiro's character. The expulsion was harsh on Ben Stiller's well-meaning character, but it made for a humorous story. Although the story centred around family dynamics, the sentiment can be applied to understand trust levels in relationships between sales teams and clients.

We can draw a circle with the team leader at the centre and the team members around the outer edges. Each member is linked back to the leader with adjoining lines, like the spokes of a wheel. This series of interconnecting lines of relationships is fully contained within the main circle, with the leader at its centre.

The controlled environment within the circle allows the members to feel trusted, protected and encouraged to participate. The leader builds a rapport with the team members based on trust, so knowing each team member is crucial. Leaders guide the team members, but the rest of the team also supports and contributes, enabling the whole team to succeed. By sharing the same values, vision and mission, each member can comfortably participate in the group.

If we focus on the relationships that maintain the circle, we can identify the attributes that make us realise that the circle is based on trust. There is a direct correlation of traits between relationships in the sales teams and the relationships within our families and friendship groups being Respect, Knowledge, Support, Protection and Rewards[55].

- **Respect:** Each member treats the other members fairly, politely and openly.

- **Knowing each Member:** Teams are formed by the relationships between the members; there is a genuine interest in knowing each other and what makes everyone tick.

- **Support:** Leaders guide and, occasionally, need to involve themselves and others when making decisions. Sometimes it may be necessary to clarify why certain decisions are taken.

- **Protection:** Psychological safety is the protective umbrella over the team that encourages openness and honesty. It allows for honest feedback without any fear of repercussions or consequences. The leader has to provide this protection for the team members.

- **Rewards:** Recognition is how we reward the results, encourage efforts, celebrate achieved commitments, and set standards within the circle.

We will explore Protection further and how it promotes psychological safety, which is the reassurance that members won't be punished for making mistakes or for taking decisions of moderate risk. One famous research project at Google showed this was by far the most important attribute of team effectiveness.

---

[55] **Paul Keijzer** . Why You Need to Create a Circle of Trust *https://www.business2community. com/leadership/need-create-circle-trust-01505068*

Fostering Team Psychological Safety

Google's internal research project from 2012, called "Project Aristotle"[56], studied the effectiveness of their teams. They recognised that focusing only on quantitative outputs such as client satisfaction rates or technical team metrics were insufficient, so they dug a little deeper and ran a combination of qualitative and quantitative tests. For the qualitative assessments, they captured inputs from executives, leaders, and team members, trying to normalise each group's bias.

They found that, while executives were more focused on results like sales numbers, team members said the team's culture and leader's vision/goals were the most important. After collecting all the data, statisticians determined that it mattered less about who was in the team and more about how they interacted and worked together. They identified psychological safety as the most important factor to a team's effectiveness.

Teams that promote psychological safety encourage their members to feel more engaged and with a sense of belonging. One of our interviewees, Cesar Cernuda, President at Netapp, explains:

"When people feel they belong, they share their knowledge, ideas, objections, energy, effort beyond what you ask. When they share, we all learn – at all levels. This builds the engine."

Trust and psychological safety also promote transparency. Every team member is encouraged to express themself freely, regardless of the subject matter. Increasing the team's psychological safety is something that everybody should contribute to, and this is where a well-intentioned leader should first set the example. Different actions can be taken to promote the team's psychological safety[57]:

- Approach conflict constructively and collaboratively

- Use emotional intelligence in conversations

---

[56] Google Guide: Understand Team Effectivenes *https://rework. withgoogle.com/print/guides/5721312655835136/*
[57] **Laura Delizonna**. High-Performing Teams Need Psychological Safety. *https:// hbr.org/2017/08/ high-performing-teams-need-psychological-safety-heres-how-to-create-it*

- Prepare for difficult conversations and anticipate the reactions

- Be neutral and curious. Avoid blaming someone

- Ask for feedback after any confrontation.

We can also measure the levels of psychological safety within a team through one-on-one conversations or surveys. These measures can be anonymous so as not to deter the employee from giving feedback and ensuring there is no employer backlash. If there is no psychological safety, employees are less likely to want to be identified. These initiatives should be implemented by team leaders or executives regularly, as they are a great indicator of team performance.

Extending our Circle to Clients or Getting into the Clients' Circles

The trust cultivated inside the circle acts as a barrier against those who are unwilling to earn their place. These barriers also represent a protective circle of trust from the client's perspective. Depending on the level of trust you've gained with prospects or clients, you could determine which level[58] you are on and make plans to advance to the next level.

These levels of trust range between levels 1 and 4, as follows:

1st Level: Indifference/Skepticism

When approaching a prospect (or as the new face to a client), their first reaction might be one of indifference if they don't know of you. Worse yet, they may regard you with scepticism if they are merely tolerating you without any real intention of purchasing your product.

For instance, if a client is conducting research to evaluate the market before making a decision, he may be sceptical of everything he hears or reads. Of course, he doesn't know you or your team, so your first task would be to start building a relationship (building trust) with your team's help.

---

[58] **Alice Alessandri** and **Alberto Aleo**. The Circle of Trust: Building and Maintaining Customer Relations *https://diariodiunconsulente.it/en/2015/09/14/circle-of-trust/*

2nd Level: Interest

Something has caught the prospect's attention, and the team may have started some conversations with the technical team. You can gain trust either directly by responding to their needs or indirectly through references, word-of-mouth, or peer conversations. The prospect needs to be confident and reassured about you before making any decisions.

3rd Level: Conditional Trust

When you are in the middle of the sales funnel, you can reach this conditional trust level with clients once you've closed the first deal or provided proof that you can deliver the promised value. Before this, the team may have spent a sales period on consultative selling activities like speeches, demos, pilots, Q&A, or Request for Proposals. The activities undertaken at this level help build a rapport with the prospect with the aim of merging your and your prospect's circles of trust.

4th Level: Trusted Advisor

In Level 4, the commitment continues after the sale. Getting into renewal/upselling cycles might generate momentum for cultivating trust that can definitely help to overcome any obstacles and issues that may appear. At this level, the client starts becoming part of your team, as discussed in Chapter 2, and you can leverage them to increase your reputation with their colleagues.

The good times enable you to increase the level of trust with your client; however, there may be times when, due to unfortunate circumstances, you drop a level or two, perhaps you failed to keep one of your promises. It may not always be possible to rebuild trust, but it is always worth the effort.

Re-establishing Trust and Getting Back the Team Power

When a team has lost trust in itself, the negative impact is felt immediately. Members lose their sense of engagement and retreat from open and honest discussions with others. Re-establishing the trust and getting back the team power may be a long road when people feel disconnected, even if it's not done maliciously or purposely to harm the team.

Team environments with a low trust coefficient can create internal and external communication challenges like misinterpretations, shallow conversations, and engaging in the blame game.

> *"In a high-trust relationship, you can say the wrong thing, and people will still get your meaning. In a low-trust relationship, you can be very measured, even precise, and they'll still misinterpret you."*[59]

When you encounter disengaged employees, you can sense their frustration and lack of motivation. Their mindset has likely done a complete 180-degree turn from when they first joined the team, when they were full of hope and inspiration.

Sadly, this deflated mindset makes individuals withdrawn; they will start looking out only for themselves and not for the team. You, as the leader, can take the first step to turn this around by identifying the cause of the problem. Sometimes all you need is a fresh start, a clean slate to start working towards a resolution. We have all been in situations where we realise that a negative situation was merely the result of a misunderstanding.

Our interviewee **Victor Antonio**, a keynote sales speaker, sales trainer, and the host of the "*Sales Influence*" podcast, told us a great story about his start as a sales manager for an international sales team.

His mandate was to build a team of former individual salespeople who had lost trust amongst themselves. How did he repair a broken team of people who had proven track records and lead them back to their former glory?

---

[59] **Stephen M.R. Covey**. *The Speed of Trust* New York Times bestseller

At the end of a 3-month assessment and reorganisation, **Victor** eagerly set about establishing new rules and a compensation plan for everybody. He announced the rules for full and partial crediting:

> *If you have a contact from another region, you can contact your team and say: 'I just found a client in your region, can I get partial credit for the sale?' And that was a respectful way of saying it, so we set up the compensation plan where there could be partial credits, where both sides had to acknowledge that there was credit due. And within a year, there was a culture change. Everybody trusted each other again. Nobody backstabbed each other. Everybody understood the rules of the game. I applied them consistently across. And they said I was kind of like, I'm the nicest guy in the world.*

In this particular case, **Victor Antonio** used his experience to establish clarity on the organisation and accountability of teams by region. The salespeople felt reinvigorated and committed again, so much so that they set new corporate sales records over the next several years.

Accountability Framework: Through Goals, Planning, Process and Coaching

When you first saw the title of this chapter, how many of you thought about sales quotas and sales goals? We call sales teams 'teams' but, when you think about it, we really remunerate the 'team' based on individual goals and objectives. Tom Watson, who essentially founded IBM, said that people respond to what and how you pay them. If you reward them based on individual behaviour, that is how the people will act.

You need to be able to create a culture of accountability. To do this, each member needs to have their own accountability structure that works for them. It starts with what each member is willing to do and commit to for the team. We try to hold people accountable for what *we* think they should be doing, but we need to hold them accountable for what *they* think they should be doing.

As we have stated throughout, the sales team is all about the "WE" and not the "I". It is the paradigm shift we are trying to introduce to the sales world.

So What is Different?

According to **Dr Solange Charas**, teams are systems, systems of themselves. A team is not a collection of individuals but a system with the multiplier effect; one and one make three, two and two make seven. As an engineer, this doesn't appear to be good math, but the team dynamic gives us this new appreciation where the sum of the parts is greater than the whole.

Dr Charas states that much research has been done recently revealing the links between financial performance and performing teams. The greater the team's performance, the greater the financial performance as an outcome. It stands to reason then that the team's goals must be goals that all team members can identify with and rally around to ensure they are all going in the same direction as a collective.

Should the team, if it is a system, not then have team goals? Exactly!

Team goals are those goals determined by the collective team. Who better to tell you what they are going to achieve than the actual team members themselves, which may include many 'I think I can' moments, and then you are there!

This is a fundamental shift from the traditional top-down approach whereby the sales manager dictates quotas based on company targets, which burden was usually only ever shouldered by one person in the team.

Another benefit of establishing team goals is that they really inspire the team when they are achieved. It gives the team a sense of ownership and belonging, a sense of wanting to do even more with the team. That feeling doesn't go away easily. Conversely, if you have an individual salesperson achieving quotas, they may be happy and elated for a short period, but the feeling soon wears off, and they have to start all over again. There are no long-term effects for achieving individual goals as there are with attaining team goals.

So, What is the Role of the Sales Manager?

With a high performing team, goals may be aspirational and seemingly unachievable. It is up to the sales leader, as the coach, to break the main goal down into achievable mini-goals. The sales leader understands who is on the team and the team dynamics and can coach accordingly to achieve the collective goals. The great thing about achievable goals is that success breeds success. The more goals the team achieves, the more successful the team is, and the more successful the team is, the more goals the team will achieve. It is one of those self-fulfilling prophecies that are elusive in the 'I' culture.

The sales leader has another role to play too: to let the team live up to their potential. A high performing sales team already knows how to think big; they have the success to prove it. However, if you are trying to create a high performing sales team, you need to encourage them to think bigger than before.

David Goggins, an ultra-athlete, motivational speaker, author, and former Navy SEAL, challenges people to look at what they have done before and figure out how to do 3x more. There are no reasons for limitations. This is the primary thought process of a high performing sales team where they think bigger than expected.

The sales leader also looks at the team's trajectory to achieve the goals they think they can achieve. Through followship, the leader will direct the team towards achieving the goals by giving them the necessary tools and support. This whole process is built on trust; the leader trusts that the goals the team are committing to are achievable, and there is collective trust in one another that the team will successfully reach the end goal.

Followship is defined[60] as '*possessing the ability to be both present and centred, following one's purpose and aligning actions around it.*'

The sales leader must be a true leader with leadership and followship skills, similar to leadership, but where you have your team in front of you, and you have paved the way for them to be successful.

Followship is true leadership in this new team-centric world. The task of bringing disparate ideas together is creating an accountability framework based on the priorities of sales teams.

What Goes into Helping a Team Identify their Goals?

First, you need to take a step back to identify the sales objectives, which must align with the business objectives. Once you have identified the objectives, you can bring in the goals to support those objectives. All the objectives should be supported with data because 'gut-feel' accounts for almost 50% of our sales decisions versus using data to inform our decision-making[61].

Each goal should encompass the following features of SMART goals:

---

[60] Fateme Banishoeib, "Followship: The Surprising Secret to High Impact Leadership" https://bestselfmedia.com/followship-the-secret-to-leadership/
[61] Forrester Research, May 2018. "The B2B Data Activation Priority"

- **Specific.** Goals should have specific endpoints and must not be vague.

- **Measurable.** You can't monitor what you don't measure, so you need measurable goals to know when goals are met.

- **Attainable**. There are realistic and stretch goals, but goals must still be attainable by the team.

- **Relevant**. In this case, the goals should be relevant to the context of the accountability framework.

- **Time-Bound**. You need some form of time frame to know if you are on track to accomplishing the goals.

The Rains group reached out to over 420 sales professionals to interview them and get their responses to specific sales challenges.[62] What is interesting about this study is that 5 of their top 10 sales enablement and leadership challenges, as listed, focused on developing team accountability:

- Implementing a consistent sales process

- Pipeline management and forecasting

- Developing sales skills

- Developing sales managers

- Coaching the sales teams.

Drawing conclusions from these observations and priorities, one can see that the sales team Accountability Framework consists of three categories. Only one of the categories actually includes sales revenue. Yet all categories are critical to ensuring that team goals are in place for the sales team. The Accountability Framework, shown in the diagram, includes:

---

[62] Global Sales Training, Rains Group. in Selling Power. https://www.sellingpower. com/2019/09/25/16602/new-study-reveals-top-sales-leadership-challenges-and-priorities

- Sales goals

- Skills goals

- Coaching

Figure 6: Accountability Framework

Sales Goals

Consistent and realistic sales goals and attainable revenue growth are always targets for any sales organisation. Just saying we are going to grow sales is merely the beginning of the story. The parts that lead up to that 'moment' are the goals that will ensure what you actually do to make the sales growth you are trying to achieve.

The best way to understand what comprises your revenue target goal is to look at the sales process that gets you to that point. Some of these metrics include:

- Sales cycle length

- Conversion rates

- Losses

- Closing ratio

- Effective channels.

Each phase and metric can be converted into a SMART goal, for example, it takes 200 leads to convert 10 opportunities. It means that every effort of the sales team that brings them closer to those critical numbers is a trackable and important goal.

These goals must be based on the company knowing its market and metrics due to the repeatability of its sales process. It won't be easy to establish these repeatable metrics for a startup. **Desh Deshpande**, one of the interviewees for this book, stated that you need at least 100 sales before having repeatable metrics.

Implementing a consistent sales process is the cornerstone of the Accountability Framework. It is a process whereby all involved know what it will take to succeed with clients and each other.

Pipeline management and forecasting is also part of the Accountability Framework. This includes the work that the team needs to do throughout the sales funnel to make the team and company successful. The actual targets vary depending on the sales team's structure, including the extended sales team and the sales funnel approach.

Examples of a team's Sales Goals are:

- Value consistently articulated across the sales funnel.

- Increasing the number of qualified leads to grow the funnel.

- Sales revenue targets, including stretch goals.

The challenge for sales managers is to constantly review the data and create goals that make the most sense to the team. This process cannot be rushed; one cannot go from zero to mature company goals overnight. The sales manager must work with the data and goals, review monthly and quarterly targets to ascertain what works and then create stretch goals based on these insights.

Skills Goals

Skills growth helps ensure the relevance of the sales team as its role is ever-evolving. It is essential to ensure that the team sees the company as supportive of its growth of skills that will change over time. Teams need to identify those skills and ensure that their team is consistently evolving in the right direction.

The sales manager role is also ever-evolving. Sales managers need to be accountable to their teams; just as salespeople grow, so too must the sales managers.

Examples of Skills Goals are:

- Ensuring that the sales team knows how to engage solely over virtual channels as they cannot travel to the client.

- Provide knowledge of how to use the available tools to make the sales team more effective.

- Managing personnel with no direct contact. The pandemic has posed further challenges for sales managers who are managing many more remote teams. Your sales management must reflect these different and new situations.

Coaching the Sales Teams

Coaching and motivating the sales team is the last piece of the Accountability Framework. You can ensure that the teams are accountable to themselves, both individually and as a team and that the coach is accountable to the team to help them all grow and be the best they can be. We will explore coaching and motivation in the next chapter.

Example

Let's look at an example of a sales team that sells high tech products in a B2B sale. We must first look at the **Sales Assumptions** that go into creating team goals. This will enable us to develop a **Sales Revenue Forecast** for the team and create the **Sales Team Composition**.

Figure 7: B2B Sales Example

Sales Assumptions

The following table includes assumptions to set the scenario:

Assumptions	Metrics/Goals	Periodicity
Sales Growth	10%	per year
Revenue per Sale	$350,000	
Product Lifetime	3	Years
Maintenance	15%	Of initial annual contract value
Retention Rate	80%	Rev
Revenue per Team	$3,000,000	per year and team
Overhead per Team	40%	
Cost per Team	$1,200,000	
Annual Sales Target	$10,000,000	
Average Number of Clients	29	
Prospect to Clients	150	

There are several key assumptions you need to make to create sales goals and the sales team composition. These key assumptions fall in the following categories:

- **Revenue** – per sale and overall revenue per team

- **Client Success** – Retention (and churn)

- **Sales Team Overhead** – % of overhead based on sales revenue

- **Marketing Success** – Prospects to Client, 'how many to make a sale'.

These numbers have all been simplified; this is simply a 'back of the napkin' analysis of what you need to understand. There are additional factors to consider, such as monthly or weekly figures, but we will keep it simple.

Sales Revenue Forecast

You can create the sales revenue forecast based on the assumptions. The most significant assumption about this process is that you know most or all of the key metrics because you have a repeatable sales process. During times of uncertainty (a pandemic!) or the company is in the early stages of growth, you must keep revisiting the core assumptions and adjust them as necessary. These adjustments should only affect the core team as a last resort – unless an individual is not performing.

4 years sales forecast example

	Year 1	Year 2	Year 3	Year 4
Revenue	$ 11,000,000	$12,100,00	$13,310,000	$14,641,000
Number of clients	32	35	39	42
Make up for churn	6	7	7	8
New clients	3	3	4	3
Total new & churn	9	10	11	11
Prospects	1350	1500	1650	1650
Monthly	113	125	138	138

The key sales team driver for this exercise is the Monthly Prospects which will be the overall team goal. The Monthly Prospects will dictate the activities the sales team need to do collectively to successfully drive prospects through the sales funnel, including marketing resources to identify prospects and sufficient sales 'horsepower' to convert the prospects into long-term clients.

There may be additional goals to enable higher client retention or less churn to drive the post-sales efforts regarding client success.

Sales Team Composition

This view lets you determine the composition of the sales team needed to support revenue growth expectations.

As the sales manager, you must try to assemble the most successful team you can, within budget. There is an additional $170K out of a budget of $1.2M for the sales team to use in this example. This gives an excellent framework for the team to be successful and be accountable as it distils the question of 'on track or not' down to team prospects to close and ensures you are doing everything to retain your clients.

Team Composition

Total Cost Rate: 100%, including overhead and commission

Roles	Salary	Total Cost
Account Executive (3)	$150,000	$450,000
Sales Engineer (2)	$125,000	$250,000
Marketing Lead (1)	$100,000	$100,000
Client Success Lead (1)	$80,000	$80,000
Team Support (1)	$60,000	$60,000
Total Team Cost		**$940,000**
Budget		**$1,200,000**
Difference		**($260,000)**

Actual vs. Planned: ($260,000) – Under budget, which means we have $260,000 additional budget available.

Coaching the Team: Keep Talent, Team and Individual Motivation High

Coaching in sales has traditionally been about creating an Accountability Framework based solely on generating revenue, even though many other factors influence the final sales revenue targets, as illustrated in the previous chapter.

We can draw parallels between a unit and its military commander with a sales team. The plans are not about one individual but about how the whole team works together to achieve the end goal. It is about winning the smaller battles ultimately to win the war–having smaller, attainable goals to achieve the ultimate goal. It highlights that an individual cannot win the battle alone but must work together with other individuals as part of a team.

We can draw further parallels with the military commander, like prioritising where to place precious resources on the battlefield, ensuring that the resources are executing against the plan, and motivating the team to work together through practice and learning from their failures and victories.

The traditional roles of coaches have been to advise on progress and to help develop the salesperson. This role has been expanded on to include:

- Getting the team to prioritise the goals and activities most relevant to achieving overall success;

- Ensuring that the team is executing against those highest priority goals; and

- Providing the motivation for the team to move towards continuously achieving their goals.

Figure 8: Sales Management Role

The role of the sales manager/sales coach now encompasses:

Advising

The old saying: '*Give a man a fish, and you feed him for a day; teach a man to fish, and you feed him for a lifetime,*' certainly advocates the merits of the advisory role. Rather than providing the team with the win, a good sales manager will look for key teaching moments that will help the sales team tap into their collective wisdom and constantly review their plans. The sales manager must 'teach the team to fish'.

The advice can also extend to how the team might do things differently to win deals. A good sales coach knows when to give the team general advice and when to give them specific advice. But a great coach will constantly work with the sales team to find those opportune teaching moments.

Being a positive leader for your team is an essential attribute of a great sales coach. The sales coach needs to exhibit leadership with flexibility and apply different leadership styles to different individuals, as needed, within the sales team.

Empathy is also an excellent coaching attribute for a sales coach; they need to be empathetic to the needs of the team. Empathy will resonate with individuals and the entire team where they know they can rely on you. This creates a safe place in which the team can thrive.

Developing

Great sales managers develop the knowledge, skills, and attributes to improve their sales team's performance. They reinforce new skills and hold the sales team accountable for applying their knowledge. The key areas to develop within teams are pushing them to do activities that will help them grow, learn about the competition, how clients are actually using the product/service, and how to articulate the value of the product or service that will compel a prospect to buy. If the sales team has bought into the shared vision, they can help develop plans and goals to support the ultimate goals through daily tactical decisions.

Prioritising

So goes the leader, so goes the team. The team needs to buy into the compelling vision that drives the company by knowing why they are doing what they are doing. Team members must also know where and how they can support the whole team. The reality for most sales teams is that the individuals seldom work together as a team. '*I want to win at the expense of someone else on my team*' needs to change to '*I want to win on a team of great people*'.

I want to be my best on a team of amazing people.

This attitude ensures that everyone's priorities and activities are aligned as a team. If the team were to track time spent on 'sales activities', they would probably be surprised to see how little of their time is actually spent on the highest priority activities that will yield the best outcomes.

The list of activities can include:

- PROSPECTING to find new clients and new opportunities

- NURTURING DREAM CLIENTS to ensure their continued support

- Making SALES CALLS to a combination of new and existing clients

- KEEP follow-up COMMITMENTS with clients

- NURTURE existing client relationships

- SALES TEAM MEETINGS

- UPDATE THE CRM.

The best sales managers help sales team members to focus their energy, efforts on those activities that yield the best returns on their time. Once these activities have been identified, the sales manager will help the sales team to maintain focus and avoid distractions that could affect successful outcomes.

Executing

Sales managers must coach their team always to execute activities with the biggest bang. Some refer to it as 'being in the zone', where all the focus is on activities that produce the most energised focus, involvement, and enjoyment. If your whole sales team is operating 'in the zone' and on the right activities, this sales team will produce amazing results.

Remember: Reward collaboration and winning against the competition, not winning against each other, and celebrate the small wins, not just the big wins.

Motivating

Sales managers must motivate their sales team to help them find and sustain their highest levels of energy and action over the long term. **Deb Calvert**, the author of "*Stop Selling & Start Leading*" and founder of *The Sales Experts Channel*, says motivation comes from helping sales team members to grow in their capacity, confidence and competence, and making them feel important.

A good sales coach knows they need to motivate the individuals on their sales team to motivate the entire team. A great way to motivate the sales team is to get them to pick their own individual incentives, those incentives that will motivate them the most. You might be surprised by what really motivates people, and you won't know unless you ask. It might be attending a conference, time off, or education, in addition to the usual monetary incentives.

You can also motivate a team with team-building exercises specifically designed to bring team members together. Team-building can be as basic as paper exercises or as exciting as crossing a river together with a rope bridge they have made. These exercises will highlight their reliance on one another to accomplish the team's overall goals and that the only way to accomplish these goals is by being part of a strong, cohesive team. The impact will carry over into the sales activities that they are collectively doing to support one another.

How to Motivate in Times of Crisis

According to Scott Ingram, challenging times can be overcome by pushing through to become better. How true! Recognising that times are challenging but that there are opportunities for everyone in the industry.

How do you innovate with something like COVID-19, for instance? When you come up against roadblock after roadblock, figure out how to do things better.

We know that certain sectors appear to be faced with insurmountable obstacles, like the travel industry. It is hard to think of anything innovative when no one is travelling. But, we believe that there are opportunities and successes out there. For example, other types of businesses, like restaurants and manufacturing, are pivoting their business models to see them through the pandemic. You might be able to create something three times better!

See it for what it is, and don't let it beat you!

The Importance of the Individual Mindset of Team Members: Hire Talent, Teach Skill

Organisations continually make mistakes when hiring due to inefficient hiring processes. As part of this chapter, we review why it is important to have efficient hiring processes for teams to grow, the challenges faced when scaling teams, skills to look for to create high performing teams, and finishing with how to apply a framework for scaling teams. Efficient hiring processes can make your hiring process agile within the team, which are also applicable to the whole organisation.

Hiring is an essential process in any organisation looking to scale in response to its growth pace. The organisation must grow horizontally by creating new teams and vertically when a team needs more people or when people are replaced. It's a recurring topic within team conversations, especially when urgent cover is needed for a position. It can be both frustrating and stressful for a team if there is no agile process in place, even more so if the team is proactively involved in the hiring process.

Facing Challenges on Hiring Talent for your Team

When recruiting new members, the main objective is finding the right candidate in a timely manner. However, the process is often complex, involving both internal and external candidates; it has to be compliant with the organisation's policies and is not always successful. We discuss some of the main challenges we've encountered later in the chapter and look at how to solve them by applying a framework for scaling teams.

237

If your organisation is growing, stakeholders within the organisation need to be vested; otherwise, you run the risk of cancelled plans, not getting the required budget approvals, and wasting everyone's time.

When establishing the need for a new hire, the process funnel can be very complex. Candidates may come from a number of different channels, like referrals, headhunting, and direct job applications, or an internal candidate can fill the role. The number of candidates can prolong the process and make alignment more difficult.

Hiring and talent management staff may not be 100% dedicated to your needs; they may be involved with dozens, even hundreds, of other hiring processes within the company. Their priorities and yours may not be aligned, which could result in unsuitable candidates and potential delays.

If the organisation's onboarding process is not adequately defined, it can take a long time for candidates to adapt, potentially resulting in feelings of disengagement and developing into a situation where the new hire does not fit in with the team.

The company's image is essential for attracting the right candidates and must be well-articulated, so candidates have a clear idea of why they want to be a part of the company.

The following is an example of our own hiring experience that resulted in a 6-month hiring period! The process was:

- HR was made aware of the need

- In-house approvals were obtained

- The job post was published

- Headhunters were engaged

- Candidates were screened, interviewed, and offers made

- The candidate was finally hired!

During this hiring period, the team's sales manager had to cover the vacant salesperson slot, which meant he could not lead the team. Instead, he dedicated his efforts to maintaining clients or completing a sales cycle to meet his overall quota. This half a year when the sales manager was not adequately leading the team had a definite impact which impact could have been minimised had the organisation applied 3 Lean methodology concepts to the process:

1. Eliminate waste

2. Optimise the whole through continuous improvement

3. Look for excellence.

And it's not just the process that posed the problem, but the output too. Even after the long and tedious hiring process, the new team member was not a fit for our team. However, this can happen during any onboarding process because of a number of personal or professional reasons. We can minimise the chances of it happening by recognising the types of team skills we're looking for to ensure that the candidate is aligned with our teams' values, understands the vision, and contributes individually to the common goal of the team.

Building Team Mindset with Individual's Growth Mindset

James Craig, one of our TWC authors, tells his children that going to university is really the start of their education journey. We couldn't agree more as, now more than ever, one's career is based on continuous learning.

You have to be personally willing to be challenged. Be able to learn new skills and grow and learn on your life's journey. This is a growth mindset.

We look for a growth mindset as one of the key skills for new hires. This mindset fosters a positive atmosphere within the team if every individual contributes and has the same attitude.

Any person who believes they can continue to grow has a growth mindset.

Jay Wright, an American college basketball coach and additional sports career coach, tells his players:

The one thing we could do to improve ourselves was to bring a great attitude, every day, to confront the challenges we faced. None of us controls what happens to us in life—but we do control our responses to those circumstances[63]

Victor Küppers, author and noted speaker of positive psychology in the Spanish community, is worth mentioning when explaining the relevance of attitude in life and applying it to our discussion. Victor presents, in his book, a formula of how much a person is valued[64]:

"Value is the sum of (Knowledge + Skill) multiplied by Attitude"

- **Knowledge:** Victor explains that everything in life requires knowledge, such as working in finance or being president. Sales teams need knowledge too, knowledge of the product, the organisation's strategy, and the client.

- **Skills:** Skills can either be soft or hard skills within the team. Soft skills are those we use to fit in with the team and the organisation, like communication, leadership, teamwork, empathy, and manners. Unlike soft skills, hard skills are easier to learn and are directly relevant to the role, like management skills, account planning skills, and the use of specific marketing or client relations management (CRM) software.

- **Attitude:** Victor says of attitude that the difference in the kind of person you are is not in your knowledge or your skills but your attitude. *"You're not amazing because of your knowledge. You're not amazing because you have a lot of experience. You are incredible for your way of being."*

[63] **Jay Wright, Michael Sheridan, Mark Dagostino**
Attitude: Develop a Winning Mindset on and off the Court
[64] **Victor Küppers** *el efecto actitud (The Attitude Effect)*

Victor explains further that he is not undermining the importance of knowledge and skills: *"Nothing worse than a useless person who's super motivated – 'I have no idea, but I'll do it!'"*. When hiring someone, we must ensure that the candidate has the appropriate knowledge and skills against the requirements of the role, but it is the candidate's attitude that will be the differentiator when making the final decision. A positive attitude derives from an optimistic, proactive and resilient mindset. These are important characteristics in life; they are also important in sales team activities where you must always be one step ahead of the client.

As remarked by **Victor Antonio**, one of our interviewees:

> *I've noticed that the most successful ones just go in, they start making calls, you know, they read a little bit to learn but they learn enough to just get going. And they're just like this constant. And the ones that come back to you with excuses all the time, are usually the ones that I really want to get rid of.*

The team needs to have a resilient mindset to overcome the many rejections they will face in their interactions.

Mike Figliuolo, through one of our interviews, expressed the importance of having a combination of resilience, patience and hunger:

> *It may not be a sale today, maybe a sale on the road: so it's that resilience on that, that persistence, that optimism and understanding, that success is not always about ringing the cash registers, success is also about building relationships.*

Proactivity and perseverance are fed by the curiosity of people willing to challenge themselves, take risks, and pursue team goals. All of these ingredients create a growth mindset. **Scott Ingram** simplified it when he said: *"Where I can grow and where I can get better, where I can improve, where I can be me and where can I push those boundaries."*

With a growth mindset, members will see inspiration when others succeed, learn from failures, and base their contributions on effort, commitment and attitude. On the contrary, a stagnant mindset won't encourage team players to have the curiosity to learn. They will not like to be challenged, and their current abilities will determine their contributions, with no desire to grow or develop.

In one of our interviews, **Marta Martinez** expressed how she likes the growth mindset as it provides the ambition in people to think big:

> *You have to build your mind thinking for impact, at life and at business. And I would like this ambition in a healthy way: thinking that you should try to do it, and if you fail, you fail. If you put the ambition very short, you will never get anything.*

A good attitude and a growth mindset are great contributors to the team mindset and should be prioritised in the list of skills required in the team as they result in potential long-term team members. Looking for these particular skills will guide you to some of the best people who will challenge, and challenge daily. This also forms part of the fit in an organisation when someone is willing to adapt continuously. We need to identify more skills for the new joiners that make for an ideal candidate for the sales team to make it more successful. We review these additional skills next.

Hiring Individual Contributors for our Dream Team

When hiring new members to the team, our objective is that they fit in with our culture and values and become individual contributors who maximise the team's performance. As **Cesar Cernuda** said in our interview: "*Don't look for someone you can just pass the baton to, but who will take that thing and run like the wind with it*". An individual contributor contributes to the team with ownership, making the team outcome a personal endeavour.

New contributors must embrace the organisation's values and culture; however, they can also enhance and enrich the team. It is a matter of ascertaining if they can be one of us, which is easy to identify by evaluating if the candidates can adapt to the team quickly. As **Dr Solange Charas** says: "*They are one of us. The more that you can look like the person you are interviewing.*"

Humility is one of those values that rarely appears in an organisations' stated values. According to **Santiago Campuzano**, one of our interviewees, this is implied in the other organisation values.

Humble people can use 360-degree listening and learn from others regardless of where they are in the organisation's hierarchy, which helps move everybody in the same direction.

Soft skills help members fit in with the team; these skills are the human qualities that differentiate people from each other and are difficult to teach, unlike hard skills.

Our interviewee, **Marta Martinez**, doesn't believe that we should distinguish between a person's personal and professional lives when assessing their soft skills; you cannot have a person who is good in their personal life but bad in their professional life, and vice versa. She also includes generosity as one of those benevolent attributes that contributes to the team; if you are generous in life, then generosity will be present in your professional activities too.

Attitude, Growth Mindset, Humility, and Generosity are all soft skills we have discussed as being the most relevant to success. Nevertheless, there are additional skills that new candidates should possess if they are to contribute to the team's performance. We've extracted the skills that are most relevant to the sales team and that employers value[65]:

- **Communication Skills:** Oral and written communications are crucial for building trusting relationships with others. Every team member will have conversations and relationships within the team, with their counterparts, their clients, and other teams. Having the communication skills for business storytelling of your value proposition will make for a more powerful presentation of the organisation and its products. Also, being consistent and assertive, when required, leads to more transparency, thereby generating more trust in these relationships.

- **Integrity:** Integrity is of vital importance in sales. It comes in many forms and is a proven attribute in many situations, both in teams and client relationships. Integrity means having strong character traits that are followed through in a person's work ethic. It is strongly related to trust, reliability, and accountability, which have all been covered in a previous chapter.

---

[65] **Alison Doyle**, *Top Soft Skills Employers Value With Examples*
https://www.thebalancecareers.com/list-of-soft-skills-2063770

- **Critical Thinking:** We want our team members to be individual contributors, accountable for their actions. This requires one to analyse situations and make the right decisions. Team members must display creativity and curiosity in problem-solving, which comes from having the growth mindset skills that we value as top attributes, as discussed before.

Our interviewee, **Victor Antonio,** explained how he identifies communication skills and integrity by looking for consistency in communication. First, he asks for a five-minute presentation on PowerPoint: "*Just pitch me anything. I don't care what it is. And then I want to see what the client is going to see. Articulation and communication skills are the big ones*". He then puts the candidates through multiple interviews to double-check the information and uncover those who are not truthful: "*I learned how to ask questions like lawyers, making two or three different ways to see if I got consistency. When it isn't a lie, you just say it, and it always comes out the same way. So with this, I always look for consistency.*"

Elon Musk, CEO of *Tesla* and *SpaceX*, uses a similar approach to Victor Antonio and explains that "*Anyone can say they're the best at what they do, but it can be hard to know whether they're telling the truth.*" Elon revealed his technique at the World Government Summit in 2017:

> *Tell me about some of the most difficult problems you've worked on and how you solved them. Because the people who really solved the problem know exactly how they solved it. They know and can describe the little details.*

When interviewing for a position, the candidate must have the combination of soft skills discussed earlier in addition to the required hard skills and experience of the role. A candidate's soft skills may be the determining factor when it comes time deciding whether to hire one candidate over another. However, it will be the candidate's experience and knowledge that dictate the first cut in incoming CVs, as some of these hard skills may be essential requirements for your sales team.

Hard skills refer to those skills people learn through academic endeavours or throughout their professional careers. Hard skills can be careers and masters topics, specific certifications from specific industries, foreign languages, marketing skills and computer skills.

Again, all of these are skills that can be learned and they all take time (e.g. two years for an MBA, one month to understand our organisation's CRM tool, etc.). There may be times that a candidate does not possess all the desirable hard skills. During the interview phase, we will review how many of these candidates can be trained during onboarding and the initial period to ensure that they are not negatively impacted during the hiring process.

Much has been written about another personality trait and whether this matters in professional situations: being extroverted versus introverted. Although extroverts are more comfortable in social situations, talented people don't necessarily have to be extroverts. According to a 2018 Yale University study[66], introverts are more astute at understanding how we behave in groups which is a skill that is very useful for measuring team performance. Being introverted can also be advantageous in certain situations where there is a team issue, like a misunderstanding that requires an understanding of behaviours to be resolved. We can definitely say that both traits are perfectly suitable for a sales team, and a combination of both traits within the team can improve team performance.

Another skill we haven't talked about here yet is leadership. Team leaders need to have strong leadership skills, but do we want a team full of leaders? Absolutely not! We can have team members who possess leadership skills and can manage situations and people. That is very important, as we want them to foresee problems, maintain the right attitude, and drive others to be positive.

Nevertheless, we also need to have followers within the team; followers who will be happy to be guided by the team leader and follow other team members' directions.

Santiago Campuzano explains how he always uses the same example to talk about the power of teams. He uses a soccer analogy on how FC Barcelona had what they called the "Dream Team" from 1988 to 1996 with Johan Cruyff as their coach. The team didn't have the best players, as recognised by individual titles, but the team achieved four league titles and a champions league championship. How? By having average players working in a top team led by an outstanding coach.

---

[66] **Anton Gollwitzer and John A. Bargh** *Social Psychological Skill and Its Correlates* *https://econtent.hogrefe.com/doi/full/10.1027/1864-9335/a000332*

The diversity of people and skills enriches a 'sales dream team': having introverts and extroverts, leaders and followers, and a combination of hard and soft skills. There should be as much diversity in a team as possible to create better relationships and better opportunities to drive business. After all, there isn't just one right way in sales–there are many, and everyone has their own way. However, the focus is not on diversity by itself; but on client diversity too. As **Elaine Teo**, Founder and managing partner of *Living Potential International*, says:

> *The diversity of your teams must reflect the diversity of your clients. Those teams who can truly empathise with their client this way are the ones who can spot opportunities that others are blind to and who possess the people skills to realise them.*

We've encountered the challenges of hiring for a team, to build a team mindset with diverse individual contributors with hard and soft skills. We wanted to include a different set of tips and tools that add to the framework and will be useful when hiring new team members to ensure a perfect fit – the 'scaling sales teams framework'.

This framework is not the ultimate hiring tool; as we all know, there are multiple ways to solve and avoid the challenges we've mentioned. Rather, it is a combination of the authors' and interviewees' experiences that we believe can improve decision-making for a better chance of success. It is up to you to review, choose and test some of the methods and create a method and process that works best for you.

Scaling the Sales Teams Framework

Our interviewee, **Dr Solange Charas**, introduced the need for a sales team framework as teams should never be allowed to lounge in the comfort zone. You should measure team performance during both the good and the bad years and constantly look for gaps in the team. The framework takes you through the steps of the hiring process from beginning to end, starting with the stakeholder's buy-in process, to finding the right people on different channels in an agile way, the rigours of the interview process, decision-making, and finally, onboarding to the team.

Stakeholders Buy-In

Involve stakeholders early on in the decision-making process when considering creating new teams or increasing the size of existing ones. This approach will ensure a smooth process and should include presenting your past achievements to justify the new investment, presenting a plan with clear expectations from new teams, new target goals, and alignment with your organisation's objectives and key results (OKRs). Be prepared for objections and be sure to respond to any questions and concerns on hiring to change their perception. This engagement will help to garner support to move forward with hiring and scaling.

Finding People in an Agile Recruiting Process

Once you've got the approval from managers or stakeholders to hire, whether a member or a whole team, it's time to begin the search to find the right people to fit the slot. You'll do this by generating a profile description of the type of person you want to hire.

The job profile is of the utmost importance. A well-structured and defined job description is crucial; the company's generic profile templates won't always suit your requirements. To avoid a flood of generic candidates, thus wasting time, you really need to be clear about the kind of expertise and experience you need in the team to fill the gap. You must, therefore, dedicate time to this task and be very specific.

Once you have the profile, you can publish it. There are several ways of finding candidates that can run parallel to one another. A well-defined process for advertising posts makes the process quicker, thereby getting candidates into the hiring funnel faster and guaranteeing a flow of candidates to be interviewed[67], for example:

1. **Public Job Post:** This may include organisation sites or social networks like LinkedIn that candidates can apply through. You'll more than likely find numerous candidates here who don't fit your needs, so it's worth limiting the number of applications (for example, 25 candidates). Limiting the number of applicants assures that the fastest get in first but that good candidates that are busy would be potentially left out.

---

[67] This is discussed more fully in **Alexander Grosse and Davide Loftsness.** Scaling teams–Strategies for Building Successful Teams & Organizations. *O'Reilly*

2. **Internal Job Post:** For current employees who may be working in other parts of the organisation. Sometimes this channel is undervalued, as the number of candidates can be low. There need to be conversations with other managers and teams of the organisation as having employees rotating teams and roles within an organisation can be a healthy way to keep talent within the organisation.

3. **Referrals:** When other employees identify potential candidates from their former experiences or network. This can be an effective way of getting suitable people on board as employees already know the organisation's values and culture. You could reward the referrals to make it a successful programme that incentivises employees to refer suitable candidates. We've seen how these programmes have been effective in both big consulting firms and smaller vendor organisations.

4. **Sourcing through social networks** is a proactive way of finding suitable candidates, and you can contact them directly. You can either participate in conjunction with HR or directly with people of the organisation or teams. In small organisations or startups, the founders can take care of this. This is very time consuming; you will find many people who are unwilling to change their jobs. Recruiters make the selection directly so, after finding a candidate with the right knowledge, experience and hard skills, the interview process only needs to focus on soft skills.

5. **Head Hunters:** You contract others to find suitable candidates through their own platforms, or social networks and sourcing is undertaken by them. Depending on the contracted services, head hunters may work on a commission basis; for example, taking the value of the first month's salary or a percentage of the annual income) as a fixed fee per candidate or a time and materials agreement.

Right Interviews for the Right Roles

When posting the job profile to these different channels, you should include a set of Questions and Answers (Q&A) for recruiters to use throughout the whole process. It doesn't matter if they repeat some of the questions in the different interviews, as the Q&A ensures consistency.

The job profile and the Q&A assessment must be thoughtfully created. For recruiters, the Q&A should be as specific as possible to the team and the ideal profile. Think of the Q&A as though you were in that interview, then write down the questions you would formulate and the answers you would like to hear from suitable candidates. The recruiters and interviewers can use this sample to confidently recommend candidates who will advance to the next phase of the hiring process.

If the role has a technical element to it, like a presales engineer, the Q&A assessments can be a mix of hard and soft skills and could be used during the first stage through an automated online test.

Making the Decision

We can use a scorecard to quantify the different hard and soft skills and experiences of candidates. This method is particularly useful if there are a number of suitable candidates who have gone through the different interview phases and have answered all behavioural assessment questions appropriately.

The Hiring Scorecard[68], shared by **Amy Volas**, is a great example that you can use as a template to create your own. According to Amy: "*That scorecard reduced my client's hiring process time by 37%, which allowed them to invest that time on other priorities instead.*" When the scorecard is defined, based on the values and other factors proven to be successful in your team or the organisation, it will help you in the decision-making process. The hiring scorecard can complement the Q&A assessment. The process might involve reviewing the scorecard before the interview (without changing it) and selecting questions from the Q&A related to each category and based on the candidates' resume.

While carrying out the Q&A assessment, you can rate the different answers, assign them a score and write it on the scorecard. Once the candidate interviews are complete, you calculate each candidate's average score and compare them with the others. You can double certain areas/questions or have a weighted score for some of the categories that reflect the more desirable requirements. You can also include a minimum acceptable threshold score for some of the categories.

---

[68] **Amy Volas** – Use This Interview Scorecard Template to Win the Top Sales Talent *https://www.saleshacker.com/hiring-scorecard-sales-process/*

Role-Play

Role-plays are highly effective ways to see how a candidate reacts to and interacts with certain situations. For each of them, you can prepare a briefing document that outlines realistic scenarios likely to happen in your team. The candidate's future line manager must participate in the role-play, although you could include different assessors from the team or organisation for a less biased decision. At the end of the exercise, the candidates' responses to the different scenarios are rated. The feedback may be factored in with the cumulative results of the scorecard to compare the candidates.

One of our authors, Andy Jaffke, uses role-play to select Account Executives. He runs these role-plays with two colleagues as assessors: one usually from the hiring team and another from a different team or department that doesn't report directly to him. This avoids bias as three people will make the final decision as a team.

Similar to what Victor Antonio said regarding presentation and communication skills, role-plays reveal several other key skills:

- How well does the candidate prepare?

- How creative are the answers when tough questions are raised?

- What levels of self-esteem are displayed?

Hiring Committees

Another complementary way of finding suitable candidates is through a Hiring Committee. Google uses this approach which has proven to be a very successful way of filtering and selecting the right candidates. Using a hiring committee promotes less bias as decisions are based on different opinions. At Google, the hiring decision is unanimous. A hiring manager can reject a candidate, but to hire a candidate, the entire Hiring Committee must say "yes".

Onboarding into the Team is not always considered part of the hiring process, which usually ends when the new hire is contracted and welcomed to the organisation. Some countries have a legal trial period for positions that can last from several weeks to 12 months. This trial period may not be sufficiently long enough to be sure that the new hire fits in with the team, has started to be productive, or contributes to the sales team.

It is crucial that the leader/manager is attentive to new members and coaches them to guarantee the team's success. If the new member was not part of the team's genesis, the team's vision, mission, values and culture must be shared with them. As Scott Ingram, one of our interviewees explains, this is important for every team member: *"It's really trying to coalesce around that vision around that idea getting bought in supporting each other and working as truly as a team to get to that shared vision that shared goal".*

The Right People in the Right Role – Who do I Need and For What?

The type of sales team you need depends on the stage of your business. One of our authors has experience working across a broad spectrum of stages with companies of various sizes. He worked on the sales teams in very specific roles like account executive, sales engineer, and sales support.

He has founded multiple companies and been instrumental in securing the first 50 sales in each of them. The types of people and the types of teams are very different at each stage. The author has admittedly made the mistake of hiring for roles that the company did not need at that particular stage of its evolution; for example, hiring a seasoned sales executive before a repeatable sales model was in place, hiring for partner managers before direct sales were completed. This hiring on spec was detrimental to company growth and a drag on expenses.

Desh Deshpande said that a founder has to make the first 50 to 100 sales to set a repeatable sales process. The people supporting you to ensure the sale goes through may not even be on your team. This is where the early-stage sales are "by hook or by crook", and you're possibly not yet thinking about what the sales team looks like until you have a repeatable process. Desh's advice is that when you know that your client wore a blue shirt and a red tie, you have a repeatable process.

If you are the founder of a start-up company and looking to bring in sales help, please don't make the same mistake the author did by bringing in a seasoned executive way too early. This move cost the company a lot of money which it could not afford, and resulted in ill will between the founder and the sales executive. The founder couldn't figure out why the sales executive couldn't sell, and the sales executive didn't have enough product knowledge with a moving target to be effective in their role. This was not fair on either party. The founder should have waited until there was a repeatable process for sales. The lesson is that you can't just 'make the team'—you have to have a team suitable for the stage of your business to make the company successful.

You really have to understand what drives clients to buy your product. This information will help you build the right team. Once you have sold to more than 50 clients, you now have a repeatable sales process.

The next phase of your growth is to hire the right sales team. We have talked extensively about Team Dynamics in this book but have not actually explored the specifics of how and what you should look for when assembling your team. The right roles. The right people. Diversity in your team. A daunting task?

"Get the Right People on the Bus" is a classic insight for team building taken from the book "***Good to Great***" by **Jim Collins**, first published in 2001. The insight is as true today as it was 20 years ago. This chapter reviews the process of seeing what types of teams might make sense to see how you can put some of these practices into play to assemble the right team.

There is a general consensus that different types of sales teams are suitable for most organisations, depending on the stage of the company.

As mentioned, the initial sales model involves the founder selling, and because they are so engaged in the sales process, they build the sales team under them.

Founder Sales Model

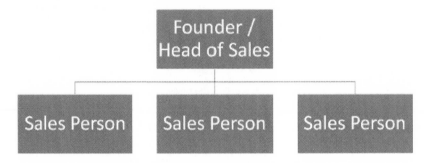

Figure 9: Founder Sales Model

The Founder Sales Model only works for a while as the founder is also usually trying to run the company. The Founder Sales Model will evolve into a traditional or dynamic sales team model, as we will explain.

The traditional sales team structure includes the traditional sales manager, a sales executive-type role that is flat, and widely used and understood.

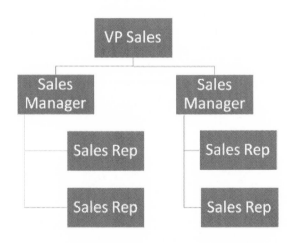

Figure 10: Traditional Sales Structure

This is a very traditional approach to sales and may be perfect for specific companies, typically where the product is easy to articulate to a client and is not a team sale. Compensation is determined by how the managers/reps are achieving their revenue target vs revenue booked. The challenge with this approach is that compensation only reflects the initial sale versus the lifecycle of a client throughout.

Many companies create more dynamic sales models, such as process sales that mimic an assembly line, and compensation is based on individual activities.

Figure 11: Dynamic Sales Model

Additionally, there are also sales pods where sales roles across the client continuum act together and are compensated, as pods.

Figure 12: Sales Pods

The types of roles you need to hire for are certainly dependent on the stage of the company but, more importantly, the roles must align with the vision of how and why you're growing the company and, as part of the sales organisation structure, you believe is best for your company. To fill your bus, you must determine what the seats on your bus look like by determining what roles you really need on the sales team. There are also new roles that might be worth investigating based on new digital models.

Typical roles in the sales organisation include:

- Founder Driven Sales – The Early Sales

- Sales Manager – The Leader

- Account Executive – Happy Client and Upsell

- Business Development Executive – The Hunter

- Sales Engineer – The Knower

- Client Success – Things Just Go Right.

Some **newer roles** might be:

- SDR – the Sales Development Rep who is dedicated to outreach for lead generation.

Let's get your bus filled with the right people sitting in the right seats and get your sales engine really humming!

The downside of not getting the right people on the bus is that it can be expensive. It is the expense of getting someone up to speed, the expense of lost opportunities where the sales just don't materialise, the expense of jeopardising clients that may not be recoverable. So, getting it right should be a priority!

You've laid out what type of organisation you are – traditional, dynamic, or a form of hybrid. You see the overall roles for each type – nothing new here. But let's go a layer deeper and see what attributes you should be looking for in these roles. Let's look at a method for hiring the right people rather than just working off a gut feeling.

The question you need to answer about your organisation is how discrete your organisation can be around the roles? Will one individual handle everything from sales to support? Probably not, but perhaps you are growing, and that is all you can currently afford.

If you are in a larger company, the actual job descriptions identify the different roles within the entire range of requirements where you might be creating individual roles based on knowledge or experience. Ultimately, revenue dictates how many people you can place in the seats. Let's revisit the roles we introduced and give them some context.

The sales funnel actually aligns with the digital sales funnel. Focusing on the skills and attributes of the person you need for each stage of your sales process can help you understand the motivation and success of various individuals on your sales team.

Founder Driven Sales – The Early Sales: This individual may actually be doing everything out of necessity. Desh Deshpande, an interviewee, believes that this is a critical role for founders as they are getting feedback from clients and are probably engaged with the first 100+ clients. This individual's skills are in market alignment and overcoming objections. Typically they will be very tenacious which is how they became an entrepreneur in the first place.

Sales Manager – The Leader: This role might initially be the CEO or the VP or director of sales within larger companies. The sales manager manages the team and ensures they have the necessary support to close business and make the tough decisions that allow the team to fire on all cylinders. The skills and attributes the sales manager will have are team building, motivation and setting expectations for the team. Typically, the sales manager will have come from sales and will also have either business development or account executive skills.

Farmer Account Executive – The Zookeeper: This role should look after the client post-sale and look for opportunities to upsell the company's new products/services. This role can be an inside sales manager where the initial relationship has been struck, and this role ensures the longevity of the client over time. The skills and attributes that are key to this role are building relationships, setting expectations with a client, overcoming objectives, and ensuring client success.

Hunter Account Executive – The Hunter: also called the business development executive, is meant to bring a new client base and potential new partners or channels into the company. The skills and attributes for this role include hunting/prospecting, active listening, overcoming objections, and closing.

Solutions Engineer – The Knower: The SE has intimate knowledge of the product and use case(s) for the client. They can hold their own with the client's technical team and demonstrate the various settings for the product. This role is typically found in larger organisations with many different technical products; they may even be the Chief Technical Officer (CTO) in smaller companies. The skills and attributes important for this role are consultative selling, product knowledge, and active listening.

Client Success Managers – Things Just Go Right: This role is vital for long-term success with clients. They ensure that the client is appropriately onboarded and is proactive in ensuring the clients are using the product and using it properly.

If there are issues, these will be corrected before they result in the loss of a client. The skills and attributes that are key to this role are relationship-building, product knowledge, and responsibility for client success.

How do you decide how many of each role you need? Based on the economics and plans for the organisation, the starting point would be to use the sales funnel as a metric for the activities and align that with the skills needed to support those activities. Then use the anticipated revenue to determine the right size team.

Or maybe you have to downsize? These are both valid questions as businesses grow and shrink, and they must react accordingly.

Now let's look at an organisation using some simple numbers and build on the context of the previous chapter around sales team goals.

Life Cycle Phases	Metrics/Measurement
Awareness / Interest / ROI Goals	Fortune 500
Lead generation / Target audience	1,000 leads (Contacts)
Prospects / Target accounts	100 qualified accounts
Evaluation / "Click" on offer	20 click through the offer
Closed deals	10 purchase orders
Upsell / Client care / Post-sales	10 clients that repeat business

For each sales account generating $200,000 of revenue, you must have a $2,000,000 objective. Determine the amounts for each sales team member using a simple math exercise:

Let's assume that the traditional model has $600,000 of revenue per sales team member. The 2,000,000 / 600,000 model gives a ratio of 3.3. Therefore, you need at least 3 people, perhaps 4, in your sales organisation with stretch goals.

The sales team/sales pod model cannot account for more than 40% of the amount of revenue it will produce. This enables one to determine the roles based on compensation to see if it is a realistic exercise to have a sales pod. In the case of $2,000,000 in revenue, the pod's overall cost cannot exceed $800,000. The sales pod may be needed in more complex sales environments.

The type of sales structure you put in place must be based on what will create the most success for your organisation.

Lastly, how do you hire and get diversity in your sales team roles? Diversity can mean any number of things, including:

- Ethnicity

- Gender

- Age

- Language

- Background

- Or such things as inclusion, culture and religion.

The bigger question, though, is why do you want diversity in your sales team?

A study by the Harvard Business Review[69] found that a team with a member who shares a client's ethnicity is 152% more likely to understand that client than another team member. You want your sales team to reflect the world.

---

69 **Sylvia Ann Hewlett, Melinda Marshall, and Laura Sherbin,**
2013. *https://hbr.org/2013/12/how-diversity-can-drive-innovation,*

Key Takeaways

1. Every role within an organisation contributes to the sales team's performance. Understanding that the roles are an extension of the team and their contribution will help you on your way to success.

2. Extending the team with indirect partners, like channel partners, and using your loyal clients as indirect sellers will expand the scope of prospects and effectiveness of sales.

3. Your sales team is part of the organisation's teams of teams.

4. Commitment and accountability will make the internal and external relationships trustworthy, durable and effective.

5. Coaching, motivating and rewarding is what keeps the team focused on success.

6. Assessing needs and challenges when hiring talent into the team will help you scale the teams within the organisation.

7. Focusing on your team members' mindset, skills, knowledge, and diversity will build an overall team mindset.

8. Acknowledging where your team fits and how the organisation sales model depends on the business stage of the organisation.

9. Getting the right people in the right roles will maximise your chances of sales success.

Appendix

Short bios of the Key Contributors to Teams Win Championships

Mike Weinberg, writer of the foreword

Mike Weinberg is a consultant, sales coach, speaker and author on a mission to simplify sales. His specialities are New Business Development and Sales Management, and his passion is helping companies and salespeople WIN MORE NEW SALES. Before launching his firm, Mike was the top-producing salesperson in three companies.

Forbes named Mike a Top Sales Influencer, and other publications list him as the #1 Sales Expert to follow on Twitter.

Mike has spoken and consulted on five continents and is the author of three Amazon #1 Bestsellers.

"New Sales. Simplified." is a 7-year bestseller and has been named the #3 most highly-rated sales book of all time.

Mike's second book, *"Sales Management. Simplified."* has been called *"arguably the best book ever written on sales management"* and named by Inc. Magazine and HubSpot as the #1 book every sales leader should read. And, his latest book, *"Sales Truth"*, became a #1 Sales Bestseller its first week on the market.

Mike is a native New Yorker who's lived in St. Louis for 25 years. He has three young adult children and has been told that his wife Katie is still the best proof that he really can sell!

Dr Solange Charas

(Interviewed by Andy Jaffke)

Dr Solange Charas is a human capital expert with 25+ years of experience as a consultant, a practice leader, a top Corporate Executive, and Board Director across all industry sectors. She is adept at the strategic C-Suite/ Board level and the "roll-up-your-sleeves" tactical level. M&A Due Diligence expert with 70+ completed transactions.

Dr Charas' PhD research proves a direct and statistically significant relationship between Boards (4% impact) and C-Suite teams (20% impact) and corporate profitability. She developed proprietary products to effectively create and manage high-performing work teams (her PhD focus) and identify organisational effectiveness and ROI of human capital investment.

She provides creative and innovative HR leadership and program design and describes herself as a culture/climate change agent. She has further experience in leading large and diverse programs and staff, plus extensive international experience, including competency in five languages. She is also a certified Team Coach.

Marta Martínez

(Interviewed by Mattia Bruzzi)

Marta Martínez is passionate about business and social innovation fueled by the combination of people's talent and technology.

Throughout her career in the IT industry, she always believed that, beyond technology, this business is about helping people, companies and institutions to live and work better, solving problems and creating new value.

Marta believes that this idea has never been as relevant as it is today. We are living in a digitally enabled world. The huge array of new, powerful and pervasive technological capabilities available today (from big data and analytics to cognitive solutions, from cloud and mobile to the Internet of Things) is urging us to explore new ways of thinking and acting in almost every process and dimension of our professional and personal lives.

As **General Manager of IBM Europe, Middle East and Africa**, she sees it as a privilege to lead an outstanding team fully focused on helping their clients successfully embrace this era of disruptive transformation.

Marta's most important mission is to understand their clients' visions, ambitions and challenges and then to engage the whole IBM team to help them to thrive.

Gururaj "Desh" Deshpande

(Interviewed by James Craig)

Gururaj Deshpande ("Desh" Deshpande) is an Indian American venture capitalist and entrepreneur, who is best known for co-founding the Chelmsford, MA-based internet equipment manufacturer **Sycamore Networks**, the **MIT Deshpande Center for Technological Innovation** and the **Deshpande Foundation**.

He is also a Life Member of the **MIT Corporation**, the Board of Trustees of **Massachusetts Institute of Technology (MIT)**, and sits on the board of the **MIT School of Engineering** Dean's Advisory Council.

In July 2010, Desh was appointed by President Barack Obama to the Co-Chairmanship of the **US National Advisory Council** on Innovation and Entrepreneurship, a group established to support the US President's innovation strategy.

Prof. David Clutterbuck

(Interviewed by Andy Jaffke)

Prof. David Clutterbuck calls himself *"The last fully active survivor of the pioneers of coaching and mentoring."*

His roles include being Special Ambassador for the oldest professional association in the field. He also co-founded the **European Mentoring and Coaching Council** and serves as a visiting professor of coaching and mentoring at four universities.

Professor Clutterbuck is a practice leader in the international consultancies **David Clutterbuck Partnership (DCP)** and **Coaching & Mentoring International (CMI)**, which specialise in supporting organisations in developing mentoring and coaching programmes and in establishing sustainable mentoring and coaching cultures. Everything David does revolves around helping people and organisations harness the power of dialogue – to have the conversations that will bring about positive change. He has written or co-written more than 70 books and recently published the second edition of his book *"Coaching the Team at Work 2–The definitive guide to Team Coaching"*.

He is visiting professor to the coaching and mentoring faculties of **Henley Business School**, **Oxford Brookes University**, **Sheffield Hallam University** and **York St John**.

In 2011, David was voted **Coaching at Work** magazine's **Mentor of the Year**. David has been recognised as the **number 1 Influencer European Coaching** by **Marshall Goldsmith Foundation**; Chartered Companion of the **Chartered Institute of Personnel and Development**; Distinguished Fellow of **The Conference Board**.

He was named one of the **2020 TOP30 Global Coaching Gurus** by Globalgurus.org.

Victor Antonio

(Interviewed by Eduardo Baez)

Victor Antonio is the author of 14 books on sales, influence and motivation who earned both a B.S. degree in Electrical Engineering and an MBA, and then built a 20-year career as a top sales executive before becoming President of Global Sales and Marketing of a company valued at $420M. He is the founder of the **Sales Velocity Academy**, an online sales training system.

Mike Figliuolo

(Interviewed by Eduardo Baez)

Mike Figliuolo is the founder and Managing Director of **thoughtLEADERS, LLC** . He is an honour graduate of the United States Military Academy at West Point, where he graduated in the top 5 per cent of his class. He served in the U.S. Army as an armour officer. Mike also spent time in corporate America as a consultant at McKinsey & Company and as an executive at Capital One and Scotts Miracle-Gro. As the founder and managing director of thoughtLEADERS, LLC, he and his team train senior executives at leading companies on leadership, strategy, communications, innovation, and other critical business skills. He is the author of three books:

1. *One Piece of Paper*: The Simple Approach to Powerful, Personal Leadership

2. *Lead Inside the Box*: How Smart Leaders Guide Their Teams to Exceptional Results

3. *The Elegant Pitch*: Create a Compelling Recommendation, Build Broad Support, and Get it Approved.

He's also one of the most-viewed authors on **LinkedIn Learning,** where he has 30 courses on a variety of leadership and management topics. His courses have been translated into six other languages and have been viewed millions of times by learners worldwide.

César Cernuda

(Interviewed by Mattia Bruzzi)

As former **LATAM President & Corporate Vice President** at **Microsoft** and now **President** at **NetApp**, a Fortune 500 company, César is passionate about developing people. He believes that only the best people can drive innovation and support the clients' transformation journeys.

What he most admires in his colleagues is humility, agility, inspiration and motivation, as well as those who stand up for their beliefs and have a strong desire to make the world a better place.

While César loves his work, he also considers himself a risk-taker. Great change requires great risks, and for him, risk is fun and motivating. He is energised by finding creative, outside-the-box solutions and encouraging people to look at challenging problems through different lenses.

But above everything else, he enjoys learning. His greatest teachers are his clients. By listening to them, he learns what they need to be successful on their digital transformation journeys.

Sami Suni

(Interviewed by Andy Jaffke)

Sami Suni is the founder and CEO of Showell, a B2B SaaS startup-company from Helsinki, Finland. Showell is a digital sales enablement platform that empowers sales and all customer-facing teams with the right content and knowledge to better engage customers at every step of the buying journey, and to close deals faster.

Sami has worked in software sales and marketing for over 15 years. His passion is to innovate and turn the innovations into sellable products and services.

Scott Ingram

(Interviewed by Eduardo Baez)

Scott Ingram is the host of the **Sales Success Stories** and **Daily Sales Tips** podcasts. He's the author of three books: "*Sales Success Stories*", "*B2B Sales Mentors*", and "*Finding Sales Success on LinkedIn*". He's also a quota-carrying sales professional, working for the professional services company Relationship One as an Account Director. Scott lives with his wife and two daughters in Austin, Texas, where he hosts the **Sales Success Summit** each October.

Santiago Campuzano

(Interviewed by Pablo Escobar de la Oliva)

Santiago Campuzano is the Senior Director EMEA Hyperscalers Alliance at **Citrix.** Santiago has led public and private organisations on their journey towards the digital workplace.

He is fully focused on leading the change of organisations for new competitive environments based on the workspace evolution as part of digital transformation. With a general background in sales, marketing, finance and a wealth of experience in IT multinationals, his goal is to lead multi-talented teams to compete successfully in new markets.

He offers his support in business strategy, sales and marketing providing a comprehensive vision for companies with a specialised background in IT companies and crucial experience in cloud computing solutions, security, mobility and workplace transformation technologies.

Chris Ortolano

(Interviewed by Eduardo Baez)

Chris Ortolano is the founder of **Outbound Edge** and is an expert in managing the "Middle of the sales funnel" and the design of the sales process.

Chris starts by raising a question around the benefits of developing an account growth plan, and he proceeds to help his clients build processes to help them achieve their sales goals.

Authors' Bios and Whys

Andy Jaffke, 7th May 1967, Föhren, Germany

Andy Jaffke, is a native German and has been living with his Spanish family in Madrid since 1999. He is passionate about leadership and coaching to help others develop to their full potential to achieve happiness and success in their lives. Andy is the author of *"Be Yourself"* and the creator of the *"Top3Planner"*. He has co-founded and founded several companies and has been working for mainly multinational software and services companies for over 20 years with a focus on Sales. Andy loves travelling with his family, going out with his friends and having good conversations, running, reading, listening to podcasts and writing.

Andy's Why

The idea to write *"Teams Win Championships"* came up in January 2020 after being inspired by the great success with the Pulsar sales team at Teradata, where he had the privilege of leading as the Area VP EMEA during 2019. Instead of writing the book on his own, Andy decided to bring together an exciting and diverse team of co-authors. Andy's shared purpose is to create a framework of great value for the global sales community by sharing practical and valuable knowledge, real-life experiences, concepts and tools; information and knowledge that actually work and can help readers to progress either as a member or the manager and leader of a sales team. Another important "Why" for Andy is to help others as best he can. It was agreed by the team that all proceeds of the book will go to one or multiple charities of the authors' choosing.

Eddie Baez, 27th February 1991, New York, USA

Born in Puerto Rico and raised in the Bronx, New York, **Eddie Baez** was a top-performing sales consultant at IBISWorld Industry Research, a leading provider of industry intelligence in the US. While at IBISWorld, Eddie achieved the "**Sales Performer of the Year**" award for 3 consecutive years. Currently, Eddie is the CEO & Co-Founder of Career Pipe PBC. Growing up, Eddie experienced firsthand the difficulties of learning the essential skills required for professional B2B sales and a lack of mentors who resembled him in the sales community. Given his voracious appetite for sales training and development and his burning desire to make sales a more accessible profession for under-resourced communities, the TWC project was an opportunity of a lifetime!

Eddie's Why

Eddie is a first-generation college graduate and a kid from the Bronx who didn't know a single thing about B2B sales growing up. No one in his immediate family or circle of friends knew a single person who worked in corporate sales. In his community, sales was not a typical career path and, unless it was tied to entrepreneurship, it wasn't highly regarded. TWC offered Eddie the ability to help people from his community who would otherwise miss their "sales calling" because of a lack of information. They could learn more about what the profession entails, and he could be instrumental in bringing some nobility back to the profession.

James Craig, 23rd September 1967, Halifax, Canada

James Craig has 30 years in the Navy and business. Armed with engineering degrees and an MBA, James worked in very large companies like Deloitte Consulting and Bell Canada and created products running in over 140 countries while at Nautel. He has started up and run two companies that he co-founded–he has extensive knowledge in small, large, public and private sector companies. James' true desire is to work with smaller companies and creating success for clients with products he has had a hand in creating.

James' Why

I remember a most serendipitous meeting vividly while visiting a client site four time zones from where I live on the other side of Canada in British Columbia. It was the same month I lost my father, Jerry Craig, to IPF, a lung disease. I was out there for a week, on behalf of the company I co-founded in 2016, to implement one of our products and carry out client training for our most strategic clients to date. It was a Saturday, and it was raining torrentially – typical weather for summer in British Columbia in summer but not winter.

I was actually up at the Whistler/Blackhomb Ski Village to snowboard for the day. Due to the rain, the hill was an hour late in opening, and it was probably the worst conditions of the year, which was extremely disappointing because I don't get the opportunity to ski one of the world's best ski hills every day. I got some runs in and was tired of fighting the ice on the hill, so I decided to have lunch. This is where I met Andy. We started talking about skiing, and then it turned to business and sales. That conversation stayed with me as Andy had some wonderful positiveness that you don't experience often.

So much to my surprise, about a month later, Andy puts out a call to his network, which I was now part of, to see who would be interested in writing a book on team sales. As a former Naval Engineering Officer in the Canadian Navy and serial entrepreneur, I knew that there was little written about the sales team even though it took on more and more importance in getting and retaining clients. Most of what was happening in the industry involved pushing our individual salespeople and not looking holistically at the team as the key to our success. So, I threw my hat in the ring to be one of the authors as I have a fair amount of sales and client success experience from my career and saw this as an opportunity to keep learning. I had also written a book in 1999 and enjoyed the process, so the thought of writing with at least 5 other people located in multiple countries was another thing that I thought I would enjoy.

And then the pandemic hit. I have to say, our weekly check-in calls throughout the writing project over the last year have saved my sanity. I have got to know each of the co-authors, albeit virtually, with the exception of Andy, and have grown to enjoy both their company and the variety of sales knowledge. The fact that we are doing this project to support non-profits worldwide is the icing on the cake. I can't wait to share a beer in Spain with all the authors when it is safe. I think that our Team has created something very special for the global sales community and believe that this is just the beginning. I hope you enjoy reading the book as much as I have enjoyed helping write it and that you walk away with a few nuggets of knowledge that will help you and your company out.

John Di Marzio, 23rd May 1966, Montreal, Canada

Born and raised in Montreal, Canada, John Di Marzio's ancestral roots go back to rural Italy in the mountainous region of Abruzzo. The red Maple Leaf is certainly home, but Italy has always remained close to his heart from afar. Family life takes precedence over all else, and despite running his own manufacturing company for the past 20 years, he ensures time is well invested with his loved ones. Never one to take things for granted, John does his best to embrace the present and make the most of what lies ahead.

John's Why

John recognises that dedication to lifelong learning and self-improvement is the gateway to life mastery. The past few years have been an especially intense commitment to self-improvement, specifically in the field of sales. By joining TWC, he hoped to write an inspirational book on sales-related material and add to his dedication to learning. Mission accomplished! The personal benefits have shown great returns with what he has learned from this brilliant group of writers. With a background in Mechanical Engineering, John tends to have a slightly different perspective than his TWC team members. Yet, sharing and embracing these distinct viewpoints have greatly enhanced the pages of this book.

When Andy first launched the idea, John was intrigued by this book-writing project. The conversation went something like this:

"What's it about?"

"A book about sales teams!"

"Who's our audience?"

"Sales teams looking to up their game!"

"But I've never written a book before this."

"That's fine!"

"But I'm an engineer."

"That could be good for us!"

"I'm a business owner."

"That's even better!"

"How much time will it take?"

"Lots!"

"How much does it pay?"

"Nothing!"

"Who will benefit from this?"

"Charitable organisations!"

Pause for about five seconds...

"OK, Andy, when do we start?"

And that, my friends, was the launch of John's writing career.

Mattia Bruzzi, 6th July 1973, Ponte dell'Olio (Piacenza) Italy

Mattia Bruzzi is a native Italian who, after 3 years in London, decided to move to Spain in 2009 with his family. He considers himself a smile dispenser as he does believe that with a smile and empathy, no wall is too hard; he is "Honesty" and "Integrity" black belt, a "prima donna" killer, and is extremely passionate about understanding and engaging with people through empathy, genuine interest and childish curiosity.

He is passionate about leadership and motivation to help others believe in themselves to give their best and contribute to greater causes. For over 20 years, he has been working in the Financial Services sector for multinational software companies focused on Sales and Business Development. He is also a Business Angel and Venture Capital investor who supports early-stage start-ups that are active on the digitalisation front.

Mattia loves travelling, sports, good food, and good wine, of course...

Mattia's Why

To write a book to show the "flip side" of the Sales coin.

Too often, the effort, the organisation and the discipline required in sales are underestimated or misjudged. Likewise, very often, the different contributions and cooperation to the Sales cycle are undervalued. This book represents a great occasion to share the experiences of the sales and management community to reflect upon the most common and dangerous mistakes.

It also presents a great opportunity to reflect on his personal experiences and learn from the mistakes and experiences of the co-authors.

Pablo Escobar de la Oliva, 2nd October 1984,

Madrid, Spain

Pablo Escobar de la Oliva was born and raised in Madrid, where he lives with his wife and son, in close proximity to the rest of his family. He's a millennial digital native who pursues his virtual dreams of living, studying and working around computers. He believes that a positive mindset transforms your life, and you will always see him with an optimistic contagious outlook. He has a constant need for achievement, which pushes him to start new challenges where he always looks to leave his mark.

He started working on startups while studying computer science and continued his career, specialising in Data and Analytics. He has been working with direct client interaction for around 20 years, with the last decade being focused on enterprise clients from multinational software providers and consulting firms.

Pablo's purpose is spending as much time as possible with his family while enjoying a healthy lifestyle; that's why his passions include travelling, healthy food, gym workouts and mountain biking.

Pablo's Why

During his career, Pablo recognised that 'going it alone' is not a long successful path for any business. His motto is: "I learn from my mistakes, but I prefer to learn from the mistakes of others".

When Pablo joined the TWC initiative, he saw it as a new challenge with multiple benefits for him while, at the same time, serving a greater purpose. He likes pragmatic books, those that serve multiple times as guidelines, so he was looking for a practical book to have on hand for multiple global sales teams' interactions. He thought joining the initiative was the best way to contribute.

Book Recommendations

A Team of Leaders – *Paul Gustavson* and *Stewart Litt*

Can't Hurt Me – Master Your Mind and Defy the Odds - *David Goggins*

Clockwork – *Mike Michalowicz*

Coaching the Team at Work – *David Clutterbuck*

Customer Centricity – *Peter Fader*

Dream Teams – *Shane Snow*

El efecto actitud (Spanish): La gestión del entusiasmo en la vida personal y profesional – *Victor Küppers y Jaime Grego Mayor*

Give and Take – *Adam Grant*

Good to Great – *Jim Collins*

New Sales. Simplified – *Mike Weinberg*

Objections – *Jeb Blount*

One Piece of Paper – *Mike Figliuolo*

Sales Management. Simplified – *Mike Weinberg*

Scaling Teams: Strategies for Building Successful Teams and Organizations – *Alexander Grosse y David Loftesness*

Start with Why – *Simon Sinek*

Spin Selling – *Neil Rackham*

Stop Selling & Start Leading – *Deb Calvert*

Straight Talk–Your Way to Success – *Dan Veitkus*

Team Genius – *Rich Karlgard and Michael S. Malone*

Team of Rivals – *Doris Kearns Goodwin*

Team of Teams – *General Stanley McCrystal*

The 7 Habits of Highly Effective People – *Stephen R. Covey*

The Challenger Sale: How to Take Control of the Client Conversation – *Matthew Dixon* and *Brent Adamson,*

The Coaching Effect – *Bill Eckstrom* and *Sarah Wirth*

The Critical Few: Energize Your Company's Culture by Choosing What Really Matters – *Jon R. Katzenback*

The First 90 Days – Michael D. Watkins

The Five Dysfunctions of a Team – *Patrick Lencioni*

The Greatest Salesman in the World – *Og Mandino*

The Ideal Team Player – *Patrick Lencioni*

The Inclusion Dividend: Why Investing in Diversity & Inclusion Pays Off – *Mason Donovan, and Mark Kaplan*

The Lost Art of Closing – *Anthony Iannarino*

The Speed of Trust – *Stephen M.R. Covey*

The Transparency Sale – *Todd Caponi*

Podcasts Recommendations

Sales Management. Simplified.–*Mike Weinberg*

Sales Influence–*Victor Antonio*

Sales Success Stories–*Scott Ingram*

Daily Sales Tips–*Scott Ingram*

Notes:

Made in the USA
Middletown, DE
17 June 2021